ALGORITHMIC CULTURE BEFORE THE INTERNET

ALGORITHMIC CULTURE BEFORE THE INTERNET

TED STRIPHAS

Columbia University Press   *New York*

Columbia University Press
Publishers Since 1893
New York   Chichester, West Sussex
cup.columbia.edu

Library of Congress Cataloging-in-Publication Data
Names: Striphas, Theodore G., author.
Title: Algorithmic culture before the internet / Ted Striphas.
Description: New York : Columbia University Press, [2023] |
Includes bibliographical references and index.
Identifiers: LCCN 2022044860 (print) | LCCN 2022044861 (ebook) |
ISBN 9780231206686 (hardback) | ISBN 9780231206693 (trade paperback) |
ISBN 9780231556606 (ebook)
Subjects: LCSH: Culture—Mathematical models. | Culture—
History. | Social history.
Classification: LCC HM621 .S836 2023 (print) | LCC HM621 (ebook) |
DDC 306.09—dc23/eng/20221223
LC record available at https://lccn.loc.gov/2022044860
LC ebook record available at https://lccn.loc.gov/2022044861

Cover design: Noah Arlow
Cover image: Rinus Roelofs, *Cuboctahedron*, wood model.
The design was made, in part, using a computer algorithm.

For Niko

CONTENTS

ACKNOWLEDGMENTS

I n 1984, near the end of fifth grade, I landed a plum role in my elementary school's spring musical. The preceding play had focused on P. T. Barnum (1810–1891), founder of the eponymous circus. The showman's relentless hyperbole and devious cons may have stirred my imagination, but I was positively gripped by the subject matter of the show my music teacher, Mr. Cousins, had chosen to produce in '84: computers. *Time*, a leading magazine of the era, had declared the computer its "Man of the Year" for 1982, and only a year later an Apple IIe landed in my home, thanks to my grandfather. The play was called *The G.I.G.O. Effect*, and the acronym, Mr. Cousins explained, stood for "garbage in, garbage out." A popular expression among programmers of the time, the phrase referred to how the quality of a computer's output was only as good as the input. If you want to listen to the musical numbers, you can find some old recordings of *The G.I.G.O. Effect* by running a quick Google search. I'd tell you to look for me in the role of Chief Glitch but, mercifully, none of the videos you'll find is of the production from my elementary school.

Nevertheless, it's only fitting that there are any videos of *The G.I.G.O. Effect* online, forty years after the fact. The play—which, if I had to guess, is set around the time of our own present day—features a benevolent, Google-like artificial intelligence named MABEL, which has become the repository of all human knowledge. But, a problem is soon revealed: with an attack of the Glitches imminent, society is threatened with the prospect of forgetting everything, and of losing its capacity to process information. The people are completely at a loss about what to do, having outsourced most of their thinking to MABEL. Transfer all the data to "the original computer," MABEL advises them—but still they don't get it. As the glitches swarm and the G.I.G.O. effect sets in, MABEL manages to eke out one last, cryptic message: "u . . . u . . . u. . . ." At last someone connects the dots. MABEL was trying to say, *Human beings, you* are the original computer! The people scramble to commit the information stored in MABEL's hard drives to their own memories, whereupon they reboot the system and restore the data. Meanwhile, and much to my character's chagrin, the Glitches are defeated, and MABEL lives on. As the play draws to a close, the audience learns that the computer age is also *our* age, the message reinforced by the heartwarming musical finale, "There's Nothing We Can't Do Together."

For preteen musical theatre of the 1980s, there's a lot, surprisingly, in *The G.I.G.O. Effect*: the tension between centralized and decentralized authority; the dangers of malware and data breaches; the foolishness of societies that overinvest in fragile information infrastructures; the cognitive effects of ubiquitous computing; the gendered history of computation; the pleasures and discomforts of dataveillance; the ontology of human and machine; the potential for error, bias, or even harm in AI; and surely more. I detect resonances with Plato's *Phaedrus* and Ray Bradbury's *Fahrenheit 451*—though the story of *The G.I.G.O. Effect* is more lighthearted than either of those works, admittedly. But, more than anything, I see in the show an effort to use the arts and humanities to make sense of what computers mean for our everyday lives, including the possibilities of connection and convenience, as well as feelings of loss and alienation. It wouldn't be far-fetched to say *The G.I.G.O. Effect* helped set me on a path to writing this book, which is an unconventional history of culture and computation, and how they converged.

The show also has me thinking about how the strengths of *Algorithmic Culture Before the Internet*, whatever they may be, owe much to the input—in all its diverse forms—that I've received throughout this project. I begin with the people who typically appear last: my partner, Phaedra C. Pezzullo, and my son, Niko Pezzullo Striphas. Chapter 4 includes a discussion of the politics of "acknowledgments." I hope, in putting my family first, that I'm managing to convey the inadequacy of the next few sentences you're about to read. Phaedra and Niko suffered through my moods and doubts, and they lifted me up. They encouraged me to press on when I was stalled—and to recognize when I was, in fact, stalled. They cared for me and for one another, giving me time and space to imagine, travel, research, and write. And they celebrated every milestone of this project with me. Phaedra talked through ideas, asked incisive questions, and delivered frank and honest criticism—the type of criticism only the closest people can provide. She has improved the quality of this book in countless ways, even if I continue to flummox her at times. I dedicated my last book, *The Late Age of Print*, to Phaedra. Niko gets this one. They lived the totality of this endeavor with me, and their love has endowed every one of the pages you're about to read.

I've also benefitted from the kindness, love, and support of my father-in-law, Vincent Pezzullo, the Courtsunis family (John, Chris, and Gus), and the Frangos family (Alexandra, George, Caroline, James, and John). An extra bit of thanks to the Courtsunises for propping me up with copious confections from the family business, Commodore Chocolatier, and to Rogue, Yoda, and Phoenix for their four-legged folly. Between *Late Age* and *Algorithmic Culture* I said goodbye to Jean and Jim Frangos, Carmen Pezzullo, and Anne Striphas, in addition to Ecco and Neptune. I miss you all, and not a day goes by that at least one of you isn't on my mind.

Glitches have a penchant for sneaking in and mucking things up, despite our best intentions. Brilliant friends, colleagues, and mentors have helped me to debug this project. Stephen Hartnett, Ben Highmore, Ben Peters, and Mehdi Semati, thank you for the invaluable feedback on individual chapters. Larry Grossberg, I'm indebted to you for reading and commenting on the whole manuscript (to say nothing of the enduring influence of your teachings). Well before there was a manuscript to debug, Charles Acland suggested I write a biography of an algorithm. I did—though perhaps not in the way either of us had imagined. Around the same time, Jason Baird Jackson prompted a decisive shift of focus for this project in recommending the work of Talcott Parsons. I'm grateful to Jason for helping me to realize that the story I was chasing exceeded Amazon, Google, Spotify, TikTok, and all the other usual algorithmic suspects.

The G.I.G.O Effect taught me much about the importance of distributed cognition. Writing this book has only reinforced the lesson. I cannot tell you how many ideas emerged over meals or in casual conversations, or how many folks emailed stories about algorithms, the details of which landed in this book. And don't get me started on the number of questions I issued on social media, and the amazing responses I received. To that end, I thank John Ackerman, Janneke Adema, Mark Andrejevic, Anne Balsamo, Ann Blair, Marcus Breen, Jed Brubaker, Andrew Calabrese, John Cheney-Lippold, Jonathan Cohn, Nabil Echchaibi,

Lori Emerson, Nathan Ensmenger, John Nguyet Erni, Lisa Flores, James Hay, Bernard Dionysus Geoghegan, Ilana Gershon, Tarleton Gillespie, Giuseppi Granieri, Ron Greene, Mark Hayward, Chris Ingraham, Chris Joyce, Michael Kaplan, Barb Klinger, Heather Klopchin, Denise Mann, John McGowan, Kembrew McLeod, Leysia Palen, Charles Parsons, Janice Peck, John Durham Peters, Søren Pold, Hector Postigo, Satish Rao, Craig Robertson, Gil Rodman, Kris Rutten, Christian Sandvig, Stephanie Ricker Schulte, Greg Seigworth, Raka Shome, Jonathan Sterne, Melissa Sutherland, Bryan Taylor, Fred Turner, Siva Vaidhyanathan, Greg Wise, and Megan Wood.

This book was initially conceived when I was on faculty at Indiana University, and it was completed at the University of Colorado Boulder. I acknowledge the support, material and intellectual, I've received from both institutions, in addition to the goodwill of Jane Goodman, Karen Tracy, Pete Simonson, Tim Kuhn, and Rick Stevens, my department chairs. My appreciation also extends to Lori Bergen, dean of the College of Media, Communication, and Information at CU, for supporting this project with a de Castro Research Award. Thanks, too, to all the students in my graduate and undergraduate "Keywords in Digital Technology and Culture" classes. Graduate advisees, past and present, have left a deeper imprint on *Algorithmic Culture Before the Internet* than they probably know. Thank you to Brandon Daniels, Mally Dietrich, James N. Gilmore, Blake Hallinan, Joe Hatfield, Michael Lahey, Chris Miles, and Bailey Troutman. Blake deserves a special mention for our collaborative work on the Netflix Prize, and for always being such a generous and astute interlocutor.

I've had the good fortune of working with Philip Leventhal, my editor at Columbia University Press, since *The Late Age of Print.* I cannot tell you how important it is for an author to connect with someone who just gets it (or, at least, is willing to go with it), someone who also knows when to tell you that your version of clever is in fact completely abstruse. I take comfort in all the ways Philip looks out for me as an author—from nurturing my ideas to coaching me through the review process, and more. Thanks too to the awesome team at Columbia University Press, without whom *Algorithmic Culture Before the Internet* wouldn't have achieved tangible form, and to the anonymous reviewers for giving me the tools to get out of my own head and to create a more approachable manuscript.

Crowd wisdom is a thing, to be sure. I prototyped a bunch of ideas on two different blogs, *The Late Age of Print* and *Culture Digitally*, and I'm grateful to the readers for their thoughtful engagements. This book has also benefitted from the input of audiences for talks I delivered at Aarhus University, Columbia College, Ghent University, Hong Kong Baptist University, Monash University, Northeastern University, Temple University, University of Alberta, University of California Davis, University of California Los Angeles, University of Colorado Boulder, University of Iowa, University of Michigan, and Vanderbilt University. Radio, podcast, and periodical interviews have been equally clarifying. Thanks to the writers and hosts of *Future Tense* (ABC/Australia), *Information* (Denmark), *Marketplace* (NPR/United States), *Pesquisa* (Brazil), *Spark* (CBC/Canada), and *Think: Digital Futures* (Australia) for providing a forum in which to make my arguments about algorithmic culture more widely accessible.

Finally, I thank Princeton University Press, Sage Publications, and Taylor & Francis for permission to repurpose snippets of my own prose from the following publications: "Keyword: Critical," *Communication and Critical/Cultural Studies* 10, nos. 2–3 (September 1, 2013): 324–28; "Algorithmic Culture,"

European Journal of Cultural Studies 18, nos. 4–5 (August 2015): 395–412; "Culture," from *Digital Keywords: A Vocabulary of Information, Society, and Culture*, ed. Benjamin Peters, © 2016 by Princeton University Press—reprinted by permission; and "Algorithms," from *Information: A Historical Companion*, eds. Ann Blair, Paul Duguid, Anja-Silvia Goeing, and Anthony Grafton, © 2021 by Princeton University Press—reprinted by permission. Chapter 3 is a significantly revised and expanded version of material first published here: "Known-Unknowns: Matthew Arnold, F. R. Leavis, and the Government of Culture," *Cultural Studies* 31, no. 1 (January 2017): 143–63. Images and quotations from archival sources appearing in chapter 4 are courtesy of the Harvard University Archives.

ALGORITHMIC CULTURE BEFORE THE INTERNET

INTRODUCTION

Welcome to the Machine

D isney Animation Studios' hit feature film *Ralph Breaks the Internet* (2018) may be the coming-of-age story of Vanellope von Schweetz, a video game character, but if you listen closely enough you might hear something else coming of age too: the word *algorithm*.

The action begins when, true to his name, Wreck-It-Ralph (voiced by John C. Reilly) breaks the controller for *Sugar Rush*, an arcade game he frequents when he's not "at work" playing the villain in his own coin-op machine, *Fix-It Felix, Jr.* The accident sets him and his best friend Vanellope (voiced by Sarah Silverman), a glitchy kart racer from *Sugar Rush*, off on an adventure into the internet to locate a replacement part on eBay. The friends quickly determine that the path to internet riches is paved with viral videos, and that they'll need to talk to Yesss (voiced by Taraji P. Henson), the stylish head algorithm of the video sharing site BuzzzTube, if they're to have any hope of securing the funds they need to purchase the new controller. Ralph and Vanellope barge into Yesss's office, where the following exchange occurs:

RALPH: Hey-o! Are you the head of Al Gore?

YESSS: I am the head al-gor-rithm of BuzzzTube, which means I curate content at the internet's most popular video sharing site, which means I don't have time to trifle with every shoeless, mouth-breathing hobo that trundles into my office. Call security, baby!

Yesss dispenses with the insensitive, Big Tech elitism once she learns Ralph is the star of an amusing series of videos attracting attention on BuzzzTube. The series proceeds to go viral after Yesss gives it an algorithmic boost on the site's homepage.

Ralph opens the dialogue with a malapropism—"Al Gore" instead of "algorithm"—whose purpose is comedic but, ultimately, didactic.[1] In doing so, he functions as a proxy for viewers who may yet be unacquainted with the term. Yesss proceeds to spell it out for them, but the explanation, tellingly, is fleeting. If lingering on the world *algorithm* is a waste of time, then it

FIGURE 0.1 Yesss, head algorithm of BuzzzTube, distributing hearts ("likes") to Wreck-It Ralph. Also pictured are Vanellope von Schweetz (*left*) and Yesss's assistant, Maybe (*right*). From *Ralph Breaks the Internet* (Disney Animation Studios, 2018).

follows that most of the audience is familiar with it already. Indeed, since the early-2000s, "the algorithm" has become a recurrent figure within the broader realm of popular culture, a pattern I've documented elsewhere.[2] In the exchange between Yesss and Ralph, the point is to get the stragglers up to speed. For everyone else, *algorithm* is an established part of everyday talk.

The presence of the word *algorithm* in a family-friendly feature film would have been unimaginable as recently as a decade or two ago, I believe, as would its embodiment in the form of a major character. Indeed, the dialogue I've quoted seems to signal the end of a process in which, slowly and gradually, *algorithm* came to be an accepted, even familiar, part of the English-language vernacular. According to Blake Hallinan, "the term 'algorithm' has become a . . . popular topic of public conversation, with references to the word in newspapers having increased more than a hundred-fold" between 1998 and 2018.[3] Before then, *algorithm* was a little-known technical term for programmed decision-making rarely heard beyond the higher levels of the disciplines of mathematics, engineering, and computer science. But even that usage was a somewhat recent development. In 1976, Joseph Weizenbaum struggled to name this type of decision-making for his colleagues in computer science, then a fledgling field. He landed on "effective procedure, or 'algorithm,' as it is also called," as if to suggest *algorithm* hadn't quite broken through to become the definitive term.[4] Peering back another couple of decades we learn "algorithm was not, apparently, a commonly used mathematical term in America or Europe" until the mid-1950s, when the Russian mathematician Andrei Markov Jr. (1903–1979) published his influential book *The Theory of Algorithms* (Теория алгорифмов).[5] In seventy years the word has gone from periphery to mainstream, from obscurity to ubiquity, from incidental to Disney.

Ralph Breaks the Internet registers something else too: culture's continuing importance as a site of investment, identification, negotiation, action, judgment, and commercial interest. Little wonder that, in 2014, Merriam-Webster declared it "Word of the Year" based on usage and online lookups.[6] At the same time, the figure of Yesss suggests that important shifts have occurred with respect to how culture is practiced and judged, and by whom—or what. Today it operates within increasingly dense socio-technical systems, or arrangements of people and machines in which neither party is the exclusive powerholder. These systems are called upon, increasingly, to settle competing claims to attention, worthiness, authority, and more. Their existence raises my curiosity: How and why have we come to abrogate this type of decision-making to automated, computational processes?

Of course, computers do far more than determine which videos will go viral, or help folks to locate buried treasures on eBay. They assist us in discovering personal and professional connections, products and services, news and knowledge, taste and opinions, and much, much more. A generation ago, this work was performed primarily by human cultural intermediaries: that is, by critics, clerks, recruiters, matchmakers, scholars, teachers, editors, curators, compilers, and librarians whose job, in part, was to determine which ideas, artifacts, and human relations deserved to stand out, and which ones did not. Now, a digital army consisting of "automatic critics and censors" has, in the vein of Yesss, assumed a growing share of the responsibility.[7] These systems operate under the auspices of platforms such as Google, Facebook, Netflix, Amazon, Apple, Grindr, LinkedIn, Spotify, Pandora, TikTok, Tinder, Twitter, and Instagram. While it's customary to recognize them as major players in the technology industry, it may be that we need to think about them in another way too: as increasingly important arbiters of culture, and thus as a new face for the culture industry.[8]

Collectively, these developments speak to the emergence of *algorithmic culture*, a term I've adapted from Alexander R. Galloway.[9] I define algorithmic culture, provisionally, in two ways: first, as *the use of computational processes to sort, classify, and prioritize people, places, objects, and ideas*; and second, as *the repertoires of thought, conduct, expression, and feeling that flow from and back into those processes*. Apropos of part one of the definition, algorithmic culture drives the movies and TV shows "recommended for you" on Netflix, Hulu, and elsewhere.[10] It's what you experience when your Twitter feed tilts towards specific individuals and interests. And it has much to do with the content, character, packaging, and delivery of the news and information you encounter—or don't—online.

Apropos of part two of the definition, consider the following: Once, a Facebook friend posted about an urgent political action, tagging it as a "life event" even though it wasn't a personal milestone. As this individual explained in the post, identifying it as such would push it to the top of their friends' news feeds, since the platform's algorithms seemed to privilege updates about the turning points in users' lives—and that's exactly where I encountered it. The incident is about more than how to trick an algorithm into surfacing a post. It's significantly about how algorithms—including tacit knowledge of how they work and of whom and what they're designed to value—are coming to orient human behavior. Tarleton Gillespie describes such actions as "the mundane, strategic reorientation of practices many users undertake, toward a tool that they know could amplify their efforts"—although the effort may be more intuitive than calculated.[11]

This two-part definition of algorithmic culture underscores the role of computers, large data sets, and mathematics in establishing, maintaining, and transforming the frameworks by means of which human beings orient our judgments, actions, and dispositions toward one another and toward the surrounding world. It's not intended to suggest algorithms have completely rewritten the rules of culture, nor that they simply define human action. Both the name "algorithmic culture" and the story behind it are about the complex interplay between "people making history" and our doing so "under conditions not of our own making," to paraphrase Karl Marx.[12] My repeated use of the word "orientation" is strategic, moreover, paying homage to Sara Ahmed, who defines orientation neither as origin nor as determination but as a more open-ended process of "feeling at home" and of "making the strange familiar."[13] Orienting is precisely what algorithms are called upon to do, at least where culture is concerned. Using complex computational mathematics, they bring us into relationship with *this* aspect of the world over *that one* and normalize the relationship.

It's not an accident that the people who design algorithms often use the language of "fitting" to describe the effectiveness of these systems. The feeling is akin to the comfort of putting on clothes tailored to your body. Yet, as Ahmed observes, orientation is hardly a fait accompli. Algorithmic culture can be ill-fitting, premised as it frequently is on flawed or incomplete assumptions about the subjects in question.[14] This is particularly true where queer, nonconforming, or otherwise marginalized bodies are concerned. Sasha Costanza-Chock describes just such an experience in moving through airport security: "As a nonbinary trans* femme, I present a problem not easily resolved by the algorithm of the security protocol." By using the word *algorithm* here they're referring not only to the institutional guidelines that will be used to determine whether a male- or female-presenting security agent should perform the requisite pat-down, but also to the computational decision-making that flagged their groin as anomalous, and thus identified them as a potential security threat, in the first place.[15]

The point is to recognize that neither computation nor culture, alone, suffices to explain where the locus of action resides in our world today. The challenge is to come to grips with their relationship, and with how that relationship is "a moving target," as Gillespie puts it: "Because algorithms change . . . the user populations and activities they encounter change as well." The nature of their "entanglement" is the real crux of the story.[16] Moreover, if the "remaking of the world in the image of the computer started long before there were any electronic computers," as Weizenbaum has suggested, then it makes sense to think about algorithmic culture as something irreducible to contemporary digital technology, the internet, social media, or other instances of the here and now.[17]

Accordingly, while this book begins and ends in the present, along the way it's a primarily historical account of how the terms *algorithm* and *culture* came to be entangled before computing became personal, mobile, wearable, implantable, ubiquitous, or otherwise—that is, before computing became "everyware."[18] The book proceeds by adopting a key-words approach that's both inspired by and revises the work of the cultural studies scholar Raymond Williams: by traveling from Cambridge, England, to Cambridge, Massachusetts, by way of medieval Baghdad; and by hopscotching across historical periods spanning the ninth century CE to the year 1975. This journey is far from exhaustive. In traversing multiple linguistic, geographical, and historical contexts, my objective is to identify and animate some decisive episodes in the *early history of algorithmic culture*, which I'll then use as a basis for reflecting—albeit in brief—on the political, economic, cultural, and technological entailments of algorithmic culture today.

In the pages that follow, I argue that algorithmic culture began to coalesce in language decades and even centuries prior to its materialization in the technological wizardry of Silicon Valley. I further contend that awareness of the critical junctures at which algorithmic culture emerged will help us to make more informed choices about the connections between culture and computation, both now and in the future. This book urges readers to look beyond the technical, to consider the literal *terms and conditions* by means of which contemporary debates about algorithms, culture, and their relationship have been structured. It's my firm belief that we cannot fully grasp what *culture* means or how it operates today, or engage in an effective cultural politics, absent this historical perspective. Moreover, this book will show how a more inclusive digital realm is unachievable if left primarily in the hands of engineers, however well-intentioned they may be. The humanities have something important to say here, too: namely, that words are key stakes in contemporary algorithmic culture, and that deliberate efforts to interrogate language must precede, or at minimum accompany, the development of "ethical algorithms" and other—primarily technical—solutions to the problem of how best to achieve algorithmic justice today.[19]

CULTURE—WTF?

Anthropologists have long understood technology to be embedded in, or an artifact of, culture. Some even go as far as to see the relationship as primeval with respect to the origins of the species *Homo sapiens*.[20] The etymology of *culture* bears the traces of this relationship. The English-language word, deriving from the Latin terms *cultura* and *colere*, first emerged in an agrarian context, where it referred to tools and techniques of husbandry. (*Technology* and *technique* both derive from the Greek root *technē*, referring to craft and contrivance.) *Coulter*, a "subsidiary" form of the word *culture*, sometimes spelled as such and designating an instrument for tilling soil, conveys the link unequivocally.[21]

All true—and yet, it would be premature to suggest there's consensus around the claim that technology "belongs" to culture. Observers who hail from aesthetically inclined approaches have tended to find the relationship more contentious, owing to the belief that technology's imprint (typically, that of industrial-capitalist machinery) corrupts human activity. Such thinking is evident in the work of the nineteenth century poet-philosopher Matthew Arnold, post-World War II social theorists such as Max Horkheimer, Theodor Adorno, and Herbert Marcuse, and other observers who've followed in their wake.[22] According to Lewis Mumford, the view that industrially manufactured cultural goods were "beneath contempt" gained traction around the mid-nineteenth century. Writing in 1958, Gilbert Simondon put the matter this way: "Culture is unbalanced because it recognizes certain objects, like the aesthetic object, granting them citizenship in the world of significations, while it banishes other objects (in particular technical objects) into a structureless world of things that have no signification but only a use, a utility function."[23]

One of the assumptions of this book is that culture and technology share a contingent—not a fixed—relationship. Because their connection depends on prevailing geo-historical conditions, we shouldn't assume that technology is, intrinsically, a product of human social interaction, however obvious that position may seem. By the same token, we shouldn't make the mistake of assuming that contingency implies pure contingency, or relationships that are so fluid as to be forever changing. Technology may indeed come to rest in culture (or vice versa), even for protracted periods of time; but always, the settlement is temporary, implying other possibilities, other forms of relationship.[24]

Further complicating the matter is the tendency to assume that au courant definitions of words—even the words themselves—apply straightforwardly to the past. Does it make sense to speak of human cultures, for instance, in describing a time when no such referent even existed? Qadri Ismail puts the problem this way: "We take it for granted, have naturalized the 'fact' that we are cultured subjects; that this matrix inside and outside us enables, conditions, constrains our subjectivity, agency, if it doesn't constitute our very being." Ismail goes on to observe that, even as late as the mid-nineteenth century, most English-language speakers would have made no such identification, given the term's agrarian overtones. "This should blow your mind," he says. "If tweeting is your thing, prompt a 'wtf.'"[25]

Little wonder that Williams characterized *culture* as "one of the two or three most complicated words in the English language."[26] He, perhaps more than anyone, documented how this once-obscure term broadened its semantic horizons, becoming a mainstay of English and neighboring languages—and, I would venture to say, a touchstone for Western self-understanding.[27] In 1952, anthropologists A. L. Kroeber and Clyde Kluckhohn assayed 164 definitions of the word *culture*. Nine years later, Williams identified three "general categories" or rubrics under which to gather this sprawl of senses and meanings:

1. the "ideal" definition, referring to the systems of valuation by means of which groups establish hierarchies, and subsequently judge the worth, of people, places, and things;

2. the "documentary" definition, referring to the whole range of artifacts, both material and immaterial, produced by a group of people;

3. the "social" definition, referring to "a particular" or "whole way of life," i.e., to customs and patterns of signification that, in aggregate, provide an "ambiance" within which unfold the daily affairs of a collective.[28]

Today, if you search *The Oxford English Dictionary*, *The Macquarie Dictionary*, *Merriam-Webster*, or other leading reference works for the entry on *culture*, you're apt to find similar words and themes: "cultivation"; "rearing"; "intellectual and aesthetic training"; "shared attitudes, values, goals, and practices"; "ideas, customs, social behaviour, products, or way of life"; etc.

The senses and meanings Williams identified with respect to *culture* remain dominant points of orientation today, more than six decades later. As such, you could easily come away from an encounter with dictionaries and thesauri with the impression that, since the early 1960s, almost nothing has changed where the meaning of *culture* is concerned. Indeed, the lack of reference to computational tools and the role they now play in processing and even producing culture is striking. At the opposite extreme, Nobel Prize-winning author Mario Vargas Llosa has argued that culture's encounter with computation has been so acute as to precipitate culture's demise.[29] Scholarly accounts are more measured in terms of talking about "cyberculture" and "technoculture," but even then the tendency has been to treat digital technology as exceptional or supplementary to the work of culture, instead of as an ordinary part of its operation.[30] It's as if one of the most dynamic words in modern English has, in our own time, become sedentary and simple, or perhaps even that it's entered terminal decline.

Yet, anyone who connects on social media, streams audio or video, shops online, dabbles in AI-generated artwork, or uses a search engine seems to grasp, at least intuitively, that the semantics of *culture* are shifting, and consequently that we cannot take for granted what the word means, much less what it's referring to. Lawrence Grossberg explains the situation this way: "The ways in which [culture] matters—and hence, its effects—have changed in ways that we have not yet begun to contextualize or theorize."[31] Another assumption of this book is that algorithmic culture may be a palpable and prevalent—and arguably dominant—phenomenon today, but its emergence continues to be in process. Thus, you might register it on a practical level without fully recognizing the degree to which it's a "thing," or without being completely aware of its relationship to established definitions of *culture*.

The question driving this book is: How did culture, the semantic and conceptual sine qua non of the humanities, become practicable and intelligible in computational terms? The question forces our attention onto the late eighteenth century. There, *culture* begins slipping the semantic confines of husbandry and entering broader usage, slowly taking on the range of meanings encompassed by the three rubrics above. *Culture* then becomes a quintessentially modern term, carving out a conceptual space for human beings apart from nature on the one hand, and from technology on the other, subordinating both in the process.[32] By the nineteenth century, there emerges an overarching view of culture as "a court of human appeal," a view that aligns with the then-burgeoning phenomenological understanding of the lifeworld as an "autonomous realm" of human affairs. This view is part and parcel of the birth of humanism, and of the humanities, the latter of which thematized culture and adopted it as its organizing motif.[33]

My intention in summarizing this history isn't to sanctify the "traditional" (white, male, Western) humanities, nor is it to advance a normative definition of culture. Instead, I offer it as a benchmark from which to gauge how far the needle has moved over the last century or so. Culture remains a court of human appeal, to be sure. This book needed to pass muster with an editor, academic referees, an editorial board, and a marketing department before finding its way into your hands— and hopefully you, the reader, will give it a favorable reception. At the risk of stating the obvious, cultural goods continue to address people, and they remain subject to human judgment. Maybe less obvious, however, are the ways culture addresses another audience—an audience consisting of machine-based, algorithmically driven systems often working behind the scenes of what, in *The Late Age of Print*, I called the "back office of mass culture."[34] There, I studied the product codes appearing on books and other types of consumer goods: sibylline features, hidden in plain sight, whose purpose is to facilitate inventory tracking and control. Literary historians tend to describe these elements as the "paratextual" parts of books.[35] Yet, it occurs to me that, in contrast to covers, title and copyright pages, tables of contents, and indices, ISBNs and barcodes are largely unintended for, and mostly unintelligible to, human readers. Twisting anthropologist Edward T. Hall's turn-of-phrase, there's now a whole "hidden dimension" of culture that both exceeds and complements human perception and sense-making.[36] Culture remains a court of human appeal, but today we must reckon with the genesis and implications of its having become a court of algorithmic appeal as well.[37]

WHY "ALGORITHMIC CULTURE?"

I first grasped the idea of algorithmic culture during an incident that occurred over Easter weekend 2009. Suddenly, 57,000 books, most of them LGBTQIA+ -themed, vanished from the Amazon product catalog after a technician reportedly altered the value of a single database attribute—"adult"—from false to true. The change spread quickly through the retailer's systems, de-listing any books that had been tagged with the corresponding metadata. Accusations of homophobia soon began to fly on social media, the hashtag #AmazonFail surpassing even the holiday on Twitter's trending topics list. But this wasn't homophobia, insisted Amazon—just an innocent slip-up by a human being whose actions were amplified by the affordances of a technical system. Maybe so, observed the late Larry Kramer, author and co-founder of ACT-UP. But, he added, "We have to now keep a more diligent eye on Amazon and how they handle the world's cultural heritage."[38]

Kramer saw past Amazon's identity as both a retailer and technology firm. In tending "the world's cultural heritage," Amazon performs curatorial work comparable to that of a museum. And as with any such cultural institution, there is a politics to whose work is showcased, whose is warehoused, and whose gets excluded from the collection entirely.[39] Responsibility for the selection process doesn't lie solely with Amazon (the company), nor, strictly speaking, with the technicians in its employ. As Kramer pointed out, the *how*—or better yet, the *what*—of the decision-making is at least as important as the *who*. Amazon may not have made a purposive choice in eliminating LGBTQIA+ -themed books from its catalog, yet those choices became manifest, the values they embodied real, due in part to the "automatic critics and censors"—the algorithms—mentioned earlier.

#AmazonFail is but one episode in a growing list of examples of "algorithmic bias," in which computational decision-making reproduces, whether by default or by design, long-standing patterns of oppression, leaving existing distributions of social, economic, political, and cultural power largely untouched. With #AmazonFail, the algorithms effectively closeted the books in question, re-instantiating, albeit temporarily, norms of invisibility, exclusion, and isolation against which LGBTQIA+ communities have long been struggling. Similarly, Safiya Noble has shown how search engines like Google have traded in racist and sexist stereotypes—outputting mugshots in searches for "Black teenagers," for instance, in contrast to the pristine stock photos appearing in searches for white teens. And in 2011, Mike Ananny discovered Google's Android app store was algorithmically cross-promoting sex-offender tracking apps with Grindr, a popular gay/bi dating app. In doing so, he argued, the automated system replicated the problematic association of gay men and pedophilia.[40]

Some of these biases have begun to be addressed, thanks in part to the advocacy of organizations such as the Algorithmic Justice League, and to the critical interventions of leading scholars and journalists.[41] Yet, as Noble, Ananny, Costanza-Chock, Ruha Benjamin, Simone Browne, Taina Bucher, John Cheney-Lippold, Wendy Hui Kyong Chun, Kate Crawford, Virginia Eubanks, Oscar Gandy, Lisa Nakamura, Cathy O'Neil, Siva Vaidhyanathan, Jacqueline Wernimont, and numerous other writers have shown, systemic bias, discrimination, inequity, and unfairness persist in many areas in which algorithms hold sway— from policing to facial recognition, threat assessment, finance, insurance, employment, social services, navigation, healthcare, human connection, the curation of news and information, and more.[42] These might seem like sinister exceptions to the apparently innocuous, often helpful, algorithmically generated product recommendations and streaming suggestions people rely on every day. In reality, they're two sides of the same coin. As James Gleick observes of information systems generally: "It is all one problem." More specifically, algorithmic culture is built on behavioral models that, as O'Neil puts it, "encode human prejudice, misunderstanding, and bias into the software systems that increasingly manage our lives." Wendy Hui Kyong Chun has taken the argument further, noting how the mathematics of correlation, prevalent in algorithmic decision-making, abides by a logic in which past patterns are made to stretch far into the future. Troublingly, this logic has its origins in eugenics: "Correlation's eugenicist history matters, not because it predisposes all uses of correlation towards eugenics, but rather because when correlation works, it does so by making the present and future coincide with a highly curated past."[43] Practically no area, it seems, is exempt. Algorithmic bias is (to invoke an overused phrase) a feature, not a bug.

"Algorithmic bias" isn't the only name observers have used to describe this condition.[44] Other names include "machine bias" and O'Neil's memorable phrase "weapons of math destruction." I value them because they center dominant technological forms unambiguously with respect to patterns of privilege, power, and difference. Mark Andrejevic speaks in more general terms of "automated media" and "automated culture," stressing how algorithmic systems increasingly "pre-empt agency, spontaneity, and risk" in their application to all manner of human affairs.[45] Both of Andrejevic's terms speak to the degree to which such systems are designed to function quasi-independently, absenting human custodians whenever feasible from the governance of our lives. Vaidhyanathan's "Googlization of everything" performs similar work, signaling not only Google's (now Alphabet's) extraordinary technological footprint, but also the degree to which tech companies in general seek to extend algorithmic rationalities into the deepest recesses of daily life.[46]

Collectively, these terms signal how the entanglement of algorithms and cultural life has become the norm over the last quarter century or so and how, in turn, observers have been searching for the most suitable name for this relationship. Every one of the preceding terms has yielded compelling insights into "how algorithms shape our world,"[47] and for that reason alone we should hold onto them.

So why *algorithmic culture*? In contrast to "algorithmic bias," "machine bias," and "weapons of math destruction," "algorithmic culture" suggests that quantitative reasoning and associated technologies are best understood within a framework that includes but also exceeds harm, one that positions the full range of artifacts, values, customs, and affects present in human societies on an equal footing with algorithms. Andrejevic's "automated media" and "automated culture" probably come closest to naming the phenomenon I'm exploring throughout this book. I prefer "algorithmic culture," however, given the accent on mathematical/computational processes and their juxtaposition with areas of life that have traditionally fallen within the purview of the humanities. The emphasis on automatism also potentially plays into the hands of neo-behaviorists who wish to claim that "we" (never they) are now programmed beings unable to resist the preponderance of algorithmic nudges presented to us throughout the day by Big Tech.[48] Similarly, while "the Googlization of everything" epitomizes the seemingly unshakable presence of leading tech firms in everyday life, the phrase lends itself—despite Vaidhyanathan's admonitions to the contrary—to attributing the major problems of our times to capitalism, generally, corporate power, more specifically, or even to a single corporation, as if economics were the irreducible, determining force behind all aspects of social life.[49]

A final note about naming: Robert Seyfert and Jonathan Roberge have proposed using the plural "algorithmic cultures," instead of the singular.[50] The point is well-taken: always, algorithmic culture is multiply articulated. My preference for the singular form is strictly a function of my interest in defining the category in general. Like Williams, that is, I'm searching for a rubric under which to gather a diverse range of practices, experiences, and expressions of algorithmic culture.

TOGETHER AGAIN, FOR THE FIRST TIME

The story of algorithmic culture isn't only about breakthrough digital products and services, nor is it just about charismatic figures from the technology industry and the grand ideas that seem to spring forth from their heads. It isn't just about Big Tech, nor is it only about homophily, filter bubbles, and the amplification of fake news.[51] Prominent though these landmarks may be, there's a more modest story to be told about how people beyond the tech world have used—and misused—words in attempting to confront changes and challenges in their daily lives.

Beyond Williams's career-long inquiry into the word *culture*, one of the works that's significantly inspired the writing of this book is Fred Turner's *The Democratic Surround.*[52] Turner places culture and technology front-and-center of a narrative about efforts to promote democratic character, both in the United States and around the world, in the aftermath of the Second World War. Among the many figures he focuses on is anthropologist Margaret Mead (1901–1978), one of Franz Boas's (1858–1942) students and, indeed, the public face of anthropology in the United States in the mid-twentieth century. Turner examines how Mead championed the cause of immersive media experiences whose purpose was to inculcate choice, individualism, participation, and other democratic values as a bulwark against authoritarianism. Significantly, her work operationalized a definition of culture in which one's personality was understood "to literally embody the symbolic order" of the social group to which one primarily belonged.[53] But the process evidently worked in reverse, too: give people the resources they need to comport themselves freely, Mead believed, and they'll disrupt a pattern that would otherwise engender a culture of conformity and its political counterpart, fascism.

The Democratic Surround helps us to see how a particular definition of culture, enacted as quasi-official government policy, played a significant role in popularizing interactive media in the 1950s and 1960s. It also provides the backstory for Turner's earlier book *From Counterculture to Cyberculture*, which explored how nonconformists like Stewart Brand, editor of *The Whole Earth Catalog*, picked up on and extended this relationship to media. According to Turner, Brand and company sought not only to popularize but to humanize computers, which up until then had been imagined largely as dehumanizing instruments of the state.[54] In this, I have no truck with Turner's account. My concern lies instead with how he treats the category, culture: as a constant, not a variable. Consider this passage, where Turner discusses Mead's involvement in the Macy Conferences on the future of social science: "The Macy Conferences . . . focused on developing new models of individual human agency in terms that were entirely consonant with theories of the democratic personality and with the theories of culture and personality that underlay them."[55] It's almost as if the word *culture* escaped unchanged from the encounter with multimedia surrounds and subsequent digital tools.

However much a consensus may have gathered around culture and personality, it didn't comprise the sum total of all thinking about culture in the United States, either before or after the war. To wit: the English "culture and society" tradition had established a foothold in North America by at least the 1880s, when the North American lecture tour of Matthew Arnold drew tens-of-thousands of listeners.[56] In the 1950s and 1960s, Williams's *Culture and Society* and *Long Revolution* received attention from major academic journals and news outlets in the United States ranging from *Political Science Quarterly* to the *New York Times*, cementing his role as one of the leading international voices on the subject of culture in the postwar period.[57] This is to say nothing of his outsize influence on the interdisciplinary field of cultural studies, which flourished in the United States and globally in the 1980s, 1990s, and beyond.

It's worth mentioning that while Williams was sympathetic to aspects of the culture and personality tradition, he harbored grave misgivings about the degree to which it assimilated the individual to culture, leaving little room for autonomy, improvisation, and happenstance. In short, it traded too briskly in abstractions. "Even in a very simple society," wrote Williams, "it is hardly ever one single 'social character' or 'culture pattern' that the individual encounters." The multiplicity of, and contradictions among, patterns were thus of paramount concern. According to Williams, they comprised a significant part of the experiential matrix out of which emerged new words, ideas, artifacts, affects, and more.[58]

The critique raises difficult questions. Among them: What to make of an historical account that not only assays but implicitly adopts a circumscribed view of culture? Indeed, the narrative trajectory leading from *Democratic Surround* to *From Counterculture to Cyberculture* suggests that Mead's thinking, however flawed, was still successfully operationalized: create enough antiauthoritarian media experiences, and, a few decades later, you end up with a free-wheeling counterculture unafraid to dabble in high tech.[59] Now, the issue isn't whether Turner's account is accurate. The work is elegantly crafted and impeccably documented. Rather, what's at stake are the broader experiential conditions I just mentioned, and where the existing research fits in with them. Later in this book, I'll turn to the language of "atmospheres" to conceptualize diffuse forms of connection, and as a stepping-stone for illustrating how the blurring of the boundaries between culture and computation wasn't strictly a countercultural endeavor. For now, suffice it to say that the story of algorithmic culture doesn't encompass the countercultural history of computing as much as it passes through and permeates it.

The same is true for what's sometimes known as "humanities computing" or, more conventionally now, the "digital humanities" (DH). Typically, DH traces its origins to the work of Father Roberto Busa S. J.,[60] who in 1946 began a doctoral thesis on the concept of presence in the writings of Thomas Aquinas. It was painstaking work. A sustained, close reading of Aquinas's oeuvre led Busa to realize presence was more pervasive in the author's work than its appearance as either *praesens* or *praese*, the principal forms of the word in Latin. Busa thus shifted gears and began transcribing each passage in which there appeared the word *in* on a 3x5-inch index card, having observed that Aquinas's "doctrine of presence is linked with" this seemingly innocuous preposition (e.g., ". . . in the presence . . ."). Sorting the cards—10,000 in all—reminded him of "grand games of solitaire" given the constant reshuffling of the columns he'd carefully arrayed across his workspace.[61] In retrospect it's clear Father Busa had created something like a sprawling, physical spreadsheet, or perhaps even a relational database. The dissertation subsequently inspired him to embark on a decades-long project in which he'd create a concordance of all the words appearing in Aquinas's writings and, later, a host of other religious and philosophical texts. But the magnitude of the Aquinas project quickly became apparent to Busa. He partnered with IBM in 1949, who provided him not only with a brigade of human assistants but also with much-needed electro-mechanical aids (a punch-card printer and reader, specifically), the corpus ultimately exceeding 10,000,000 words. Later he'd turn to faster, fully electronic digital computers to expedite the coding and processing.[62]

Despite the work, Father Busa rejected the title of "pioneer of the computers in the humanities," having discovered comparable initiatives already proposed in law and literature after he'd started in on the Aquinas project.[63] Furthermore, Busa seems to have been unaware of Russian mathematician Andrei Markov Sr.'s (1856–1922) study of vowel-consonant patterns in Alexander Pushkin's poetical novel *Eugene Onegin*, which Markov presented to the Imperial Academy of Sciences in St. Petersburg in January 1913. Markov's handcrafted tables, consisting of 200, ten-by-ten arrays he'd culled from the first 20,000 letters of the text, are reminiscent of Father Busa's "grand games of solitaire"; David Link describes them as "Markov's mathematical crosswords."[64] Three decades later, Markov's innovative conception of probability chains, deriving from the Pushkin study, would prove foundational for Claude Shannon's mathematical theory of communication and, thus, for information theory.[65] The Russian mathematician's punctilious exercise in literary decomposition suggests another plausible point of departure for DH, or, better, a more temporally and geographically dispersed view of the emergence of the field than is customary. As Busa himself observed in 1980: "Isn't it true that all new ideas arise out of *milieu* when ripe, rather than from any one individual?"[66]

Busa's comment underscores the importance of attending to the complex conditions under which computation and culture—what I am calling algorithmic culture—converged on one another, rather than attempting to establish a singular point of origin. Regardless of how it's conceived, Busa's fifty-six-volume *Index Thomisticus* was undoubtedly a prototype for what David M. Berry has termed the "computational turn" in the humanities, a move that came to define DH throughout much of the 1990s and early 2000s. The scholarship of that period consisted primarily of "the application of the computer to the disciplines of the humanities" (DH v1.0), which in turn provoked a more fundamental rethinking of their theories, methods, epistemologies, objects of study, boundaries, and systems of scholarly communication (DH v2.0).[67] Berry contends that DH has since entered a new phase (v3.0), wherein researchers must now come to terms with the degree to which the convergence of computation and culture has been achieved and how, then, the latter is becoming inconceivable absent the former. That is, we can no longer naively apply computers to culture, as if the one were exogenous to the other. Channeling Lev Manovich, Berry says the key question now confronting DH is: "What is culture after it has been 'softwarized'?"[68]

It's a compelling question, one that presses DH scholars to dive deeper into the intricacies of code, to explore the nature of computationality, and, as my colleague Lori Emerson has observed, to think with and about the physical devices that mediate culture, "softwarized" or otherwise.[69] It's also profoundly forward-looking. If the answers prove as valuable as the question, then surely there's a bright future ahead for DH 3.0. Yet, it seems to me there's a complementary question DH scholars ought to be asking, one that can and should provoke a more sustained interrogation of the field's own origins and, hopefully, a broader recognition of the people, places, artifacts, systems of thought, and orientations constitutive of DH. The question is a variation of the one I mentioned earlier was driving this book: What needed to happen to culture (the idea, the word) for it to be amenable to being "softwarized?" Again, there's no necessary reason why this fusion should have occurred in the late twentieth century, particularly when some of the key thinking had suggested the cold, calculating world of technology was fundamentally incommensurable with the buzz and the bloom of culture. The challenge is to answer this question in such a way as to avoid relying on "supersigns" (e.g., *capitalism*) that explain away the problem more than they manage to explain it.[70]

STRANGER THAN FICTION

Lawrence Grossberg opens *Caught in the Crossfire: Kids, Politics, and America's Future* with a pithy epigraph from Mark Twain: "Why shouldn't truth be stranger than fiction? Fiction, after all, has to make sense."[71] Although the quotation passes unremarked, it's safe to say that it epitomizes Grossberg's approach to cultural studies, as well as my own, here. Cultural studies is an intellectual endeavor that eschews theoretical, methodological, and political "guarantees" in favor of a more malleable approach to matters of historical and contemporary concern.[72] It assumes that the world doesn't uniformly abide by the conventions of narrative storytelling or render itself easily in the medium of writing, and this complexity is precisely what cultural studies endeavors to let in. It does so by relying minimally on the aforementioned supersigns, whose tendency is to arrest the world, and by turning instead to more elastic frames such as "contingency," "orientations," and the like. Cultural studies seeks ways of interfacing with objects of study that will allow them to stretch out, spill over, contract, twist, turn, flex, fold, extend, retract, tighten up, and unwind again. The approach shares much in common with the reactions against representationalism in painting (e.g., abstract expressionism, cubism, surrealism, etc.), which, through painting, sought to challenge the notion that you could straight-forwardly depict reality on canvas.

Algorithmic Culture Before the Internet draws inspiration from science and technology studies, history of science, media stud-ies, digital humanities, anthropology, communication, and information science. The work may be interdisciplinary, but my primary scholarly orientation is cultural studies. This has as much to do with my putting the history, meaning, and politics of the word *culture* front and center as it does with the broader approach, which is more constitutive than conventionally nar-rative, and more episodic than historically comprehensive. Some-times, the book follows well-known figures and clearly defined socio-semantic pathways. At other times, the connections between the chapters, and among the examples within each chapter, are more inferential. *Algorithmic Culture Before the Inter-net* isn't an experiment in avant-garde writing, but I do take seriously the conceptual and stylistic challenges of "grasping . . . real relations" in their complexity, rather than imposing textbook understandings on them.[73] Thus, my effort to contextualize algo-rithmic culture requires a narrative style that aligns with these values. One term that I've invoked thus far, "history," is close but insufficient given the tendency of historical accounts to slide into historicism. Dipesh Chakrabarty defines the latter as "a mode of thinking about history in which one assumed that any object under investigation retained a unity of conception throughout its existence and attained full expression through a process of development in secular, historical time."[74] In contrast, the style that I employ throughout this book foregrounds biographical details, instances of lexical "misuse," and historical ephemera, as

well as the protracted, dispersed, and often unintentional processes of their assembly into a "teeth gritting harmony" called
algorithmic culture.[75]

Williams's *Culture and Society: 1780–1950* is perhaps closest to
the approach that I'm following here. Consider Stuart Hall's
description of the book: "*Culture and Society*—in one and the
same movement—constituted a tradition (*the* 'culture-and-
society' tradition), defined its 'unity' (not in terms of common
positions but in its characteristic concerns and the idiom of its
inquiry), itself made a distinctive modern contribution to it—
and wrote its epitaph."[76] In other words, in gathering together
an eclectic group of eighteenth, nineteenth, and early-twentieth
century poets, novelists, critics, polymaths, and theoreticians
from Britain, *Culture and Society* created a syllabus where previously there was none. The book, however, didn't purport to
represent a coherent school of thought. The culture and society
"tradition" was connected neither by a commonality of perspective nor by a shared institutional location, but by a subterranean
network of watchwords including *democracy, industry, art, class,*
and, most importantly, *culture.* These words thematized the
social, political, economic, and technological realignments taking place with respect to England's rapid industrialization, Williams observed, providing grist for Edmund Burke, Matthew
Arnold, William Morris, T. S. Eliot, F. R. Leavis, George
Orwell, and other leading writers of the period who sought to
take stock, and maybe steer the course, of the changes transpir-
ing all around them.[77] Culture, they argued, should be the means
to that end. And while they never arrived at a consensus definition of the word, the definitions they did offer tended to privilege implicitly gendered and racialized assumptions about quality and tradition, and to position culture as the antithesis to the
emerging "mass" society.

The culture and society "tradition" is typically remembered as conservative, even though the roster of writers also included Marxists, socialists, social reformers, utilitarians, liberals, and romantics.[78] Whatever the case, the purpose of *Culture and Society* wasn't to hold this tradition aloft, but to bring it back down to earth. "It is indeed the peculiar audacity of the book that it builds on conservative argument rather than belittling it," Raphael Samuel states, "taking on reactionary social thinkers, but turning their perception to radical and democratic ends."[79] Such is the case with the present book, which, though hardly exhaustive, draws together scattered elements of an algorithmic culture "tradition," or "assemblage."[80] In doing so, my objective is to contextualize its "characteristic concerns and idiom of inquiry" and, where needed, to rearticulate elements that reinforce the status quo to more progressive ends. *Algorithmic Culture Before the Internet* is significantly historical, moreover, but like *Culture and Society*, history isn't the ultimate end. "Our object," Williams observed in 1958, "was to enquire into and where possible reinterpret this tradition which the word 'culture' describes in terms of the experience of our own generation."[81] Likewise, this book is ultimately more about what we might *want* from history moving forward than it is *about* history per se.[82]

Now, I'm aware of the contradiction of having just criticized textbook examples, only then to pay homage to Williams. I see his oeuvre not as a model but as a heuristic with which to ask questions about the historicity of *culture* and to experiment with ways of answering them. Williams's work would hardly be reproducible today, anyway. Gary Hall once mused about how different cultural studies' foundational works would be, had they been produced in a context in which digital technologies prevailed over paper. "What if Richard Hoggart," founder of the

Birmingham Centre for Contemporary Cultural Studies, "had had e-mail?" Hall pondered.[83] The question affirms Friedrich Kittler's more general point about the degree to which our historical "situation" depends on media. Indeed, the culture and society tradition was legible to Williams, but also something of an enigma, because he caught the tail end of the discourse network—the characteristic media, institutions, and infrastructure—that had produced it.[84] He then felt compelled to bury it, as it were, owing to the pressures electronic media and new computational tools were, by mid-century, beginning to exert on the traditional humanities.

This isn't to suggest a clean break, however; the culture and society tradition doesn't end once algorithmic culture starts to emerge in earnest. It's better to imagine a metamorphosis in which aspects of the former persist, but within an altered situation or context. Algorithmic culture is an opportunity for cutting new pathways through culture and society—for rediscovering neglected sources and for accenting familiar ones differently. Determining "the best which has been thought and said" is precisely what Google's algorithms do billions of time each day, for example, however much Matthew Arnold—whose definition of culture this is—would have scoffed at the company's means and ends.[85] But algorithmic culture isn't only about running over the same old ground. It also presents opportunities for pushing beyond the parameters of culture and society by following different figures, taking in their experiences, and listening for instances in which language expands in relationship to the turbulence of existence.

The pages that follow constitute an effort to piece together a story about algorithmic culture and its conditions of possibility. One thing to point out is that this isn't a technical history, nor a history of technicians. As Bruno Latour has observed, the history and sociology of science has tended to be written as if it were reducible to the history and sociology of scientists—figures who, typically, made their mark in laboratory or clinical settings.[86] Even more traditionally, the focus has been on major technological breakthroughs. Though people and their experiences are an ostensible focus of the book, and while this book is, on some level, a history of science and technology, the figures discussed here hail from such places as literature and literary studies; sociology and anthropology; comparative philology; and, in one case, mathematics—although, as we'll see, that category is retroactively imposed. The goal is to explore what they've had to say, but to do so in a worldly way that exceeds the professional setting. The idiom of algorithmic culture is equally the object of concern. This book is about the relationship of language and experience, and it seeks to explore, historically and on a human scale, how it ever made sense to bring culture and computation together. And for that reason the primary narrative ends right around 1975, on the cusp of the explosion in personal computing that would, within a decade or two, secure the hegemony of Silicon Valley and prompt the materialization of algorithmic culture.

Nevertheless, you'll see that a contemporary instance of, or controversy pertaining to, algorithmic culture frames each of the subsequent chapters. The purpose of including this material is threefold. First, the examples are meant to further acquaint you with the subject matter, at least as it exists in the present day. Second, my hope is that the examples will help you to find your bearings amidst the historical material, where the familiar landmarks of algorithmic culture will mostly slip away. To that end, I've chosen each of the frames strategically—significantly, based on its resonance with the major themes of the chapter to which it corresponds. Finally, in accumulating across the book, the examples are there to demonstrate the breadth of algorithmic culture and, by extension, to further justify the claim that it's a "thing."

Chapter 1 reflects on the concept Williams developed to explore the relationship between language, experience, and social change, which is also the conceptual touchstone of this book: "keywords." Here, I endeavor to move beyond colloquial understandings and scholarly implementations of the term, which tend to reduce it to a signifier for important or emblematic words. Keywords are that, but they're also so much more. By indexing sometimes subtle shifts of sense and meaning, they register not only changes in a language but also incipient shifts in our shared conditions of existence. As I demonstrate in chapter 1, Williams engaged extensively in keywords research, including in *Culture and Society*, but only briefly did he reflect on the concept of keywords itself, and rarely, if ever, did he consider the complex methodological entailments of performing this type of work across time, setting, and media. A major purpose of the chapter, then, is to start addressing those gaps by spending time with "keywords" and, indeed, subjecting Williams's concept to something resembling a keyword analysis of its own. The result is a revision to that project whose new name, "key-words," simultaneously honors Williams's theoretical legacy and confronts its abiding limitations.

Although chapters 2, 3, and 4 focus primarily on the ontogenesis of algorithmic culture, theory and method remain significant concerns throughout. For Williams, instances of keywords (his usage) manifested primarily in dictionaries, literary artifacts, and the published writings of white males residing in Northern Europe, typically England. This book would have been impossible to write had I abided by such a circumscribed methodology. The word *algorithm*, the focus of chapter 2, has a long and complex history that traverses South, Central, and West Asia, a history in which handwritten manuscripts and oral communication are decisive. Chapter 3 focuses on the word *culture* in Britain but does so by dwelling primarily on anecdotes, an evidentiary form often blasted by critics for being too personal and, thus, antithetical to the cause of "rigorous" scholarship. Chapter 4, on *algorithmic culture*, examines institutional case files, private letters, and other types of documents that typically reside out of view of the public eye. Because I'm engaging with objects, settings, words, and identities that have been subordinate—even illegible—to the project of keywords, each of these chapters includes a brief methodological reflection, whose purpose is to extend and complicate some of the discussion appearing in chapter 1.

Empirically, chapter 2 focuses on procedural mathematical computation, instanced, as noted above, by the word *algorithm*. The etymology of *algorithm* leads almost unfailingly to Moḥammed ibn-Mūsā al-Khwārizmī, a polymath who lived and worked in Baghdad in the ninth century CE, whose surname is the purported source of the word.[87] Instead of accepting this account, which posits an irreducible point of origin for *algorithm*, I explore the relations of power and authority that produced it. The process begins by digging deeper into al-Khwārizmī's life and, more specifically, into the history of conquest, coloniality, and ethnic and religious persecution that may have landed him in Baghdad. Next, I follow al-Khwārizmī's treatises on algebra and the Indo-Arabic number system as they wound their way west into Europe and eventually to Britain, where, in the nineteenth century, they were taken up by Orientalist scholars who produced the first English-language translations of al-Khwārizmī's work. The objective is to show how the standard al-Khwārizmī "story" was forged under conditions of British colonialism and, more specifically, an Orientalist desire to imagine al-Khwārizmī's Asia as Europe's proto-logical past. Moreover, I argue that al-Khwārizmī's translators mischaracterized the texts in regarding them strictly as elementary mathematical treatises. The chapter concludes with a close reading of al-Khwārizmī's *Algebra*, highlighting the text's intricate mapping of relations of kith and kin under conditions of slavery, in addition to some nascent affinities between culture and computation.

The content of chapter 3 may be the most familiar to readers who are acquainted with Williams. The cast includes two of the more frustrating characters from his work on culture and society: Matthew Arnold and Frank Raymond (F. R.) Leavis. They are figures who—rightly, to some degree—are accused of advancing an elite, and ultimately conservative, view of culture, one that's deeply at odds with industrial modernity and, by extension, algorithmic culture. This chapter offers a different take on these figures. Inasmuch as Williams talked about the relationship of language and experience, he gave scant attention in his writings on keywords to the actual—or, for lack of a better way of putting it, the biographical—conditions under which *culture*'s senses and meanings stretched out. Thus, I linger not only on the published works of Arnold and Leavis but also, significantly, on anecdotes about their lives, especially Leavis's, in an effort to tell a story that doesn't simply reinforce the conclusion that they were prigs who bemoaned modern technology. Despite the assimilation of their writings on culture to patrician interests, both figures were, in their day, outsiders who observed the violent effects of state power, and in Leavis's case suffered them bodily. And those experiences in turn led them to define *culture* as a flexible and critical resource for governing human relations peaceably. Significantly, Leavis's definition also emerged out of a sensual connection to technical artifacts, not in spite of them. Thus, the story I tell is not about high culture evangelism but about how, even among so-called aesthetes, the definition of *culture* comes to share a positive association with the government of human affairs, an association mediated by complex—even technical—processes of discernment and judgment.

Having established these connections, chapter 4 explores the conditions under which they came together to produce, in incipient form, the characteristic idiom of algorithmic culture. The focus here is on the third quarter of the twentieth century, at the height of the Cold War and in the throes of the hunt for clandestine communists in the United States. The setting for the chapter is Harvard University. There, key figures associated with the university's Russian Research Center and the Department of Social Relations were scrutinized by government intelligence agencies owing to fears they'd succumbed to communist influence, or else that they were poised to do so. Even their families were implicated. For Clyde Kluckhohn and Helen and Talcott Parsons, the loyalty investigations underscored how there was potentially no limit to state-sponsored surveillance and coercion, even in the United States, and that totalitarianism remained a palpable threat despite the recent defeat of the Axis powers in the Second World War. They offered a programmatic response in the form of the graduate curriculum in "social relations," which sought a "common language" for the social sciences and installed *culture* at its center. Hundreds of graduate students, many of whom would go on to become the leading voices in their fields, learned that *culture* referred not only to pattern and meaning but to an array of informal techniques for governing human affairs. In principle it was a way of executing state functions, but without the state's propensity for physical and spiritual violence. The anthropologist Clifford Geertz, an alumnus of the

Department of Social Relations, would later add symbol processing to this political theory of culture, thus analogizing culture to computer software and to the structured decision-making characteristic of computer algorithms.

The framing examples mentioned earlier all build toward the epilogue, which recenters the narrative in the present day. I open by reflecting on the Cambridge Analytica affair of 2018, in which algorithms and misappropriated data were purported to have swayed the outcomes of the UK "Brexit" vote and the United States presidential election, both having occurred in 2016. The goal isn't to accept these claims at face value, but to use the scandal as an occasion for reflecting on the idiom of algorithmic culture, past and present, and for tracing its movements and articulations from the Global South to the Global North. Indeed, the definition of culture was—and remains—a critical stake to be won or lost with respect to the Cambridge Analytica scandal. The broader objective is to think through what an historically driven key-words approach might offer in terms of understanding the relationship between culture, technology, and politics today. We're not prisoners of language, I contend, but neither are we alone in history. Like the statues installed in public squares, words like *algorithm* and *culture* are monuments freighted with historical ambivalence. Listening closely to their terms and conditions is a necessary first step in reclaiming definitional agency, I argue, and in building a more just and inclusive algorithmic culture.

1

KEY-WORDS

Language isn't a zero-sum game, except when it is. That much became apparent in early 2015, when a group of authors and word-watchers wrote to Oxford University Press (OUP) in protest. It had all started around 2003, when OUP began dropping existing terms from the *Oxford Junior Dictionary* to make way for words it deemed more relevant to seven-year-olds coming of age in the new millennium. *Sin* was out, and so were other terms associated with Christianity including *abbey, disciple, nunnery*, and *vicar*. Also gone were words pertaining to the British monarchy and English imperialism including *coronation, duke, duchess, emperor*, and *empire*. But the largest swath of excised words—at least 117 of them—referred to plants, animals, and environments. Between 2003 and 2012, the *Oxford Junior Dictionary* bid farewell to *acorn, adder, apricot, beaver, bramble, bray, brook, buttercup, cauliflower, crocus, fungus, goldfish, heather, lark, magpie, nectarine, pasture, tulip, starling, sycamore, weasel, willow, wren*, and many others. Even *bacon* got the cut. They were replaced with words like *bilingual, biodegradable, bungee jumping, cope, dyslexic, emotion*, and *endangered*. But these weren't the words that troubled the protestors. They were disturbed by the addition of *analogue, attachment, blog, broadband, chatroom, cut and paste, database, email, export, MP3 player, voicemail,* and other technology terms "associated with the indoor lives of modern childhood," as one of the protestors put it.[1]

In contrast to the standard edition of the *Oxford English Dictionary,* which boasts more than a quarter-million entries spanning twenty physical volumes, the junior edition includes less than 10,000 words encased in a compact volume amenable to small hands. Because space is a premium, OUP is forced to make difficult choices about whether to include new words, which ones to include, and what to do with the existing entries. And OUP has defended those choices, suggesting that at least some of the changes reflect a more multicultural Britain, and thus the need to decenter the white, Anglican, English experience. The publisher has been less forthcoming about the inclusion of terms associated with contemporary digital technology, however, and about the decision to excise so many terms referring to plants, animals, the countryside, etc. The selection had something to do with word frequency as reflected in OUP's corpus of texts, and with the impression that the population of Britain is no longer as rural as it once was.[2] Whatever the case, it would be easy to dismiss the controversy: this is a dictionary intended for seven-year-olds, and it's not like they won't eventually graduate to reference matter containing both *buttercup* and *broadband.* But that's not the point. The point is to appreciate how the unique constraints of the *Oxford Junior Dictionary* compel choices about which words matter and how, in doing so, they might tell us something about the conditions under which certain words come to assume priority over others.

Words may be the obvious stake in this controversy, but the larger issue concerns the politics of inclusion and representation, and also then the relationship between history, experience, and "relevance" as determined, significantly, by the algorithms used to parse the Oxford children's corpus. I'm not suggesting those algorithms are predisposed to favoring tech terms. It seems reasonably clear, however, that a purportedly "objective" system tends to surface and indeed helps to sanctify dominant patterns of usage. It thus provides cover for not stopping to ask: Why have those patterns become dominant in the first place?[3]

The controversy surrounding the *Oxford Junior Dictionary* is a study in what can happen when people and machines reckon inadequately with the complex temporality of words. The British Empire may be a residual point of reference, lexically speaking, but the aftereffects of empire and settler colonialism are deeply felt to this day. All those recently toppled monuments have fallen for a reason. And yet, somehow, *empire* is less palpable—less present—than *email*? Once again, we find ourselves in the gap between language and experience, which was a starting point for this book. There, I suggested that culture may be operating in new ways, or perhaps in older ways that have been operationalized anew, and yet the reference matter that's supposed to account for these shifts has yet to catch up with the new algorithmic reality. The lesson here is that the task of defining words like *algorithm* and *culture*, or of writing the story of language more broadly, isn't the sacred duty of lexicographers and their kin. Their methods may be powerful, but they take us only so far in understanding the kaleidoscopic life of words.

This was precisely the recognition that brought Raymond Williams to the project of keywords, as well as my own in revisiting his approach here. Keywords isn't an anti-lexicography. It is, I argue, a methodology for centering questions of power, politics, mediality, experience, and conditions of existence with respect to the movements of words through time. I further contend that keywords has been widely misunderstood, or applied in ways that sometimes disregard important aspects of the project's underlying philosophy. Before moving on with the story of algorithmic culture, therefore, I wish to pause and reflect on what a keyword is, and on the entailments of undertaking research in that vein. This is, on some level, an obligatory chapter on theory and method. On another level, it's a critical if somewhat oblique component of the larger story of algorithmic culture. The culture and society tradition became legible to Williams in and through the project of keywords, specifically; the one went hand-in-glove with the other. As Alan Durant puts it, "neither the word itself nor the concept of culture, [Williams] found, could be understood without referring to a cluster of words with which it interacts."[4] Other approaches to language could have surfaced some of the major plot points of the culture and society tradition, but generally they were ill-equipped to connect the dots. The same is true for algorithmic culture, whose story not only lends itself to keywords but also, critically, to an overdue refinement of the project.

KEYWORDS, KEY WORDS, KEY-WORDS

Keywords give voice to the experience: "something's different around here." This was the feeling Williams registered upon his discharge from the army in 1945, having served as commander of a small tank brigade in the Second World War.[5] He returned to Cambridge University to find "a new and strange world" had taken hold, one that bore little resemblance to the home he'd left four and a half years earlier. He mused with historian Eric Hobsbawm, a friend and fellow war veteran, that the people there "just don't speak the same language" anymore, as if to say those who'd remained on the home front had abandoned the familiar vernaculars of the 1930s.[6] The bewilderment was enough to prompt Williams to embark on a series of projects on the relationship of words, historicity, experience, and social change. Formally it would span a quarter-century, from *Culture and Society* (1958) to the original (1976) and revised editions (1983) of *Keywords*, and it would suffuse many other aspects of his research. The objective, broadly, was to identify "a general pattern of change" in specific terminological clusters, and thus to create "a special kind of map" of the material and symbolic transformations those changes both referenced and embodied.[7]

This is what I am calling "the project of keywords," which encompasses but is also larger than the two editions of the book bearing the title *Keywords*. Indeed, it's critical to recognize that, for Williams, keywords existed as a single effort distributed across two different but related approaches. One thread, exemplified by *Culture and Society*, was quasi-intellectual-historical and consisted of close readings of major figures, mostly literary, whose published writings seemed to nudge the semantics of *culture* (and related words) toward a modern usage. The other thread, exemplified by *Keywords*, was quasi-etymological (sometimes it's described as "historical semantics") and consisted of terms whose semantic vicissitudes retold the story of *Culture and Society* from a predominately lexical perspective. It had all begun as a unified endeavor, however, an early draft of *Keywords* initially comprising an appendix to *Culture and Society*.[8]

The second (historical-semantic) approach, in particular, has been widely emulated, resulting in an ample secondary literature that now also lays claim to keywords. It consists of omnibus volumes such as *New Keywords: A Revised Vocabulary of Culture and Society* and *Keywords for Today: A Twenty-First Century Vocabulary*, as well as works addressing keywords in particular settings such as public health, environment, disability, information, media/technology, popular culture, and identity.[9] The authors and editors of these volumes seem to invest differently in keywords. Some follow closely in Williams's footsteps, while others begin with him, only to pursue a somewhat different pathway in the end. Despite differences in content, there's near-universal acceptance of the form of a keywords book. The vast majority of the secondary literature abides by the same basic structure as Williams's *Keywords*, which consists of an introduction followed by alphabetically arranged and internally cross-referenced studies of particular words. One of the few exceptions is *Keywords Re-Oriented*, which endeavors to decenter the entire keywords project by placing it in dialogue with scholarship, literature, and terminology from China.[10] Another is *Pluriverse: A Post-Development Dictionary*, which pushes the decentering impulse into the realm of the decolonial. While "keyword" is invoked repeatedly throughout the volume, and while the structure is reminiscent of *Keywords*, Williams isn't identified as a reference point for the project at all. Instead, the goal is to "challeng[e] the modernist ontology of universalism in favor of a multiplicity of possible worlds . . . a pluriverse."[11]

There's a sizeable tertiary literature on keywords, moreover, addressed primarily to readers in the areas of business and religion/spirituality, which also typically displays no tie whatsoever to Williams. Titles like *Chocolate Covered Keywords: Getting a Taste of SEO*, *Beyond Basketball: Coach K's Keywords for Success*, *Keyword Research: SEO Domination*, *Astrological Keywords*, *Qur'anic Keywords*, and *Hebrew-Greek Key Word Study Bible* suggest a more generic understanding of "keyword" prevails outside of academe. There, it seems to denote a term of unspecified importance, a buzzword, or even metadata whose purpose is to capture and manipulate the attention of search engines, as in the case of Search Engine Optimization (SEO). The last of these senses is critically important, reminding us that language now addresses both people and machines and that "keyword," however defined, is a relative designation, not an absolute one: "Chocolate covered" to whom or what, and in what context?

Part of the difficulty in answering the question "What is a keyword?" thus boils down to the fact that, as Alan Durant observes, "the meaning of 'keywords' itself changes. Current prevalence of a 'search' sense for 'keyword' challenges any obviousness we might presume in the 'Williams sense' among readers coming to *Keywords* for the first time."[12] While I wouldn't describe Williams's understanding of keywords as "obvious," the point still stands: we cannot take for granted what a keyword is, or simply assume commonsense definitions apply. This is as true for the secondary literature as it is for the tertiary literature, even in cases where an author may refer directly to Williams. Bennett, Grossberg, and Morris note the "overly academic reception of *Keywords* in recent years," suggesting that at least some of the literature has strayed too far into the realm of technical language. The purpose of the project, they argue, is to provide "a useful, intellectually and historically grounded guide to *public* questions and struggles for meaning shared by many people in the field of culture and society."[13]

The separation of the two dimensions of the project is a source of additional confusion. Had Williams been allowed by his publisher to include his initial foray into keywords as an appendix to *Culture and Society*, as he had intended to do (I revisit the incident in chapter 4), a broader, more robust sense of how to research and write about keywords would have been in place from the beginning. That is, *Keywords* might not have come to stand in for the totality of the project, a situation that's apparent in the form adopted by much of the secondary literature.

Keywords is about shifts of meaning, conflicts over usage, and complexities of etymology, but it's no less about people and the ways they wrestle with language in response to changed or changing—or even troublingly static—circumstances. The challenge of keywords lies in documenting the *dynamic relationships* that exist between and among people, regimes of experience, particular words, technological forms, and possibly more, and in doing so *creatively* rather than formulaically.

In other words, the unique structure Williams developed for *Keywords* shouldn't be taken as a model but as an imaginative, contextually bound solution to the problem of how to isolate the language layer of the story of culture and society. Here I'm reminded of Stuart Hall's warning about "the danger of . . . high formalism" present in the theory of articulation, or assembly, in cultural studies, which lends itself to cookie-cutter applications.[14] Similarly, important additions to the terminology and critical reflections on Williams's numerous omissions have not, for the most part, provoked an equally sustained interrogation of the methodology and modes of presentation of keywords in the secondary literature.[15] I'm also reminded of Gary Hall's provocation, noted in the introduction, about what cultural studies might have looked like had its founding figures come of age in the era of ubiquitous digital technologies. Hall wondered about Richard Hoggart and email.[16] For my part I'm curious to know: What if Raymond Williams had had Facebook or LinkedIn? I pose this question in part because, as Moses Boudourides has shown, the cross-referencing structure Williams created for *Keywords* is akin to a social network, albeit one consisting of words.[17] Imagine if Williams had had at his disposal the concept of the social graph, which maps human connection much as *Keywords* maps lexical relationships. It's possible books like

Culture and Society and *Keywords* would have looked radically different. Perhaps they would have been one and the same.

The final source of confusion about keywords lies with Williams himself. Despite being widely recognized as an authority on the subject, Williams had surprisingly little to say, explicitly, about keywords; or, to put a finer point on the claim, he was far more inclined to practice keywords than he was to reflect on the practice itself. By my count, he dedicated less than thirty pages to conceptualizing this, one of his signature theoretical and methodological contributions. The material includes a few indirect references in the introduction to *Culture and Society*, plus a footnote in the foreword; fifteen pages of introductory material appearing in *Keywords*, his most sustained statement; a page or so in *Marxism and Literature*; and another ten pages, in the form of an interview, appearing in *Politics and Letters*.[18] Thirtyish pages are hardly insignificant, but then again Williams published more than two dozen books in his lifetime (fiction, nonfiction, and drama), along with scores of essays and interviews. His reflections on keywords are scant relative to this extensive body of work and disproportionate to the influence of the paradigm. The lopsidedness is even more pronounced where the formatting of keywords research is concerned. Williams addressed the topic in just the final two pages of the introduction to *Keywords*.[19] With a dearth of material to draw on, one can hardly fault subsequent authors and editors for having fallen back on the mostly alphabetical, glossary-like form. That said, Williams seems to have been ambivalent about it. "In writing about the field of meanings," he noted, "I have often wished that some form of presentation could be devised in which it would be clear that the analyses of particular words are intrinsically connected, sometimes in complex ways."[20] It's a strange, almost out-of-body statement, as if Williams were distancing himself from the very framework he'd spent decades developing.

The point of this discussion is to invite you to embrace experimentation in both the research and the writing of keywords. Williams himself invited "other kinds of connection and comparison" in thinking through matters of form.[21] Yet, for all this, what remains unclear is the extent to which he understood keywords as specific, or at least adjacent, to the culture and society tradition. For Williams it apparently existed in public— mostly white/male/British—print culture, which in turn begs the question: How capable is keywords when it comes to recognizing other traditions, figures, vocabularies, and forms of relationship? That is, how well is it suited to surfacing the story of the emergence of algorithmic culture?

The answer is, in short, imperfectly, as books like *Keywords Re-Oriented* and *Pluriverse: A Post-Development Dictionary* make clear. I'll have more to say about specific adaptations needed to tell the story of algorithmic culture in the chapters to follow. For now, I wish to return to—and further complicate—the distinction I introduced between the text of *Keywords* and the broader project encompassing it. Just as I'm reluctant to reduce keywords to *Keywords*, so too am I hesitant, moving forward, to use the label "keywords" to refer to something other than theoretical and methodological principles for studying the culture and society tradition. That is, I wish to define something like a practice of "keywords" for algorithmic culture, specifically, and to find a way of conveying the situatedness of the project unambiguously. Throughout this book I employ "key-words" (hyphenated) to signal that usage, and "key words" (spaced out) to refer to the totality of projects operating within a more general methodological horizon, one that would include Williams's work, the secondary and tertiary literature, and this book as well.[22] In landing on key-word, I've chosen to hold on to a form of the original term that indicates the indebtedness of my approach to the existing literature. I've tweaked the orthography, however, as a way of reminding readers that key-words is neither trans-contextual nor comfortable within the parameters of conventional usage.

- key words: A general methodological horizon in which researchers explore words, their meanings, and/or relationships between and among those words in determinate contexts.
- keywords: A specific practice of key words operationalized by Raymond Williams, by means of which he explored the ontogenesis of the culture and society tradition across multiple projects.
- Keywords: A specific instance of Raymond Williams's practice of keywords; a book in which he sought to isolate the language layer of the culture and society tradition and map the tradition's internal structures.
- key-words: A specific practice of key words, operationalized in this book and inspired by Raymond Williams's practice of keywords, by means of which to explore the ontogenesis of algorithmic culture.

WHAT'S IN A NAME?

The decision to use "key-words" to describe the general approach of this book is methodologically strategic. There are, however, historical grounds for doing so as well. Today the standard orthography is *keyword*, but when the term first appeared in written British English, around 1762, it was the hyphenated form, *key-word*, that made the initial breakthrough. In other words, I'm deliberately reactivating a supposedly passé form whose definition, according to the *Oxford English Dictionary* (*OED*), is "a word that serves as the key to a cipher or code." Building on this definition, I want to define *key-word*, provisionally, as a semantic figure that provides unique entry into some aspect of reality that may be obfuscated or otherwise challenging to discern.

This form, *key-word*, meshes remarkably well with the subject of algorithmic culture. I'd venture to say they belong to the same general vocabulary, by which I mean the tissue of historico-semantic relations that binds complexes of words together. At the risk of getting ahead of myself: it's through the work of Moḥammed ibn-Mūsā al-Khwārizmī (c. 780–850 CE), the purported namesake of the word *algorithm* and the subject of chapter 2, that the number zero winds its way into the English language. Both *zero* and *cipher* share a common etymon in the Arabic word *ṣifr* (صفر), and there was a period, ending about a century ago, where zero was referred to in English as a "cipher in algorism" (the latter term, an alternate spelling of *algorithm*).[23] There are also intriguing resonances with the cryptanalytical dimensions of information theory and the algorithmic processes used to decipher secret messages, though I won't go into them here.[24] For now, suffice it to say that just as Williams's keywords was entangled with the culture and society tradition, so too is the project of key-words entangled—etymologically, if nothing else—with algorithmic culture. This relationship is important to acknowledge: research methods are best conceived not as instruments to be applied to problems exogenous to them, but as analytical and interpretive resources endogenous to the very problems to which they're addressed.[25]

The *OED* goes on to indicate that the spelling of *key-word* remained stable for the better part of 150 years, only then to differentiate with the introduction of *key word* (1907) and *keyword* (1926). Both variants, suggests the *OED*, were outgrowths of two novel definitions to have emerged during the second quarter of the nineteenth century: "A word, expression, or concept of particular importance or significance" (c. 1848); and "a word (usu. one of several) chosen to indicate or represent the content of a larger document, text, record, etc." (c. 1827).[26] The latter form, *keyword*, would go on to become a frequent traveler within the realms of science and industry and, later, information storage and retrieval.[27] I doubt it's a coincidence that, through keywords, Williams sought to historicize the cultural politics of a "selective tradition" that suddenly faced new questions owing to the industrialization of printing at the end of the nineteenth century.[28]

The Google Books database tells both a similar and a different story in charting instances of both *key-word* and *key word* back to 1805, and *keyword* to 1819.[29] Initially the orthography was inconsistent, the database shows, each spelling enjoying around a decade of dominance. But whatever the spelling, the term remained peripheral with respect to the English language as a whole, appearing on average only about once per million printed words throughout the first quarter of the nineteenth century. By 1840 *key-word* had settled in as the conventional written form, only then to be overtaken in 1915 by *key word*, whose ascendance had begun in earnest in 1907. *Keyword* reached the number two spot in 1961, and by 1977—a year after the first edition of Williams's *Keywords* was issued—it managed to overtake *key word* in terms of frequency of usage. As of this writing, instances of *keyword* outpace those of *key word* by a ratio of more than five to one, and those of *key-word* by a ratio of nearly ten to one—evidence that affirms the *OED*'s acceptance of *keyword* as the standard orthography today. And although the term is hardly central to the English language, its various spellings now appear approximately four hundred times per million printed words.[30]

These changes in spelling might seem like trivial developments—first a hyphen, then a space, and finally a union—but they tell a story about subtle, if critical, shifts of sense and inflection that have made it more difficult to appreciate the uniqueness and complexity—the "keywordiness," if you will—of key-words. According to the *OED*, which I believe to be accurate on this point, *key-word* treats both elements of the compound as nouns, and thus as equally substantive partners. Until roughly the early twentieth century, the term was no less *key* than it was *word*. But the relationship has grown lopsided now that *key word* and *keyword* have established themselves. Today *key* functions more often than not in the supporting role of adjective, its purpose, to shore up the type of *word* in question.[31] You can hear the hierarchy in the pronunciation of *keywords*, with the stress typically falling on the second syllable. The result, consequently, is an attenuated sense of their "keyness." English speakers of the eighteenth and nineteenth centuries might have understood *key-words* as *decisive and revelatory semantic figures*. Today keywords tend to be approached, conventionally, either as *generally important terms* or as *linguistic avatars*.

It's for this and the aforementioned reasons that, for purposes of this book, I want to shift the semantic baseline back to the earlier form, key-word. A key-word isn't simply a word that performs "key" functions, however the latter may be defined; it's a unique class of words in which the "keyness" is an inherent part of the "wordness," and vice versa. I'll have more to say about what this means momentarily. For the time being, the hyphen is meant to alert you to this relationship and, indeed, to restore an equal partnership to both sides of the compound. It's also meant to cue your inflection when you say the word out loud: the stress should fall on both words, with the hyphen signaling a momentary pause in between the two. Also, they should be said slowly and deliberately, in contrast to the tendency in U.S. English to slur the two parts of the compound *keywords* together. Williams clearly preferred *keyword*, moreover, but he occasionally employed the other two spellings. The table of contents for *Culture and Society* lists "The Key Words—'Industry,' 'Democracy,' 'Class,' 'Art,' 'Culture'," and in *The Long Revolution* Williams notes the import of the "key-word . . .'imagination'" in eighteenth century Romantic thought.[32] While these variations could have stemmed from vagaries in copyediting, they also might suggest Williams's own struggle to pinpoint the right term for the endeavor.

Whatever the case, it's worth pointing out that Williams, as far as I can tell, never sought to bring the resources of his approach to bear on *keyword* itself, much less any of the variants. This is precisely what I wish to do now. I begin with *key*, whose brevity belies a long and contested history. Written evidence of *key*'s existence in proto-English language discourse dates back a millennium, although some observers assert the word existed in the vernacular well before it appeared in manuscripts.[33] In the *OED*'s version of the story, *key* derives from the Old English word *cæg*, a term of Germanic inheritance imported by the Anglo-Saxon tribes who conquered England after the collapse of Roman rule in the fifth century CE. Even then it referred to an instrument for opening locks,[34] although the possible cognates *keel* (German form *Keil*, meaning "wedge") and *cleaver* are also intriguing for their signification: devices for dividing, splitting, or tearing asunder.[35]

Etymologist Anatoly Liberman challenges this history, however, claiming instead a Scandinavian origin for the word. He hones in on a now rare instance of *key* present in the dialects of northern England, *key-legged*, connoting twistedness, awkwardness, crookedness, or bentness, which appears to have derived from terms pertaining to the left-hand side present in older Swedish, Danish, and Icelandic dialects.[36] The earliest English-language key, he argues, must have been "a stick (pin, peg) with a twisted end."[37] Liberman also dismisses efforts to isolate a Latinate origin for the word, calling them "futile" and "obviously doomed to failure," although the results of those efforts persist in other etymological resources, the *OED* included. Here the root in question is *clāvis*, Latin for *key*, from which the English language may have developed musical terms like *clavichord*, *clef*, and *keynote*, all evidently linguistic kin of the keyboard on which I'm composing these words.[38]

What to make of this back-and-forth? I'll leave it to the linguists, etymologists, and lexicographers to settle historical accounts with *key*, though doubtfully ever once and for all given the contested origins of the term. Still, it's worth putting a finger on some themes more or less consistent across the corpus of arguments and evidence. First, there's the preoccupation with form, explicit in Liberman's account, but also apparent in the Latin- and German-inspired roots and cognates (clavichords, keels, cleavers) whose wedge action is apt to leave an impression. Second and relatedly is the emphasis on passage, not only in the sense of opening a lock, but also in the sense of ontological transformation—a passage or division between orders of existence. Such is the difference between singing on key (music) or off (cacophony). So it also goes when a butcher applies cleaver to cow, whereupon a creature once ambling about the pasture becomes steak, chops, beef, or meat.[39] A sense of instrumentality pervades these accounts, moreover, as in the case of locks and musical instruments and also, maybe less obviously, Liberman's example of the twisted pins. Two additional themes, though inconsistent across the evidence, are worth underscoring as well. The sense of *key* present in *keynote*, also in *keystone*, suggests a unifying function, prominence, or authority vested in the capacity to set the tone for others. But there's also something like a contrasting view embodied in the northern Frisian word *kei*, an offshoot of the Scandinavian forms connoting awkwardness, that also suggests "inarticulate[ness]" or "lack . . . [of] fluency."[40]

Like *key*, *word* dates back to Old English, though its etymological roots sink even deeper into the linguistic tilth of Europe, and perhaps beyond. The *OED* lists it as of Germanic origin, and likely then a token imported to Britain by the invading Anglo-Saxons. Cognates exist throughout many northern European languages, both past and present, including *waurd* (Gothic), *orð* (Old Icelandic), *woord* (Dutch), *ord* (Swedish and Danish), and *Wort* (German), "all denoting both 'an utterance' or 'an element or unit of speech, a word'."[41] More compelling than any particular instance of *word*, however, is the Indo-European base they purportedly share in common, *wer-*, leading candidate as the source of the ancient Greek forms *rhēma*, (ῥῆμα, word), *rhētor* (ῥήτωρ, speaker), and *rhetoric* (ρητορική, verbal arts), also the Latin form *verbum* (word)—all terms connoting debate, public discourse, and the capacity of words to induce and embody action.[42] Also intriguing is the semantic drift one finds as *wer-* winds its way north into the Baltics. There it appears to have developed into the Lithuanian *vardas* (a given name or title) and the Latvian *vārdas* (a given name or promise), both connoting structures of social obligation. Moving backward in time, the

OED speculates that *wer-* itself may have derived from the Sanskrit *vrata*, meaning "behest" or "command," suggesting words delivered in the imperative.[43]

Many of these senses are available in contemporary English. Yet, they tend to take a backseat to the prevailing definition of *word*: an utterance, or the nominative designation for some person, place, idea, action, or thing. Their niche seems to be colloquialisms, where, for instance, the promissory sense is captured in the expression, "you gave me your word"; the imperative by the phrase, "say the word and I'll do it"; and the argumentative by one of the richest instances of understatement present in the English language, "they're having words." One might also point to the interjection "word!," now a somewhat passé expression hailing from Black American music and speech. A relative of the imperative form, it indicates "a response of affirmation" and, by extension, conveys respect for the figure about whom the phrase is uttered.[44]

In all of these cases, and many of those present above, a movement away from the nominative or signifying function of words is palpable. Instead, the usage more closely resembles that of a *mot d'ordre*, an "order-word." As Gilles Deleuze and Félix Guattari explain:

> We call *order-words*, not a particular category of explicit statements (for example, in the imperative), but the relation of every word or every statement to implicit presuppositions, in other words, to speech acts that are, and can only be, accomplished in the statement. Order-words do not concern commands only, but every act that is linked to statements by "social obligation."[45]

Order-words, thus, are terms, phrases, or statements that bear uniquely on the architecture of social relations. They help establish, maintain, and transform relational hierarchies and also, then, the more abstract domains (e.g., culture, law, economy) in which those hierarchies are embedded. Brian Massumi puts it straightforwardly: order-words are "word[s] or phrase[s] creative of order." The military dimension of *mot d'ordre*, Massumi continues, endows the term with additional subtlety: not only that of a directive, but also that of a watchword—a definition for *word*, incidentally, the *OED* claims is "now rare."[46] *Mots d'ordre* help sort enemy from friend, allowing the latter to gain access to territory from which all others, in principle, are barred.

If that sounds a lot like what keys do, then you already know where this discussion is going. The purpose of this etymological exercise is to demonstrate how *key* and *word* share more in common with one another, semantically, than might seem obvious at first—a commonality that becomes apparent when we proceed from the more archaic or peripheral definitions of each term, rather than from the preferred ones. Furthermore, the discussion of *key* and *word* encompasses a range of senses and meanings essential to defining key-words and, by extension, to clarifying the nature of the work they perform.

A MISPLACED PART OF SPEECH

The provisional definition of *key-word* I introduced earlier accords with the sense of access associated with keys. You might also think about key-words as familiar (and, sometimes, novel) terms whose connotation or character has, as if all of a sudden, become twisted or awkward with respect to established usage. This isn't to suggest existing definitions of words suddenly fall by the wayside, but instead that nascent senses and meanings recontextualize established understandings and usages. This phenomenon is sometimes known by the technical term "cata-chresis," denoting an incidence of lexical misuse in which some-one struggles to find the right word, only then to distort the meaning of the word they've happened upon.[47] Lexicographers, for their part, are apt to disparage such incidences as "corrup-tions," but from the perspective of key-words, there's no such thing. Language cannot be corrupted because it's never pure to begin with.[48]

Put differently, there's no mechanism internal to language that would cause key-words to twist all by themselves. Their semantic shifts embody broader changes in social reality. Typi-cally, words operate within the realm of "the residual" or "the dominant." Williams introduced these concepts late in his career to challenge rigid notions of economic determination, though they have broader applicability with respect to the philosophy of history underlying his work as a whole, and to my own under-standing of key-words. The residual refers to aspects of social reality held over from some earlier historical moment. Though ostensibly out of time, they're nonetheless active in the here and now. Language, for example, is filled with so-called archaisms, the sum total of which bear witness to how linguistic elements from the past persist in, and thus continue to enframe, the pres-ent.[49] The dominant, meanwhile, refers to "a central system of practices, meanings, and values"—the de facto touchstone of a society by means of which a majority of its members organize and make sense of their lives.[50] Dictionaries are the most visible manifestations of the dominant, lexically speaking, insofar as they codify the existence of particular words, canonize usage, and stigmatize aberrations.

Key-words are a special class of language, however, and they typically relate to a different dimension of time and reality: what

Williams calls "the emergent." Just as the residual refers not to some abstract past but to the effectivity of older elements within a present-day social formation, so too does the emergent refer not to some abstract future but to the effectivity of nascent elements within the here and now. The emergent thus names that which has begun to exert substantive bearing on human thought, conduct, and expression, though the effects are often not widely generalized, or even recognized.[51] Key-words are emergent phenomena in the sense they're either critical terms newly introduced into the lexicon (Williams gives the example of the word *capitalism* in the early nineteenth century) or, more typically, existing words whose unexpected twists and turns betoken shifts in the architectonics of the world around us.[52]

But key-words are more than just emergent language, strictly speaking. They're junction points between the emergent and a fourth category Williams introduces, "the pre-emergent," or aspects of reality that are "active and pressing but not yet fully articulated."[53] From a methodological standpoint, key-words are important not only because they're semantically and temporally complex, but also because they mediate access: specifically, to incipient forms of social experience that exceed the discursive. This is precisely what I chart across the next three chapters with respect to algorithmic culture: the *pre-emergence* of what is today a dominant, or at least well-established, aspect of reality. The sense of inarticulateness expressed in the Frisian form *kei* embodies the inchoateness typical of the experience of pre-emergence. Or, as Vilém Flusser puts it: "There are . . . words that seem unwilling to fit so organically; they demand an almost extra-linguistic effort in order to be thought and articulated. When we think them, we feel a barrier, and when we articulate them, we are tempted to grunt, shout, or make a gesture."[54] Key-words thus operate at the edges of language, helping us to carve new discursive pathways through a world whose changes we may have yet to fully cognize. As such, they may be the closest we come to grasping the ineffable.

Consider, for instance, the experience of responding to a Facebook post prior to 2016. It was only then that the company added a range of possible reactions ("love," "care," "haha," "wow," "sad," and "angry") to the venerable old "like" function—an effort, no doubt, to mitigate the discomfort of having to like a negative announcement, as in when a friend shared news about the death of a loved one. The experience of liking something negative was awkward enough just prior to the rollout of the new reactions feature, but remember how fraught it was at the dawn of social networking—back when people still fretted over whether social media "friends" were worthy of the name? At what point did it become possible—sensible—to affirm something that you disliked in order to show support or solidarity for someone whom you've quite possibly never met? The example illustrates the complex movement of key-words, in which established meanings collide with emergent senses that may seem so awkward and unfamiliar as to border on nonsense.

Key-words not only index the becoming-sensible of nonsense. More importantly, they signal the "languaging" of emergent— often felt—regimes of social experience, and in doing so they underscore the broader stakes of adopting a key-words approach. Here, language isn't an end in itself but a vehicle for adducing the conditions that produce shared and often bewildering experiences of change—conditions that may be abstruse but that are nonetheless lived with sometimes crushing immediacy, or even deadening tedium. This is why the heuristic "structure of feeling," which Williams defined as the "characteristic elements of impulse, restraint, and tone" that are prevalent in a time period, figures prominently within the framework he devised for keywords.[55] More recently, Ben Anderson, Kathleen Stewart, and Dora Zhang have each turned to the language of "atmospheres" in an attempt to account for the affective dimensions of everyday life that so interested Williams, while moving away from the rigidifying language of structure. Anderson defines "atmospheres" as the "collective affects that . . .'envelope' [*sic*] and press upon life." Stewart describes them as "force fields in which people find themselves . . . a capacity . . . that pushes the present into a composition, an expressivity, the sense of potentiality and event." Zhang, meanwhile, emphasizes that, despite being "elusive and vague . . . atmospheres have real effects."[56]

The power of these concepts resides in their helping us to identify unities among seemingly disparate phenomena, particularly incidences in which people who are socially and geographically far apart begin using the same novel senses, meanings, words, phrases, and expressions as if coincidentally.[57] Williams's analysis of the word *jargon* is instructive in this regard. He notes the term's derivation from Old French, where it referred to "the warbling of birds, chatter"—apt descriptors for how conversation grows indistinct at scale and apt metaphors, then, for imagining the chaotic cross talk that both suffuses and conditions experiential atmospheres.[58] So conceived, *jargon* refers not to some insular, intimidating, or even alienating terminology but to the lively, atmospheric warble that can, under the right circumstances, condense into key-words, prompting familiar terms to change their tune.

Key-words are not, therefore, the result of creative geniuses performing unprecedented work on language. Neither are they effects or representations of reality becoming something other than itself. They're elements integral to this process of differentiation. A "central aim" of Williams's approach to keywords, and,

indeed, of my own in this book, is "to show that some important social and historical processes occur *within* language."[59] This
necessitates taking a step beyond the usual referentiality of
words. According to Deleuze, signs typically refer to "worldly"
objects and their accompanying mental images. Some signs,
however, embody an order of truth or reality exceeding the
bounds of readily observable, empirical propriety. "Perception
supposes that reality is to be seen, *observed*; but intelligence supposes that truth is to be *spoken, formulated*."[60] The reference here
to form isn't accidental, given how, in their deep etymological
recesses, *key* and *word* suggest shape, order, and unity. Key-words
are implicated in the constitution of the very realities they then
help us to explicate. Taking a cue from Deleuze, it might be
worth imagining new aspects of reality as though they were
crumpled up pieces of paper—complicated ("folded with") initially, in the sense that the random intermingling of edges, cor-
ners, and surfaces yields an amorphous, undifferentiated wad.
Key-words are like the tensile fibers that slowly stretch out the
wad, giving it contour and definition, and thus rendering it sim-
pler (from the Latin *simplex*, "one fold") to recognize.[61] The
logic here is neither linear nor dialectical but recursive, a function of the immanence of words to processes of historical change.
Williams, for his part, describes this as the "binding" and "indicative" function of keywords,[62] which seems to me equally applicable to key-words. This is also more or less what keystones and
keynotes do, for whatever it's worth.

There are no master keys, however, nor keys to the city—if
by that one means terms so central to a language (or to "language," period) as to provide full and unfettered access to the
movements of reality writ large. The critique of universalism
present in *Pluriverse: A Post-Development Dictionary* is an urgent
reminder of the expansionist impulse that can take hold of even

well-intended efforts to identify this or that word as "key."[63] For this reason I want to insist that key-words are more limited in scope, referring always and only to specific contexts or "existential territories."[64] This is why Williams's *Keywords* has a subtitle: *A Vocabulary of Culture and Society*. It's meant to signal that he's not surveying the most important words in the English language. Instead, the terms he assembled in the book tell a story about decisive shifts in the definition, and more broadly the experiences, of culture in the North Atlantic region. These shifts helped to usher in modern-day anthropological and aesthetic understandings of the term, endowing it with categorical status so that it became possible to identify ourselves as cultural beings. This further suggests that key-words are not trans-historical. They come, they go—some, like *culture*, enduring for longer and shouldering more critical weight than others. Hence, Williams's decision to issue a revised edition of *Keywords* just seven years after publishing the first one, in 1976: some words, he reflected, "have become more important in the period between that original list and the present time," among them, newly added terms like *ecology* and *technology*.[65] Because key-words are bounded in space, time, and idiom, it's critical to indicate to which specific "fragments of reality" they correspond.[66]

Colin MacCabe mischaracterizes Williams's endeavor, then, in describing it primarily as philological.[67] While there are elements of philology, and while there's also a clear etymological component, neither approach comports with the agnostic disposition characteristic of Williams's project, as well as my own. By "agnostic," I don't mean uncritical or politically neutral. Key-words is indeed a critical project, in the last instance, as I explain below. In the first instance, however, key-words rejects what Williams called the "sacral attitude" typical of philology, etymology, and lexicography.[68] It's not about revering historical documents, much less about exalting their authors. Nor is it about using historical methods to recover the authentic, original meaning of a word—as if such a thing existed. Neither is key-words about using scholarly authority to consecrate hierarchies of usage. However helpful philology, etymology, and lexicography may be, all of these disciplines are ultimately too insular. The tendency to focus on *a* word often comes at the cost of exploring the nexus of "connection and interaction" among terms.[69] This is why the approach is always key-words, plural.

One of the curiosities of Williams's work was his occasional use of "semantic figures" as a synonym for key-words.[70] In a language with few obvious choices for naming the "thing"—*word*, *term*, *expression*, and, at the outer limits, *phrase* or *concept*—I sympathize with the need to find a suitable workaround. But "semantic figures" also encourages us to think differently about the tokens we usually call words. They're bearers of meaning, to be sure. Yet they're also, as we've seen, instruments with the capacity for action—specifically, for helping to figure new regimes of existence. In this, the project of key-words draws upon the shared etymology of *word* and *verb*, an overlap that begs the question: Why, at what point, and on whose authority did the latter become a subclass of the former? Maybe "semantic figures" isn't so much a circumlocution as a sign of Williams grasping to name a misplaced part of speech, one that exists in a transversal relationship to the taxonomies beloved by modern grammarians.

English teachers (or maybe *Schoolhouse Rock!*) tell us that "a noun is a person, place, or thing"; that a verb is "what's happening"; and that "hooking up words and phrases and clauses" is the function of a conjunction.[71] Yet, for all their apparent facticity, these categories are not empirically given; there are other ways of thinking about the division of labor among words.

"Traditional grammar," Flusser writes, "generally unconscious of its fundamental ontological function, classifies the words of a given language according to a supposed correspondence between words and 'reality'." Flusser goes on to describe this view as "naïve."[72] Williams himself may not have towed the hard line, but even so the entries populating *Keywords* both cut across and test the limits of familiar grammatical categories. The lion's share of the entries are ostensibly nouns, or substantives as they're sometimes known, but there are also adjectives (*creative, mechanical, structural, subjective; ethnic* and *formalist*, too, when they are not behaving as nouns); verbs (*determine, improve*, and, depending on usage, *labour, taste, work*; one might include the verbal nouns *development, generation*, and *liberation* here too); and even one suffix (*-isms*) whose presence in the collection has not, to the best of my knowledge, provoked a broader rethinking of keywords's object of study. In any case, Williams occasionally correlates these semantic figures with particular parts of speech, but looking at the entries all together raises questions. Why do so many words operate across parts of speech? Are the existing categories adequate or exhaustive? What might we discover about language by putting prefixes, suffixes, and other linguistic bits and pieces on the same plane as word stems? And what about numbers, typographical symbols, and iconic images for that matter?[73] Can they ever be key?

Key-words is a grammatical undertaking less in the modern sense, then, and more in the classical sense of coming to terms with how people literally *come to terms*. Its purpose is to apprehend both the existential and everyday conditions under which human beings acquire and sometimes improvise the language necessary for engaging in public discourse (rhetoric) and, more abstractly, for reflecting on their own being-in-the-world (philosophy).[74] There's a critical component, moreover, one that raises the stakes on the whole endeavor. Indifference to the usual worries of grammarians doesn't mean turning dispassionately toward language. Words, Williams argues, are "elements . . . of problems"; they're part and parcel of the myriad "controversies and conflicts" that arise as both human and non-human actors partake of the difficult work of living together.[75] There is, in short, a politics to key-words—not only regarding the vocabularies in question, but also with regard to the outcomes of the analysis. The aim, specifically, is twofold: first, to provide readers with a unique set of intellectual and narrative resources with which to grasp, better than they might otherwise, the confluence of forces affecting their daily lives; and second, to use those tools to strategize about where best to direct political energy, now and in the future.

Despite drawing inspiration from grammar, linguistics, and adjacent disciplines, key-words doesn't follow in the vein of claiming to be an objective science. This is due, in part, to the critical disposition characteristic of the approach. It also has to do with the degree to which key-words is a speculative endeavor. The focus on the incipient stages of historical change, when there arises the feeling "something's different around here," demands letting go of the expectations and assurances of traditional empiricism. You cannot sustain orthodox epistemological realism in the face of emergent aspects of reality, where evidence is apt to be scarce, unauthorized, ill-formed, widely dispersed, or seemingly nonsensical. A signature feature of key-words is that they mediate the gap between people's felt experiences of change and the eventual transcription of those experiences into the official organs of discourse—a gap Meaghan Morris has referred to as "reality lag."[76] Sexual harassment comes to mind here, a phenomenon that was widely experienced long before it was ever named, much less entered into dictionaries or law. The same is true, currently, of "stealthing," which refers to the non-consensual, often surreptitious, removal of a condom during sexual intercourse, which has only recently been named, identified as a form of sexual assault, and considered as a matter of law.[77] A key-words approach necessitates epistemological and methodological heterodoxy precisely because it must reckon with incongruities of this kind—what Williams described as "the very common . . . phenomenon of an extraordinarily shocking innovation of discourse . . . which yet produces elements of *recognition.*"[78]

Writing in 1930, Antonio Gramsci reflected on the rise of the fascist dictatorship that had landed him and countless other members of the political opposition in prisons throughout Italy. "The crisis," he determined, "consists precisely in the fact that the old is dying and the new cannot be born; in this interregnum a great variety of morbid symptoms appear."[79] An interregnum: technically, the period between the death of a sovereign and the crowning of the successor, although now the term can refer more generally to gaps or periods of transition in which the usual rules may no longer apply.[80] Key-words thrive under such conditions. They're one among many types of "morbid symptoms" to arise when the familiar contours of daily life begin to strain under the pressure of the unfamiliar. And yet, key-words hold a special place insofar as they're elements of the transition itself, cleaving the solid present and providing definition for a reality yet to come.

A BIOGRAPHY OF WORDS

Earlier in this chapter, I noted the intimate relationship between the culture and society tradition and white/male/public print culture in Britain. Paul Gilroy has observed how the narrowness of this "tradition" yielded "strategic silences in [Raymond Williams's] work" around questions of race;[81] one could say much the same thing regarding gender, sexuality, dis/ability, and numerous other identity categories. I mention this here, in the closing pages of this chapter, for two reasons. First, inasmuch as this book is inspired by the writings, concepts, and imaginativeness of Williams, I want to be clear that I don't consider his work to be unassailable, or a model to emulate. I say this with due acknowledgment of his working-class background and, indeed, of his upbringing in Wales, close to the English border. (The Anglo-Saxon term from which "Wales" is derived—*Wealh*, meaning "foreigners"—is an enduring reminder of how the Welsh people, traditionally of Celtic origin, can be considered colonial subjects.[82]) Part of what I wish to do in this book, moving forward, is to explore ways of opening up keywords so as not to reproduce endemic silences.

This leads me to my second point. The question of silence isn't only about traditions and canons, strictly speaking. It's also about the media technologies and associated discourse networks in which, as a researcher, you go about searching for words, artifacts, figures, stories, and more. As Friedrich Kittler observed of the work of Michel Foucault: "His concept of the archive—synonymous with the library in Foucault's research methods, if not in his theory—designates a historical a priori of written sentences." As such, Kittler concludes, "Foucault's research did not progress much beyond 1850."[83] It's not lost on me that keywords is similarly invested and bound, although the endpoint is about a century later.[84]

This chapter, thus, is only the beginning of the methodological reappraisal of keywords, and of the journey from there to key-words. Across the next three chapters I stage a series of encounters with voices, figures, artifacts, contexts, technologies, and other phenomena that test the limits of the existing paradigm and define in greater detail this book's primary theoretical and methodological objectives. I've only painted the broad strokes in this chapter, and necessarily so. Because the methodology of key-words is, on some level, coextensive with the story of algorithmic culture, it would have been impossible to fill in the missing details any sooner.

A few observations about what key-words will look like. Though each of the next three chapters ostensibly focuses on a key-word (*algorithm, culture, algorithmic culture*), they don't take the form of the entries you'll find in *Keywords*. Nor do they exactly follow the approach of *Culture and Society*, in which authors and their polished, published writings take center stage. While you can expect to find elements of both approaches in the coming chapters, my primary goal is to reconstruct the diffuse experiential atmospheres within which particular speaking subjects dwelled and, more to the point, to explore the processes by which those atmospheres are "completed" in and through key-words.[85] What you shouldn't expect, maybe counterintuitively, is a "big data" or corpus linguistics approach to the subject of algorithmic culture. I've already noted the limits of such an endeavor in discussing the controversy surrounding *The Oxford Junior Edition*. Similarly, Deborah Cameron and Ben Highmore each have noted the dangers of conflating word frequency and relevance (i.e., "keyness"), as though power had nothing to do with why certain terms appear more regularly in public discourse than others.[86] You can definitely expect an ample amount of biographical material, but be aware that what you're encountering is not biography in the conventional sense. Recall what I said in the introduction to this book, about "people making history" and their doing so "under conditions not of our own making." What follows, accordingly, is a *biography of words as told through the lives of particular, embodied people*—people whose experiences have had something to do with how meanings emerge and come to make their way in the world.

2

ALGORITHM

Virginia Eubanks's *Automating Inequality* is a stunning account of how algorithms disproportionately impact impoverished persons. The book focuses on the social services sector in the United States and, more specifically, on the delegation of critical decisions about eligibility, benefits, risk, and policing to computationally based decision systems. The change-over has occurred in the name of "modernizing" social welfare, Eubanks argues, and in the process it's diminished the authority of the human caseworkers who once handled the bulk of the decision-making. There's bitter irony here: high-tech digital solutions for the problem of how best to manage social services have produced conditions reminiscent of the poorhouses of old. Both systems "divert the poor from public benefits, contain their mobility, enforce work, split up families, lead to a loss of political rights, use the poor as experimental subjects, criminalize survival, construct suspect moral classifications, create ethical distance for the middle class, and reproduce racist and classist hierarchies of human value and worth."[1] The book, like so many accounts of algorithmic bias, is an urgent reminder of how vulnerable populations are often among the first to be fitted to computational decision systems whose logic may undercut their lives and livelihoods. Indeed, as Eubanks points out, the talk of high-tech "disruption," rampant among the Silicon Valley elite, is generally ill-suited to persons desperately in need of support, sensitivity, and stability.[2]

At the heart of Eubanks's story of algorithmic inequality are families, including her own. She opens the book with a horrific anecdote about how a mugging left her partner, Jason, with extensive jaw and facial fractures. To add insult to injury, and for reasons that were never explained, the insurance company denied many of his medical claims, resulting in emotional distress and financial hardship for the couple. "My instinct," writes Eubanks, "was that an algorithm had singled us out for a fraud investigation" owing to the newness of the insurance policy, the sudden volume of claims, and the fact that she and Jason maintained a domestic partnership; that is, they were not legally married. I highlight this anecdote as a probable instance of the ways in which algorithms are routinely called upon to parse human connection. Or, as Eubanks puts it: "Our world is crisscrossed with informational sentinels like the system that targeted my family for investigation."[3] That is, they're not only rendering decisions about how to process insurance claims, or making determinations about eligibility for vital social services. They're programmed to make more fundamental judgments about who gets to count as important in our lives, how, to what extent, and in what specific contexts. If Eubanks's instincts are correct, then an algorithm must have found her relationship with Jason "weighed" less than it would have had he been identified as her legally wedded husband. Never mind how they felt about one another, or the shared life they'd built up for over a decade. Algorithmically, Jason mattered less than if they were married.

What to make of this anecdote? Clearly, it speaks to how algorithms are administering the boundaries between familiar

ALGORITHM ೦ 69

and family, kith and kin, in apportioning economic resources, healthcare, and social services. In other words, they're performing critical, cultural work, as most social networking technologies do. At the same time, it speaks to how a fixation on the latest technological developments can obscure what else is at stake when algorithms enforce inequality: in this case, struggles over the meaning of the word *family*. In *Keywords*, Williams identified *family* as a term with "an especially significant social history," given how the boundary it delineates is subject to episodic—sometimes radical—shifts, as well as to protracted periods of settlement.[4] Understandably, automation never factored into Williams's account, much less the computational dimension, since he was writing when computers were just starting to become widely available, processing power was paltry compared to today, storage capacity was relatively small, and networking was the exception, not the rule. The challenge thus lies in finding a way to consider all the layers—the algorithmic, the cultural, and the semantic—together. Of course, it would be easy enough to say that a brilliant (or villainous) computer scientist simply woke up one day and decided to apply algorithms to all manner of human relations, thereby creating a template for the systems that now routinely automate inequality. The iconic algorithm scene in *The Social Network* (2010), a film about status seeking and the creation of Facebook, embodies such thinking.[5] What it neglects, however, are the conditions that led to connecting all those dots in the first place. Accordingly, this chapter asks: How did algorithms, definitions of kith and kin, and what Eubanks calls "hierarchies of worth and deservingness" all come to be entangled?[6]

Inasmuch as keywords helps to open up this question, it can only take us so far toward an answer. Central to the question is the will to impose mathematical formulae on human relations,

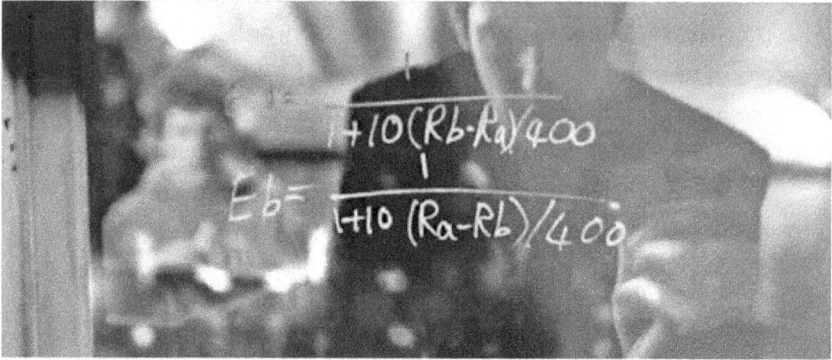

$$1+10(R_b-R_a)/400$$
$$E_b = \frac{1}{1+10(R_a-R_b)/400}$$

FIGURE 2.1 The iconic algorithm scene from *The Social Network* (Columbia Pictures, 2010). Pictured are Eduardo Saverin (Andrew Garfield, *foreground*) and Mark Zuckerberg (Jesse Eisenberg, *background*).

an impulse that was practically unthinkable for Williams. Because culture purportedly maps the qualitative dimensions of human experience, reflecting on terminology addressed to life's quantitative dimensions was apt to seem superfluous, even nonsensical to him.[7] The entry for *equality*, maybe the most obviously mathematical term in *Keywords*, is telling. Williams opens by observing that the word's "earliest uses" in the English language referred to "physical quantity." He abruptly pivots into a discussion of its relationship to political and social theory, however, a connection that sustains most of the entry. Only near the end does the quantitative element re-emerge. Williams acknowledges "the persistence of *equal* in a physical sense, as a term of measurement," as well as how it "has obviously complicated the social argument."[8] He demurs from thinking through this sense of *equality*, however, its "obviousness" apparently reason enough to submerge it.

The difficulties run deeper still in that the primary mathematical term under consideration here—*algorithm*—appeared in some form about nine hundred years prior to the constellation of senses and meanings Williams identified as characteristic of *culture*'s modern usage, and well before print culture was a thing. To tell the story of *algorithm*, keywords must metamorphose into key-words. Only then will the mathematical subtext of the culture and society tradition begin to emerge, and only then will the necessary methodological tools fall into place for exploring the entanglement of culture and computation. Apropos, Michel de Certeau once spoke of "a mobile language of computations and rationalities that belong[s] to no one."[9] I cannot think of a more fitting description for the idiom of algorithmic culture. The central claim of this chapter is that the process of entextualizing *algorithm* reduced it to a mere token of mathematics and, along the way, papered over a long history of people dispossessed of their lives and livelihoods, to say nothing of the methods they devised for endowing the world with order. The objective of this chapter is to peel back the paper, as it were. And perhaps, then, in the stories of people struggling to extricate themselves from the digital poorhouse, you'll not only hear voices echoing from the poorhouses of old; you'll also be able to listen for a fainter and more distant warble, that of a plural, disappeared "someone" for whom the "no one" of algorithmic rationality stands in.

MATHEMATICS IS ORDINARY

In researching the word *algorithm*, a term whose history spans at least 1,200 years, you quickly discover how difficult it is to put flesh on the bones of speaking subjects for whom scant historical records exist. Under such circumstances, historical conditions become paramount, as opposed to letting the figure of the individual become their proxy. You also discover the degree to which language and meaning become almost unnervingly unfixed the more you slip the reliable reference points of print culture and the many disciplines it's helped to inspire, particularly philology, lexicography, and orthography.[10] And then there's the whole matter of mathematics, a formation whose present shape owes an equally significant debt to print, and one whose past persists in a host of vernacular forms. Writing about the word *algorithm* and its conditions of emergence means accepting that "numbers were once among words," as Friedrich Kittler put it, and then possibly expanding the methodological ambit of key-words to include mathematical units, concepts, operations, and more.[11] It might even make sense to rename the whole endeavor "key-terms," since *term* not only functions as a synonym for *word* but also designates an element of a mathematical expression.

All that is to say, the challenges of writing about *algorithm* as a key-word are manifold, among them ethnocentrism, methodological individualism, and historical anachronism. Apropos of the latter theme, say the word *math* today and you're apt to conjure a host of familiar associations: numbers, notation, symbol manipulation; special tools like compasses, protractors, graph paper, slide rules, calculators, and spreadsheets; maybe even the mathematics classroom, or a composite image of the math teacher. Or the word might provoke more diffuse recollections— say, of a type of abstract (and for some, headache-inducing) mental discipline consisting of steps methodically taken and techniques painstakingly applied, any departure from which will land you in the valley of partial credit.

Whatever the case, for the purposes of this chapter it's critical to recognize that the academic discipline of mathematics, along with the institutions and apparatuses that have grown up around it, is but one way of formalizing the practices and modes of thinking referred to as such. Indeed, they need not be formalized at all. "Mathematics itself is only a particular formation of the mathematical," observed Martin Heidegger. This is why, etymologically, the word *mathematics* refers not only to a specific craft and discipline, but also to knowledge and learning more generally (hence, the *polymath*).[12] Similarly, Helen Verran has challenged the positivistic basis of Western mathematics, noting that so-called "natural" numbers (i.e., the positive integers, and sometimes zero) are about "as 'culture-free' as a rock."[13] Her objective isn't to deconstruct the underlying metaphysics, however, but to explore, anthropologically, the emergence of mathematical concepts and modes of thinking within specific communities of practice. Jens Høyrup, one of the leading historians of mathematics, has also developed this point. His research into the "social basis" of mathematics has led him to distinguish between "scientific" and "sub-scientific" frameworks for organizing mathematical knowledge:

> Scientific knowledge is knowledge which is pursued systematically and for its own sake . . . beyond the level of everyday knowledge. . . . Sub-scientific knowledge, on the other hand, is specialists' knowledge which . . . is acquired and transmitted in view of its applicability. Even sub-scientific knowledge is thus knowledge beyond the level of common understanding, and it may well be much more refined than "scientific" knowledge.[14]

The point is to recognize that significant aspects of the mathematical endeavor, historically speaking, have been driven by "surveyors, architects, master builders, and the like"—that is, by a laity whose practices and priorities need not have aligned with those of mathematicians, more strictly defined.[15] Indeed, both the label "mathematician" and the accompanying figure seem to have emerged only around the sixteenth century. Earlier, one was more likely to have been called a "geometer."[16] Høyrup's research has also shown how, time and again, the people whom we now identify as professional mathematicians raided the "vast supply— anonymous and ubiquitous—of [sub-scientific] mathematical problems and techniques," incorporating these precious resources into their own repertoires only then to disavow the very groups that, for generations, had been developing and refining them.[17]

Mathematics also used to look considerably different than it does now. Joseph Mazur has pointed out that, numerals not-withstanding, the notation people now typically identify as math (e.g., $+$, $-$, $\times$, $\div$, $=$, $>$, $<$, Σ, $\sqrt{}$, $\int$, etc.) largely didn't exist before the sixteenth century. Its prevalence today is attributable to a host of factors, among them inexpensive paper, which came to exist alongside, and to a certain degree displaced, abacuses, counting stones (*calculi*), and other tools that allowed merchants to perform mathematical calculations quickly and publicly, and with minimal need for written symbols. Notation was signifi-cantly affected by the affordances of print media, moreover, par-ticularly in the early modern period when typesetters struggled to reproduce elements of mathematical expressions in the inter-stices between lines. For example, Gottfried Wilhelm Leibniz (1646–1716) accommodated publishers by ceasing to use the vin-culum, or overline, to indicate mathematical grouping, substi-tuting inline parentheses that are common to this day.[18] But the story here isn't about mathematics diving ever deeper into the depths of symbolicity. To the contrary, the purpose of the story is to grasp how "the use of symbols . . . does not make" an expression mathematical "any more than words do."[19]

Indeed, the dividing line between mathematical expression and written or spoken language was less distinct before the six-teenth century. As Mazur has shown, European mathematical texts from the preceding two centuries tended to use alphabetically and phonetically inspired abbreviations to indicate mathematical variables and operations. Instead of today's ubiquitous x, Italian texts often employed the letter c, meaning *cosa* or "thing," to signify an unknown value. The letters *ce*, short for *censo* or "square," informed readers to multiply a value by itself. Other texts drew inspiration from Latin, employing the letters p and m to indicate addition (*plus*) and subtraction (*minus*), respectively.[20] Mathematical expressions, so rendered, bore only a passing resemblance to their counterparts of the present day. At the risk of imposing some anachronisms of my own, their style was more akin to the stripped-down staccato of telegraphic communiqués, or possibly even to that of text messaging. K?[21]

Indeed, the deeper you delve into the history of math, the better able you are to appreciate how far the locus of mathematical discourse shifted over the modern period. "Rhetorical" is an umbrella term that historians of math use to describe one of the leading forms of pre-modern mathematical discourse, particularly the narrative or expository style often seen in manuscripts produced before the sixteenth century CE. If notation was present at all, it tended to be minimal.[22] The writings of Moḥammed ibn-Mūsā al-Khwārizmī (c. 780–850 CE), the subject of the next sections of this chapter, are a case in point. Consider this passage from his treatise on algebra, written around 830 CE:

> Of the case in which *squares are equal to roots*, this is an example. "A square is equal to five roots of the same"; the root of the square is five, and the square is twenty-five, which is equal to five times its root.
>
> So you say, "one-third of the square is equal to four roots"; then the whole square is equal to twelve roots; that is a hundred and forty-four; and its root is twelve.

Or you say, "five squares are equal to ten roots"; then one square is equal to two roots; the root of the square is two, and its square is four.[23]

Tellingly, the first complete English-language edition of the manuscript, published in 1831, not only renders the original Arabic text in English but also contains footnotes further translating the author's rhetorical style into notation more comprehensible to modern readers.[24]

The gap between then and now isn't insignificant, clearly, and it seems only to widen as lyrical and oral forms of mathematical expression are introduced into the mix. Imagine, for a moment, the challenge of trying to explain even a middling mathematical operation to the uninitiated: say, how to calculate the square root of a fraction. Now, imagine trying to do so without modern notation—and in the form of metered verse. Such was the style in which the Indian mathematicians Aryabhaṭa (c. 476–550 CE) and Brahmagupta (c. 598–668 CE), both writing in Sanskrit, composed their major works. Laden with rhythm and rhyme, their writing appealed not only to the eye but to the ear. Surely, they wrote with the mnemotechnics of non-literate persons in mind.[25] The work is all the more impressive in that both figures didn't just recapitulate existing mathematical knowledge; they also pushed the boundaries. Thirteen centuries before *Schoolhouse Rock!* delivered the catchy jingle "My Hero, Zero" (1973), Brahmagupta's magnum opus, the *Brāhmasphuṭasiddhānta*, lyricized the then-unorthodox notion that zero was a number and, indeed, one of profound mathematical consequence.[26]

But how expansive, really, is the gap separating antiquity from today? Contemporary mathematicians may have opted out of verse (not all of them, it turns out), but that doesn't mean orally inclined modes of mathematical expression have disappeared altogether.[27] The challenge, again, is to rediscover mathematical concepts and operations in places other than the ones that are professionally sanctioned. For example, parents and caregivers routinely use song and verse to lay mathematical foundations for pre-literate children:

> One, two, buckle my shoe;
> Three, four, close the door;
> Five, six, pick up sticks;
> Seven, eight, lay them straight;
> Nine, ten, a big fat hen.

"This Old Man" also comes to mind here, as do calendar rhymes like "Solomon Grundy" and "Thirty Days Hath September."[28] They're not far removed from the quasi-rhythmic mathematical riddles you might have encountered in adolescence or adulthood, such as: If a hen and a half lay an egg and a half in a day and a half, how many eggs will half a dozen hens lay in half a dozen days? (Twenty-four, in case you're wondering—and why all the mathematical hens?) These examples, along with magic squares, Sudoku, and other instances of "recreational" math, point to the endurance of vernacular mathematical traditions. That is, they demonstrate how math maintains an intimate connection to everyday life, beyond textbooks and classrooms, and thus how it participates actively in "the adventure of lived ideas."[29]

Williams famously insisted that "culture is ordinary."[30] In hindsight, maybe he should've suggested that mathematics is ordinary too. Williams never managed to say that, of course, nor exactly did Marcia Ascher and Robert Ascher. Yet, in inaugurating the field of ethnomathematics in the 1980s, Ascher and Ascher complicated the relationship between culture and calculation. They acknowledged anthropology's longstanding interest in mathematical thought and practice but sharply criticized the discipline's treatment of the subject matter: "Most anthropologists were limited in their understanding of mathematics and have seldom asked relevant questions. . . . The category mathematics is our own, and so we cannot expect to find anything so labelled by other peoples."[31] Overstated, perhaps, but the point is nonetheless compelling. You shouldn't presume to know what mathematics is, where to find it, how and by whom it will be conducted, by what means it will be recorded and transmitted, nor even for what purpose it exists in a given place or time. Ascher and Ascher then go on to distinguish between "explicit mathematics," referring to formalized/professionalized ideas and operations (including, presumably, Høyrup's "sub-scientific" dimension), and "implicit mathematics," referring to concepts and practices immanent to a host of ordinary "areas and activities."[32] The former endeavor tends to be self-reflexive and cumulative; the latter tends to arise with respect to specific, everyday phenomena and, though abstract in its own right, generalizes little beyond the context at hand.

Importantly, Ascher and Ascher do for culture precisely what they do for mathematics: hold its facticity in abeyance. Granted, Ascher and Ascher employ the word *culture* throughout their landmark paper on ethnomathematics, using it in standard fashion to refer to human social groups and accompanying ways of life. Near the end, however, they offer an example of implicit mathematics, the significance of which they may not have fully appreciated. "Ordering human relationships is certainly as fundamental as imposing order on space," they write. "In our [presumably Western] culture, interest in the logical structuring of kinship is minimal; in others, it is a much more elaborate and dynamic element of daily life."[33] The example is startling in that

it suggests how kinship, one of the most fundamental and abiding concerns of anthropology, is irreducible to the culture concept. One can make sense of purportedly "cultural" relationships
mathematically, that is, without respect to the culture concept.
So, on the one hand, Ascher and Ascher's work underscores the
conceptual, semantic, and functional proximity of culture to
mathematics (or, at least, to a certain type of mathematical imagination). On the other hand, it raises difficult questions about
how much the word *culture* explains, and how much it potentially explains away.[34]

Moving forward, the objective is to resist the temptation to
see mathematics strictly as a tool for abstraction, and to re-embed
fundamental aspects of mathematical thought, practice, and
expression in the everyday. But there's something even more
counterintuitive going on here: Per Ascher and Ascher, what if
we resisted the impulse to use culture as an explanatory vehicle
for mathematics, even if only initially? Is it possible, or desirable, to conceive of "cultural" relationships absent the culture
concept? If so, what might those relationships consist of, and
what methods would be used for making sense of them? Moreover, if *culture* is a touchstone for Western self-understanding,
as I argued in the introduction to this book, then what are the
historical and political entailments of conceiving of algorithms
as instances, expressions, or manifestations of culture, particularly with respect to figuring relations between "the West and
the rest?"[35] After all, *algorithm* is a loanword traceable to Central Asia, the establishment of Islam, and the consolidation
of the Persian Empire. In pointing to this history, I'm inviting
you to let go momentarily of the "guarantee" of culture, to embrace
the fact that *algorithm* long predates *culture*'s modern senses
and meanings, and thus to consider *algorithm*—at least for a
little while—on its own terms.

IMAGINING THE ALGORITHM

Eubanks is right to point out how, currently, "we have remarkably limited access to the equations, algorithms, and models that shape our life chances."[36] Perhaps that will change in the years and decades to come, as the struggle for algorithmic justice continues. But for now, we're mostly left filling in the blanks on what algorithms are and the mysterious ways in which they work. Little wonder—as I noted in the introduction to this book—that the figure of the algorithm has grown increasingly widespread in and beyond popular culture.[37] Its presence is indicative of the emergence of what Ed Finn has called an "algorithmic imagination," although I'm bending the concept, admittedly. Finn is interested in describing how computational systems such as Google engage in forms of imaginative thinking when, for example, they seem to predict what we want to search for.[38] Without diminishing the importance of predictive analytics, my use of "algorithmic imagination" is closer to C. Wright Mills's concept of the "sociological imagination," which he used to describe the epistemological conditions whereby individuals may become self-conscious of their positions in, and movements through, a society.[39] Similarly, by "algorithmic imagination" I'm referring to instances in which people become aware of, and possibly self-reflexive about, their relationships to computationally based decision systems. This definition aligns closely with Taina Bucher's understanding of the "algorithmic imaginary," by which she means "the public's beliefs, experiences, and expectations of what an algorithm is and should be."[40]

The emergence of an algorithmic imagination is a positive development, generally, particularly when it's understood in this "sociological" sense. Compared to 2010, when I first began writing about algorithmic culture, I can now safely assume some cognizance of the word *algorithm* and of the issues pertaining to the relationship between algorithms and culture.[41] Yet, as discourse on the topic proliferates, it becomes too easy to assume too much about what it takes to situate algorithms, or *algorithm*, in context. This is as true of academic scholarship as it is of journalism and popular culture, all of which and more participate in constructing an algorithmic imagination.

For example, what to make of writers' oft-repeated invocation of Mohammed ibn-Mūsā al-Khwārizmī, the figure from whose name the English-language word *algorithm* purportedly derives? It seems enough to say that he was a Persian mathematician who, in the ninth century CE, introduced the basic principles of algebra in his book *Al-Kitāb al-Mukhtaṣar fī ḥisāb al-jabr wa-al-Muqābala* (roughly, *The Compendious Book of Calculation by Restoration and Balancing*) and, in another untitled volume, the Indo-Arabic numerals.[42] This bit of historical detail establishes a human origin for the term *algorithm* and its association with mathematics. It also, importantly, underscores how any account of algorithmic culture necessarily exceeds Western history. "It is something beyond irony," observes Tarleton Gillespie, "that *algorithm*, which now drops its exotic flavor into Western discussions of the information society, honors an Arabic mathematician from the high court of Baghdad."[43]

The impulse to acknowledge al-Khwārizmī is an admirable one. The political climate in the United States and elsewhere, often hostile to Islam, renders any such acknowledgment a political act of inclusion, one undoubtedly aimed at troubling normative canons and maybe even racial stereotypes. By the same token, the "al-Khwārizmī story," as I call it, bespeaks a tendency among writers to arrest a term that is now everywhere and in motion.[44] In providing a seemingly stable set of etymological, textual, corporeal, and ethno-religious bearings, the al-Khwārizmī story renders *algorithm* manageable in much the same manner as the word's subsumption under the rubric of *culture*. While there's nothing inherently wrong in invoking the figure of al-Khwārizmī, doing so shouldn't come at the cost of asking questions about the story's explanatory power. Among them: To what extent is it appropriate to locate al-Khwārizmī as *algorithm*'s human point of origin? Given what we now know about the history and sociology of mathematical knowledge, is it right to label someone working in al-Khwārizmī's time a "mathematician?" Or, better still, what relationship, if any, might his work have shared with sub-scientific, vernacular, or implicit forms of mathematics? What does it mean to identify al-Khwārizmī as "Persian" or "Arabic?" What more might we learn about al-Khwārizmī, *algorithm*, and perhaps even *culture* by reading—instead of referring indirectly to—his manuscripts and other relevant artifacts? Is the al-Khwārizmī story sufficient to ground a truly robust algorithmic imagination?

These are difficult questions—more difficult than they might at first appear. The challenges are not only substantive, but methodological. The historical record on al-Khwārizmī is sparse, as I mentioned earlier; it's also, significantly, the product of a combined oral-manuscript culture in which the referential guarantees—the "fixity"—of print didn't yet exist.[45] In the ninth century CE/third century AH, the lexical landscape was molten. Thus, in studying material from al-Khwārizmī's time, we cannot take terms, definitions, or other points of orientation for granted. Witness the frustration of historian George A. Saliba in attempting to trace the etymology of major terms in premodern Arab mathematics:

Arab algebra used the word *jabr* to mean more than one operation, which resulted in terminological confusion. The word *muqābalah* was used in an equally inconsistent manner. And to add to the confusion these two words, *jabr* and *muqābalah*[,] were also used to denote operations that were commonly denoted by the terms *radd* and *ikmāl*.[46]

With regard to al-Khwārizmī specifically, mathematician Asuman Güven Aksoy attributes the muddle to al-Khwārizmī's having "invent[ed] language to communicate with others." Historians Jeffrey A. Oaks and Haitham M. Alkhateeb provide a more nuanced analysis, noting how "the Arabic words *al-jabr* and *al-muqābala* were appropriated from everyday language into arithmetic and algebra in nontechnical ways."[47] Whatever the case, the endeavor here is akin to gazing to the edges of the known universe, where space, time, matter, and every other constant becomes suddenly, disarmingly fuzzy.

The point of testing the adequacy of the al-Khwārizmī story isn't simply to see how well it holds up but, more importantly, to bear witness to the power dynamics endemic to the process of expropriating and entextualizing mathematical knowledge, and in drawing links between racialized individuals and contemporary technologies. "High-tech Orientalism," observes Wendy Hui Kyong Chun, "would seem to be the limit case for race as technology, for it literally figures the raced other as technology."[48] Apropos, what to make of the claim that al-Khwārizmī is the authoritative source of the word *algorithm*? In Finn, for example, we learn:

The word [*algorithm*] itself derives from Abū 'Abdallāh Muḥammad ibn Mūsa al-Khwārizmī, the famed ninth-century C.E. mathematician (from whose name *algebra* is also derived). *Algorismus* was originally the process for calculating Hindu-Arabic numerals. Via al-Kwarizmi, the algorithm was associated with the revolutionary concepts of positional notation, the decimal point, and zero.[49]

Or consider this passage from Christopher Steiner's *Automate This*, appearing in a section entitled "Where Did Algorithms Come From?":

> The word *algorithm* comes from Abu Abdullah Muhammad ibn Musa Al-Khwarizmi, a Persian mathematician from the ninth century who produced the first known book of algebra. . . . Algebra's name comes straight from the *al-Jabr* in the book's title. As scholars disseminated Al-Khwarizmi's work in Latin during the Middle Ages, the translation of his name—"algorism"—came to describe any method of systematic or automatic calculation.[50]

The conclusion seems straightforward enough: *algorithm* derives from al-Khwārizmī. When the name says it all, what more is there to say?

The issue here is prevalent in the history and sociology of science, which, as I noted in the introduction, has a habit of mistaking its endeavor for the history and sociology of scientists.[51] This slippage is particularly troubling where al-Khwārizmī is concerned. In identifying him as the irreducible point of origin for the word *algorithm*, observers seem to believe they're bearing witness to complex cultural and ethno-religious traditions. They are, however, actively effacing them. As Stuart Hall reminds us: "It was the silences that told us something; it was what wasn't there. It was what was invisible, what couldn't be put into frame, what was apparently unsayable that we needed to attend to."[52]

Lest we forget, surnames are no less given than are first or "given" names. Though their specific sources are often lost to history, many surnames were coined on the basis of physical or moral attributes, occupations, skills, resemblances (to animals, plants, and objects), social standing, patronymy, matronymy, and possession (as in the case of slave ownership). Toponymy, still another source, applies to al-Khwārizmī, whose name references the place from which his family is believed to have hailed: Khwarizm, an area in Central Asia situated near the South Aral Sea.[53] Straddling parts of present-day Uzbekistan, Kazakhstan, and Turkmenistan, Khwarizm is a refuge from the surrounding terrain. The source of the name "Khwarizm" is contested, referring variously to "low," "nourishing," or even "abject" land.[54] There, parched deserts and sweeping plateaus give way to the nestling waters and loamy silt of the Amu Darya River Delta. By one account, "Khwarizm must from the earliest times have been of importance for the development of civilisation in Central Asia." Herodotus, the famed Greek historian, attested to the area's significance in the fifth century BCE, and Alexander the Great is believed to have received the King of Khwarizm, Pharasmanes, about a century later.[55]

Important, yes, but hardly idyllic. As a crossroads of Asia, it was, and remains, strategic territory for rulers intent on empire-building. Archaeological records for Khwarizm date back to about 6,000 BCE, although relatively little is known about the region's early inhabitants. Evidently, they were hunter-gatherers who fished and eventually herded livestock, established agriculture, and engaged in metallurgy. Legend has it that Khwarizm became a stronghold for Turkish peoples and a "thriving kingdom of antiquity" around the thirteenth century BCE.[56] It fell to the first Persian (Achaemenid) Empire in the sixth century BCE, however, and remained under imperial control for about two centuries. The Persian conquest of Khwarizm helped to solidify the prevalence of Zoroastrianism in the region starting with Darius I (c. 550–486 BCE), the earliest of the Persian emperors to have adopted the religion.[57] Independence from Persia was punctuated by episodic incursions by nomadic tribes, leading to ongoing political unrest.

Nevertheless, inhabitants of the area maintained their own spoken language, Khwārazmian, and by the first century BCE they'd established their own script, a derivation from Aramaic, which had been "brought to the region by the administration of the Achaemenid empire."[58] The history of empire may well be the history of writing things down.[59] Later, the Khwārazmian people introduced their own calendar, inspired by its Zoroastrian counterpart, possibly to signal the end of Parthian rule.[60] Year one of the "Chorasmian [*sic*] era" seems to have occurred somewhere in the second quarter of the first century CE.[61] Modern historians may have imposed the label, yet their having done so shouldn't diminish the significance of the Khwārazmian assertion of calendar-power.[62] Khwārazmian time endured for 800 years, despite the return of Persian control to Khwarizm in the second century CE, this time under the Sasanian Empire.

Today, the Khwārazmian language is all but extinct. Traces of the written form persist on rare coins, pottery pieces, and ossuary inscriptions excavated from archaeological ruins; in scholia appearing in a lone Arabic dictionary from the twelfth century CE/sixth century AH; and in the form of about four hundred sentences preserved by Arab legal scholars in texts from the thirteenth century CE/seventh century AH. The spoken language, so-called "old-Chorasmian," is basically lost. Owing to a general absence of vowels from the written artifacts, "it is possible to represent the language only in unvocalized transliteration."[63] In contrast to other purportedly "dead" languages such as Latin, whose grammar and pronunciation are nonetheless still with us, Khwārazmian appears to be (if you'll pardon the colloquialism) "dead-dead." But the Khwārazmian language and accompanying calendar didn't simply fade out over time. Instead, "the brilliant culture of the Kharezm [*sic*] Province was discriminated out of existence" starting around 712 CE/93 AH, when Qutaybah ibn Muslim, the Arab governor of nearby Khorasan, invaded in the midst of a Khwārazmian civil war.[64]

"Discriminated" may be putting it lightly. Despite the Muslim principle of *dhimma*, which offered a measure of protection for Jews, Christians, Sabaeans, Zoroastrians, and Hindus dwelling in Muslim or Muslim-occupied territories, people who hadn't accepted Islam were in this period subordinated and marked as other. Though they were allowed to maintain their faith and participate in public affairs, opportunities for social and economic mobility were restricted: "Non-believers were often considered to be 'internal emigrants' and not permitted to rise to the same rank as Muslims." Jews and Christians were uniquely singled out with identifying badges—yellow and blue, respectively—they were forced to wear on their clothing.[65] An account by the Khwārazmian intellectual al-Bīrunī (c. 973–1050 CE/362–440 AH), penned three centuries after Qutayba's invasion, suggests daily life under Arab rule was beset with psychological, epistemological, and physical intimidation. "Qutayba did away with those who knew the script of Khwarezm [*sic*], who understood the country's traditions and taught the knowledge of its inhabitants; he submitted them to tortures so that they were wrapped up in the shadows and no one could know (even in Khwarezm) what had (preceded) or followed the birth of Islam."[66]

Algorithm refers to a person, then, but also to a place laden with imperial, colonial, and ethno-religious history. And it's this context into which al-Khwārizmī—both the figure and the story—must now be enfolded. Was he Persian? Perhaps, but the label seems to identify him primarily with the city where he came to settle, Baghdad, or with an area nearby, Qutrubbull, possibly his birthplace.[67] Other accounts suggest he may have hailed from Khiva, formerly the city of Khwarezm, which took its name from the surrounding region.[68] Alternatively, the label "Persian" may refer to al-Khwārizmī's relationship to Khwārazmian, a language he or his ancestors were likely to have spoken. But speaking a Persianate language doesn't make someone Persian any more than speaking French, Portuguese, or another Latin-derived language makes someone else Roman. All of al-Khwārizmī's major writings were in Arabic, moreover, further complicating any straightforward ethno-linguistic identification. There's also some question as to whether he was a Muslim for his entire life, or if he'd converted from Zoroastrianism. If al-Khwārizmī did convert, he may have done so to curry favor at the court of his patron, Caliph al-Mamun (c. 813–833 CE/198–218 AH), or possibly to avoid the *mihna*, an inquisition of non-believers.[69] It's also worth mentioning that the epithet "ibn-Musa," or "son of Moses," suggests an indeterminate connection to Judaism.[70]

Periodizing al-Khwārizmī's life is no less vexing. It was uncommon to be aware of one's birth year in al-Khwārizmī's time.[71] More important for record-keeping purposes, where such practices existed, were the names of family members and possibly the location of one's birth. Any knowledge we may now have about al-Khwārizmī's birthdate is a reconstruction by later historians, often by the very type of Orientalist scholars whom Edward W. Said criticized in his magnum opus, *Orientalism*.[72] But the issue runs deeper than the epistemology of birth records, or even the ways in which the modern West produced the "Orient" as an object of knowledge. The claim that al-Khwārizmī was born in the ninth century CE of the Gregorian calendar, or even that he was born in the third century AH of the Islamic calendar, says more about the exercise of power in defining time and structuring human "time-sense" than it does about al-Khwārizmī's biography. What to make of the fact that virtually no one mentions his having been born in the eighth century of the Khwārazmian calendar? "Whoever sets the time rules the society," observes John Durham Peters. Or, as Stephen Nissenbaum puts it, "the power to *name* time was also the power to *control* it."[73]

If anything is clear about al-Khwārizmī, then, it's that he or his ancestors emigrated from the steppe land of Central Asia to Baghdad, and while he may have enjoyed some privileges as an intellectual working at the court of al-Mamun, he was not of the preferred background.[74] But the point isn't really to correct the al-Khwārizmī story with the "facts." Rather, the point is to appreciate the degree to which the story as such perpetuates a long-standing pattern whereby a people, a place, a language, and a time system are actively disappeared not only through physical conquest, but also through symbolic annihilation. The contemporary imperative to etymologize al-Khwārizmī bears an uncanny resemblance to earlier practices of entombing fragments of the Khwārazmian language in the pages of authoritative Arabic texts. In both cases, the sanctification of origin and meaning occurs through processes of entextualization whose very condition, ironically, is the eradication of whole repertoires of minoritarian discursive practices. This is precisely what Siraj Ahmed means by the phrase "philological power," or what you might call, alternatively, the will to philologize: the evisceration of communicative traditions through their apparent preservation.[75]

DIXIT ALGORIZMI?

As examples from the preceding section show, contemporary authors are often quick to recognize al-Khwārizmī for having introduced both the Indo-Arabic number system and key principles of algebra. Giving credit where credit is due is, evidently, part of the modus operandi of the al-Khwārizmī story. But so too is the tendency among present-day observers to mention al-Khwārizmī's manuscripts on numeration and algebra without ever discussing the substance of those books in detail, much less considering their historicity as media/material objects. Perhaps the omission has something to do with their "rhetorical" style, which can be alienating to readers unaccustomed to expository mathematical writing. Or perhaps it has something to do with the authority ascribed to the figure of al-Khwārizmī, both in and through these books. The most well-known copy of the manuscript on numeration, a thirteenth-century Latin translation housed at the University of Cambridge, opens with the invocation "Dixit Algorizmi," or "al-Khwārizmī said." The phrase is repeated several times in the manuscript. Another version of the manuscript opens similarly: "Incipit prologus in libro alghoarism" ("Here begins the book of algorism"), as if to consecrate the author's words, insights, and authorial status.[76] Whatever the case, it's worth exploring what these and other texts not only say but *do* apropos of the will to philologize.

Al-Khwārizmī is believed to have been born about thirty years after Chinese papermaking techniques had wound their way into West Asia. The story of how this came to pass is the subject of speculation. By some accounts, Chinese prisoners of war, captured during the Battle of Tallas (751 CE/133 AH), may have revealed the new arts of papermaking to their Muslim captors as a condition of their freedom.[77] However the techniques were passed on, the new process carried significant advantages over earlier ones. Instead of reeds (used in the production of papyrus), which required specific growing conditions, or expensive calf skin (the basis for vellum), papermakers could now utilize rags or wood pulp for raw material. Paper became cheaper and more plentiful thanks to these everyday resources.

The change was particularly welcome in Baghdad, where the climate was less than ideal for supporting large-scale production of papyrus. Al-Fazl, brother of a high-ranking member of the Abbasid caliphate, reportedly established a paper mill in the city in 793 CE/177 AH, which utilized Chinese techniques. Al-Khwārizmī probably would have been a teenager at the time. It's worth noting that Baghdad had been installed as the capital city of the Abbasid Empire only three decades prior (previously, the capital had been Damascus), and that it was still actively under construction when the mill was founded. The latter may have been more than just the artifact of a fledgling industry; it may also have been a physical extension of the Abbasid dynasty's growing imperial power. The existence of a type of paper, *Ma'muni*, named for Caliph al-Mamun, would seem to confirm the mill's material and symbolic importance. Clearly, it was a critical element of the industrial infrastructure for what would become a thriving textual culture under the reign of al-Mamun.[78]

Al-Mamun is believed to have founded Bayt al-Hakima, the "House of Wisdom," a think tank dedicated to the pursuit of what would now be described as scientific and philosophical knowledge. It's the institution from which al-Khwārizmī received patronage and under whose auspices he produced works on astronomy, trigonometry, geography, the Jewish calendar, and possibly history, in addition to the manuscripts already mentioned. The House of Wisdom was a linguistic crossroads, moreover, serving as a key site for what contemporary historians label the "translation movement." It's doubtful figures now associated with the movement would have identified themselves as such. Nevertheless, from about the eighth until the thirteenth centuries CE (roughly the second to the seventh centuries AH), a desire for intellectual, religious, and military superiority fueled intense interest among Muslim rulers in translating texts written in Latin, "Greek, Syriac, and Persian languages . . . into Arabic by expert Arabists."[79] Given al-Khwārizmī's work on the "Hindu art of reckoning," a title often ascribed to the manuscript on numeration, it seems reasonable to surmise there was interest in translating or adapting material from South and perhaps East Asia as well. The period 750–850 CE/132–235 AH, which spanned al-Khwārizmī's association with the House of Wisdom, was particularly active where the production of textual matter was concerned.

Appreciating the densely layered textuality of al-Khwārizmī's work is critical to understanding both the constructedness of the al-Khwārizmī story and the conditions of emergence of contemporary algorithmic culture. What's the significance of crediting him for having authored books on Indo-Arabic numeration and the foundational principles of algebra? Or, as John N. Crossley and Alan S. Henry put it in the preface to their English-language translation of the manuscript on numeration, "What is this text?"[80] The question couldn't be more apt. Until the early twentieth century, it was common practice to bind multiple manuscripts—sometimes unrelated—together in a single volume. Such is the case with the manuscript on numeration, which occupies a single edition alongside several other manuscripts, only some of which pertain to the subject of mathematics.[81] Perhaps this is splitting hairs, but the suggestion that al-Khwārizmī produced "books" is something of an anachronism. It may be more accurate to say he produced writings on leaves of paper that were subsequently produced and presented *as books*—which is to say, as coherent and authoritative textual artifacts—by binders, translators, commentators, librarians, and other interested parties. Furthermore, it's difficult if not impossible to ascertain the degree to which the manuscripts composed by al-Khwārizmī ought to be considered singularly *his*. This isn't to suggest misattribution of authorship. Rather, the point is to appreciate the degree to which we're dealing with objects whose being-in-the-world is a product of what book historians sometimes refer to as "textual corruption" (which is only corruption from the standpoint of modern readers who expect rarefied texts). Consider this description of the work on numeration: "Essentially all we have is an incomplete 13th-century copy of what is probably a 12th-century translation from Arabic into Latin; the original Arabic may well have been considerably different," as evident, if nothing else, in the translator(s), scribe(s), or illuminator(s) having struggled to represent the concept of place value using Roman numerals.[82]

The manuscript on algebra is in a comparable state, although at least eleven known copies of it exist. The list includes six editions in Arabic, three in medieval Latin, and one each in Italian and Hebrew.[83] The Arabic edition that resides in the Bodleian Library, Oxford University, is the basis for the standard English-language translation of work. Frederic (Friedrich) Rosen, the translator, described the manuscript thus:

It is written in a plain and legible hand, but unfortunately destitute of most of the diacritical points: a deficiency which has often been sensibly felt; for though the nature of the subject matter can but seldom leave little doubt as to the general import of a sentence, yet the true reading of some passages, and the precise interpretation of others, remain involved in obscurity. Besides, there occur several omissions of words, and even of entire sentences, and also instances of words or short passages written twice over, or words foreign to the sense introduced in the text.[84]

Ironically, Heinz Zemanek, writing in 1981, faults the Rosen translation of 1831 for its numerous "shortcomings" and laments the lack of an "improved edition and revised translation."[85] Try as they might, translators and scribes seem eternally condemned to charges of infidelity.

The words *algorism* and, later, *algorithm* wound their way into the English language most likely along circuitous pathways. Linguistic innovation is often oral before it's textual, and particularly so during the period under consideration here. Nevertheless, the significance of the Latin translations of the material on numeration, both of which invoke al-Khwārizmī by name, shouldn't be underestimated. Nor should two of the extant Latin translations of the *Algebra* manuscript (as I will henceforth refer to it), the first attributed to Robert of Chester (c. 1145 CE/539 AH), the second to Gerard of Cremona (c. 1170 CE/565 AH), both of whom resided in Moorish Spain.[86] "The translations," observes Barnabas Hughes, "were the . . . vehicles that carried algebra throughout much of medieval Europe"—and, presumably, prompted a burgeoning familiarity with a semantic figure that would eventually coalesce into the word *algorithm*.[87]

The name "Algus," evidently referring to al-Khwārizmī, appears in the poem *Le Roman de la Rose*, written in Old French in the thirteenth century CE/seventh century AH:

| Bien la vous vosisse descrire, | I would willingly describe her to you, |
| Mès mi sens n'i porroit soffire, | but my sense is not equal to it. |

Mi sens! qu'ai-ge dit? c'est du mains,	My sense! What have I said? That's the least one could say.
Non feroit voir nus sens humains,	No human sense would show her,
Ne par vois vive, ne par notes,	Either vocally or in writing,
Et fust Platon ou Aristotes,	Even if it were Plato or Aristotle,
Algus, Euclides, Tholomées,	Algus, Euclid, or Ptolemy,
Qui tant orent de renommées	Who now have such great reputations
D'avoir esté bon escrivain,	For having been good writers,
Lor engin seroient si vain,	Their wits would be so useless,
S'il osoient la chose emprendre,	If they dared undertake the task,
Qu'il ne la porroient entendre.	That they could not do so.[88]

The stanza is intriguing if for no other reason than it raises doubts about the ability of "algorithm" to reckon with and represent gendered subjects. Chaucer is believed to have read and translated *Le Roman de la Rose*, work that may have inspired two references to al-Khwārizmī in his own poetry. The first instance, spelled "Argus," appears in *The Book of the Duchess* (c. 1368 CE/770 AH) and is perhaps the oldest extant use of the name in written Middle English:

That thogh Argus, the noble countour,	That though Algus, the noble counter,
Sete to rekene in his countour,	Had set to reckoning that encounter,
And rekene with his figures ten—	And reckoned with his numerals ten—

For by tho figures mowe al ken,	For by those numerals all may ken,
If they be crafty, rekene and noumbre,	If they be skillful, all the sum there
And telle of every thing the noumbre—	And tell of everything the number—
Yet shulde he fayle to rekene even	Yet even he would fail to reckon
The wondres, me mette in my sweven.	The wonders that in dream did beckon.[89]

Here again, the algorithm fails in its task. Al-Khwārizmī makes another cameo in *The Canterbury Tales* (c. 1400 CE/802 AH), specifically in the Miller's Tale where "hende [clever] Nicholas," a pedant and scoundrel, tutored in the arts, is consumed by mathematical calculations:

And koude a certeyn of conclusiouns,	And he knew a certain (number) of operations,
To demen by interrogaciouns,	To determine by scientific calculations,
If that men asked hym, in certein houres	If men asked him, in specific hours
Whan that men sholde have droghte or elles shoures,	When men should have drought or else showers,
[. . .]	[. . .]
His Almageste, and bookes grete and smale,	His Almagest, and books large and small,
His astrelabie, longynge for his art,	His astrolabe, belonging to his art,
His augrym stones layen faire apart,	His counting [algorithm] stones lie neatly apart,

On shelves couched at his   Arranged on shelves at
beddes heed;   his bed's head;[90]

The stanzas are significant for a couple of reasons. Substantively, they raise questions about the nature of scientific calculation, which, in this rendering, overly intellectualizes the repertoires of daily life. Everyone already knows when to bathe or have a beer. Grammatically, they instance a shift of cases: the proper noun Argus from *The Book of the Duchess* has transformed into the adjectival form, "augrym." Rarely are such shifts innocent, and such is the case here given Chaucer's reputation as a chronicler of vernacular English. He may have been privy to people talking into existence a term roughly equivalent to the modern form, "algorithmic."

The point is to appreciate the complex genesis of the terms and conditions of algorithmic culture and, more specifically, the degree to which its emergence depended on historically freighted processes of entextualizing (arresting, circumscribing, authorizing) ordinary thought, conduct, and expression. Nowhere is this pattern more evident than with respect to Rosen's translation of the al-Khwārizmī *Algebra* book. What to make of the attribution "Printed for the Oriental Translation Fund" appearing on the title page?

Rosen was born in Hanover, Germany, in 1805 and died in London, England, in 1837. His life, short in years, was long in textual matter. After an initial foray into law he came to study under Franz Bopp, who was renowned for having developed comparative philology and, eventually, the Proto-Indo-European hypothesis, which posited a common "Aryan" basis for Asiatic and European languages.[91] Rosen himself set about producing works on the origins of Sanskrit, a translation of the *Rgveda* (a collection of sacred Vedic hymns), and, of course, an

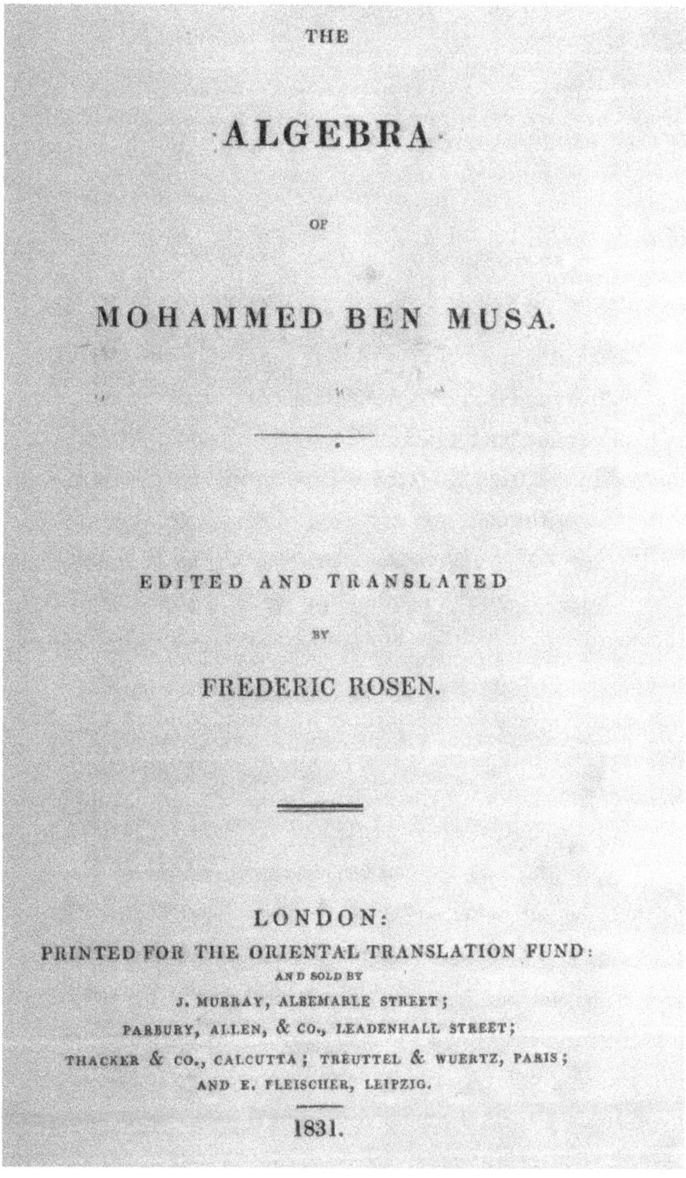

THE

·ALGEBRA·

OF

MOHAMMED BEN MUSA.

EDITED AND TRANSLATED

BY

FREDERIC ROSEN.

LONDON:
PRINTED FOR THE ORIENTAL TRANSLATION FUND:
AND SOLD BY
J. MURRAY, ALBEMARLE STREET;
PARBURY, ALLEN, & CO., LEADENHALL STREET;
THACKER & CO., CALCUTTA; TREUTTEL & WUERTZ, PARIS;
AND E. FLEISCHER, LEIPZIG.

1831.

FIGURE 2.2 Title page of *The Algebra of Mohammed Ben Musa*, edited and translated by Frederic (Friedrich) Rosen, 1831.

English-language edition of al-Khwārizmī's *Algebra*, among other notable writings. Much of this work happened after he'd moved to London, where, for two years, he was chair of philology at London University (now University College London). He taught Persian, Arabic, Hindi, and Urdu to students bound for the English colonies.[92]

The move to London placed him deep in the trenches of English colonial-philological power. It was there that he fell in with Henry Thomas Colebrooke, whose father, Sir George Colebrooke, had served as chairperson of the British East India Company, following a stint as a member of Parliament. Henry began working as a civil servant in India at age seventeen and was stationed there for more than thirty years.[93] By age forty, he'd risen through the ranks to become head of the Court of Appeals of Calcutta. In that capacity he authored, among many other documents, a legal brief in 1812 legitimating the continuation of slavery in India, even though Britain had abolished the slave trade five years earlier. Colebrooke believed there was a particularly important need to maintain the enslavement of children, a practice he likened to a social welfare program for destitute Indian families, for whom child-selling could become a source of income.[94] Moreover, while it's unknown whether Colebrooke owned enslaved persons himself, "it was common for British residents in India to have household slaves and to have no more than fleeting qualms about them," as Rosane Rocher and Ludo Rocher have written.[95] Colebrooke is also known to have fathered at least three children—Eliza, Sophia, and John Henry—with one or more Indian concubines, women whose names went unrecorded on the children's birth records.[96] According to Rocher and Rocher, the "children were whitewashed, as it were, of their Indian mothers and extirpated from their mothers' culture and religion."[97]

Colebrooke's interest in the law, and the connections he drew between law and philology, closely paralleled those of Sir William Jones, whose work Ahmed traces in *Archaeology of Babel*: "Colonial textual authority was . . . Jones's remedy for the evil of native clerical authority." Typically, this "remedy" took the form of "the substitution of a historically authoritative text," prepared by one or more European scholars, for the "heterogeneous manuscripts and performances" that for generations had guided autochthonous juridical practices.[98] The entry for Colebrooke, published in the *Dictionary of National Biography* (1887) fifty years after his death, affirms he was similarly inclined: "The difficulties attending the administration of justice among natives [in India] according to their own law made a study of the latter essential to the proper exercise of judicial functions with which Colebrooke was now entrusted."[99] Colebrooke even completed Jones's translation of *A Digest of Hindu Laws on Contract and Succession* (1797), the project almost having been scuttled after Jones's sudden death, in 1794. Colebrooke's pursuits exceeded the law, moreover, extending into the realms of astronomy and mathematics. In 1817 he published the first English translation of the work of Brahmagupta and that of another Indian mathematician, Bhāskara (c. 1114–1185 CE), both of whom had written in Sanskrit.[100]

While in India, Colebrooke became a member of the Asiatic Society of Calcutta and an avid reader of *Asiatic Researches*, the society's journal. Jones had established the organization in 1784, with Colebrooke later serving as president. For more than forty years, the society was open only to persons of European descent.[101] Colebrooke sought similar company upon returning to London in 1814, founding the Asiatic Society of Great Britain and Ireland and its journal, *Transactions of the Asiatic*

Society, in 1823. The group consisted largely of colonial scholar-administrators like himself, and in 1824 it was issued a royal charter by King George IV, a patron of the society. The Oriental Translation Fund, inaugurated in 1828, would provide London's budding philological community with financial and institutional resources with which "to publish, free of expense to the Authors, translations of the whole or parts of such works in the Oriental languages as the Oriental Translation Committee shall approve." Its purpose was archival, moreover, with the broader aim of fostering social reproduction through education: "These translations are generally to be accompanied by the original texts printed separately, and such illustrations as may be considered necessary. By the publication of the original text it is intended to multiply copies of such works as are scarce, and to furnish students at a moderate expense with correct copies of the best Asiatic works, to which they might not otherwise have access."[102]

But what type of subject, exactly, did the Royal Asiatic Society hope to produce through exposure to these texts? It seems the point wasn't merely for readers to consume "Oriental" texts on their own terms. Instead, it was to imagine the texts as proto-logical sources of European culture, and therefore as sources whose intellectual, spiritual, and moral worth had long since exhausted itself. From a philological standpoint, Asia amounted to nothing less and nothing more than Europe's pre-civilizational past.[103] The prospectus for the Fund addressed this theme explicitly:

> Whatever may be our present superiority over Asia in the arts and sciences, it cannot be uninteresting to the inquiring mind to recur to the sources from which we derived the first elements of our

knowledge. In this respect Asia must be recognized as the elder sister and instructress of Europe; and although the hordes of barbarians, which poured forth like a torrent from her northwestern regions, effectually extinguished the light which she at first imparted, yet we are indebted to the Mohammedan courts of Cordova, Grenada, and Seville, for its restoration, as it is to them that Europe owes the rudiments of many of her now highly cultivated arts and sciences.[104]

Such was the atmosphere in which Colebrooke approached Rosen, suggesting he undertake a translation of the al-Khwārizmī *Algebra* manuscript residing in the Bodleian Library.[105]

Colebrooke knew of the manuscript having translated part of the work himself: the material comprising a prefatory section of the Brahmagupta/Bhāskara volume entitled "Progress and Proficiency of the Arabians in Algebra."[106] Though neither complete nor definitive, Colebrooke's translation of the *Algebra* was likely the first instance of the work to be published in English. It was also, quite possibly, the first of *any* of the mathematical works attributed to al-Khwārizmī to appear in the language. Like virtually all of these writings, moreover, the circumstances surrounding the translation were hardly unambiguous. As Colebrooke admitted:

The rules of the library, though access be readily allowed, preclude the study of any book which it contains, by a person not enured [*sic*] to the temperature of apartments unvisited by artificial warmth. This impediment to the examination of the manuscript in question has been remedied by the assistance of the under[-] librarian Mr. Alexander Nicoll; who has furnished ample extracts purposely transcribed by him from the manuscript.[107]

To put it in no uncertain terms: the mathematics of "the Khuwárezmí," as Colebrooke referred to him, initially appeared in English in the form of a nineteenth-century translation of a nineteenth-century transcription of a fourteenth-century Arabic transcription of material composed in the ninth century CE/third century AH—notwithstanding whatever else may have happened in between.

Given Colebrooke's aversion to chilly rooms, one can only wonder about the degree to which environmental factors have affected the history of media, the will to philologize, and indeed the biography of the word *algorithm*.[108] In any case, his express purpose for including the al-Khwārizmī excerpt was to establish what he believed to be the irreducibility of Indian algebra, and thus the point of origin for European mathematics.[109] It would fall to Rosen to translate the manuscript, duly demoted, in its entirety, but even Rosen could scarcely execute the task: "A highly distinguished friend of mathematical science . . . has with great patience and care revised and corrected my translation, and has furnished the commentary, subjoined to the text, in the form of common algebraic notation."[110] The standard English-language edition of the *Algebra* was twice translated, in other words: once into contemporary English prose, a second time into modern mathematical symbolism.

But what, exactly, did Rosen and company believe they were translating? At the heart of the question lies a passage appearing in al-Khwārizmī's preface to the *Algebra*: "The Imam al-Mamun, the Commander of the Faithful . . . has encouraged me to compose ["compile" in Colebrooke's translation] a short work on Calculating by (the rule of) Completion and Reduction, confining it to what is easiest and most useful in arithmetic, such as men constantly require in cases of inheritance, legacies, partition, law-suits, and trade, and in their dealings with one another."[111] Rosen and Colebrooke are in general agreement as to the interpretation of the statement: if al-Mamun was aware enough of algebraic principles to commission a "useful" work on the subject, then there must have been less accessible "treatises" already in circulation.[112] They part company only on the extent to which Indian sources may have inspired the work. Rosen, in contrast to Colebrooke, saw greater originality in al-Khwārizmī's presentation.[113]

Knowing the Orientalist predilection for textual authority, it's hardly surprising that both figures assumed existing tomes must have inspired al-Khwārizmī's *Algebra*. From a philological standpoint, any other explanation for the genesis of the manuscript was practically unthinkable. But what if other explanations are possible? What if other types of discursive practices had played a role? Both Colebrooke and Rosen assumed, furthermore, that they were engaging with an instance of "Arab" mathematics, and hence an exemplar of "the culture of the sciences among the Arabs."[114] (The appearance of the word *culture* in conjunction with the name, al-Khwārizmī, is worth noting here.) But what if they misrecognized the object of their encounter? What if the *Algebra* wasn't strictly a manuscript on mathematics, which is to say "mathematics" as defined by normative (modern, Western) understandings of the term?

Writing in 2007, Jeffrey A. Oaks and Haitham M. Alkhateeb provide an opening. They note that while al-Khwārizmī and another Muslim polymath, Ibn Turk, were among "the first to write books on algebra, they did not invent the method." So far the authors appear to be on the same page as Colebrooke and Rosen, even citing the identical passage from the *Algebra* as evidence for the claim. They go on to note, however, that the basic principles of algebra were "most likely transmitted orally before

being recorded in writing," thus raising the possibility that sub-
scientific and even implicit mathematical influences were at play.
Høyrup takes the hypothesis one step further in identifying references to *ahl al-jabr* and *aṣḥâb-al-jabr*—respectively, "algebra
people" and "followers of algebra"—in Arabic texts produced in
close proximity to al-Khwārizmī's tenure at the House of
Wisdom. "It is clear," he concludes, "that the company of *al-jabr*
must be a group which was *not inspired by al-Khwârizmî*; instead,
it *supplied him with inspiration*."[115]
  Al-Khwārizmī is not so much a point of origin, then, as he is
a boundary figure mediating more and less formalized mathematical practices. His work is decisive with respect to the
transformation—the entextualization—of the latter into the former. Høyrup observes that within a century after al-Khwārizmī,
"the idea of a special group of *al-jabr*-people seems to have
disappeared. Instead, the subject is now understood as the discipline of al-Khwârizmî's" algebra, which itself had come to settle into *"mathematics* understood as a unified field" associated
chiefly with books.[116] This shift is critical with respect to the Orientalist misrecognition of al-Khwārizmī's *Algebra*. Orientalist
scholars, and indeed those who have followed in their wake, tend
to view the object as a book of mathematics. It's better approached
as "a tissue of quotations drawn from . . . innumerable centres of
culture" whose subject matter exceeds and even scrambles definitions of the mathematical, conventionally speaking.[117]

IMPARTING LEGACIES

At last we've arrived at the *Algebra* manuscript. It's a relatively
compact if thematically sprawling document, including sections on basic algebraic principles and operations, paradigmatic

problems, the computation of commercial transactions (including material on geometry), and the application of algebraic techniques to problems of estate and legacy. The manuscript consists of 122 handwritten pages. Of those, the final section comprises almost half (58 pages) of the manuscript. The proportion isn't insignificant. This is a text as much about algebra, strictly speaking, as it is about forms and degrees of human relation, customs of dividing property, and "hierarchies of worth and deservingness," to recall Eubanks's memorable phrase.[118]

The section "On Legacies" opens with the following problem: "A man dies, leaving two sons behind him, and bequeathing one-third of his capital to a stranger. He leaves ten dirhems [a unit of currency] of property and a claim of ten dirhems upon one of the sons."[119] The question, which could easily appear on a contemporary algebra exam, is: How much of the deceased father's property should each son receive? The problem gets worked out, in narrative form, over the next several pages, along with variations in which the number of heirs and the amount of debt are altered. Mathematical operations seem to be front-and-center throughout, the matter of kinship fairly straightforward (from a patriarchal standpoint) and thus seemingly incidental to the examples. Yet, the examples grow increasingly challenging the further one ventures into the manuscript. Subsequent pages introduce wives, fathers, mothers, daughters, brothers, sisters, and in-laws, along with increasingly diffuse shares of credit, debt, and bequest. For instance: "A woman dies and leaves eight daughters, a mother, and her husband, and bequeaths to some person as much as must be added to the share of a daughter to make it equal to one-fifth of the capital and to another person as much as must be added to the share of the mother to make

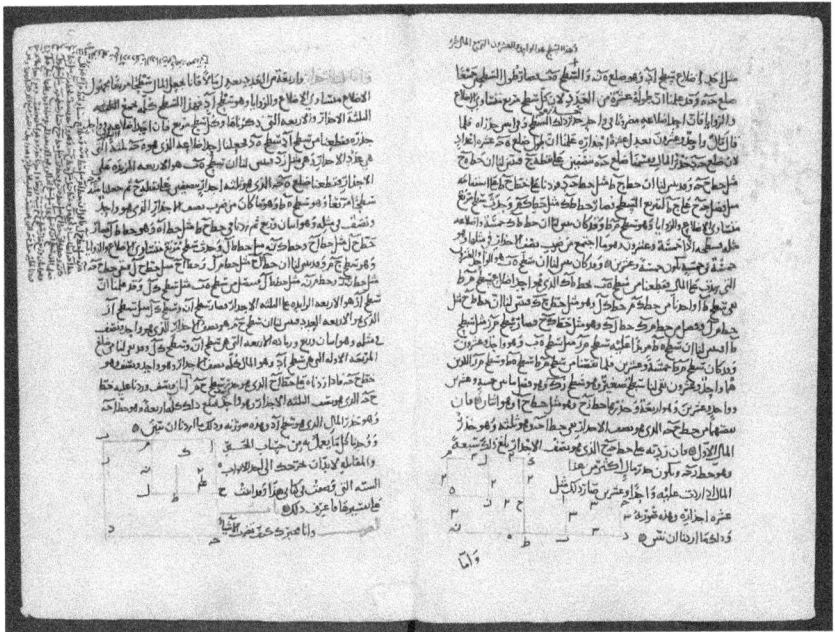

FIGURE 2.3 Pages from al-Khwārizmī's *Algebra*, from the manuscript residing in the Bodleian Library. © Bodleian Libraries, University of Oxford, used under Creative Commons License CC-BY-NC 4.0.

it equal to one-fourth of the capital."[120] While the problem undoubtedly concerns the apportionment of the deceased woman's estate, it also seems to address the problem of how to conceive of relations between generations of immediate family *with respect to* relations between kith and kin.

However ramified these relationships may appear, they are, from the standpoint of the manuscript as a whole, still relatively unambiguous. The latter parts of the work introduce a series of complications that test the boundaries of human relationality and the art of imposing order on it. For example: If a marriage occurs in the midst of a terminal illness, is that marriage legitimate? If so, to what extent? Who should possess what remains of a dowry once a recently wedded, terminally ill husband has died? If the husband has children from a previous marriage, what portion of the estate do they deserve? Are they entitled to any of the woman's assets once she dies? If the woman has children from a previous marriage, are they entitled to any of the deceased husband's assets?[121] Algebra may be a means for solving such problems, but it's surely not the end here. What's also at stake is the parsing of kinship: At what point and under what circumstances can someone claim to have become *family*?

Gender and generation, friends and family, partners and pretenders: the *Algebra* is rife with the challenges of parsing human connection and of endowing it with sense, value, and meaning. The section on estate and legacy closes with maybe the most complex relationship of all, that of masters and slaves: "Suppose that a man on his death-bed were to emancipate two slaves; the master himself leaving a son and a daughter. Then one of the two slaves dies, leaving a daughter and property to a greater amount than his price."[122] Surely this is more than a math problem. It's nothing less than a moral drama—a drama, tellingly, Colebrooke and Rosen ignored in their respective presentations of the manuscript. The portion translated by Colebrook comes from the section on basic algebra.[123] Perhaps the "ample extracts" with which he was provided didn't include the ones on enslavement. Then again, to the extent those extracts were "ample," it may be reasonable to conclude that enslavement was so unremarkable for Colebrooke that it registered, at best, as an incidental theme. Rosen, for his part, never once mentions enslavement in the preface to his own, complete translation, nor really anything about the substance of the manuscript, choosing instead to focus on its condition and origins.[124] Their silence on the subject of enslavement speaks volumes about the extraordinary burden words like *mathematics, science,* and *algebra* bear in their commentaries on the text, and about the ways nonwhite bodies are absorbed into, and in effect become, Western media apparatuses, as Armond Towns has demonstrated with respect to the Black African diaspora.[125]

Here it's worth pausing to reflect briefly on slavery—or rather, slaveries—under Muslim societies, and more specifically during the Abbasid Empire.[126] Slavery had existed in Central and West Asia (and indeed throughout much of the world) long before al-Khwārizmī, but the period in which he was writing was significant for the expansion and intensification of this abhorrent institution. "Around 800 C.E. [184 A.H.] there was a noticeable shift from the more humanistic sentiments in the Quran and the hadith to a more commercial and punitive approach, as [male] slaves began to be used increasingly as soldiers, entertainers, and, under Abbasids, laborers."[127] These individuals, many of them taken from the east coast of Africa, were delivered by slavers to the Empire's eastern reaches where, in backbreaking feats of civil engineering, they transformed dreary swampland into arable farmland. (These conditions culminated in the Zanj Rebellion of 869 CE/255 AH, which resulted in a free state that existed for fourteen years.) The new arrangement didn't displace, but added to, the mainstay of domestic servitude, where enslaved women endured the drudgery of daily household chores in addition to expectations of sexual availability on the part of the patriarch, and possibly his sons. According to one source, "the gratification of the master's pleasures" was "the commonest motive—lawful in Muslim eyes" for acquiring enslaved persons.[128] Countless children resulted from these forced couplings, raising difficult questions about kinship and estate, those categories confounded by the status of slaves as both persons and property. "Obviously some major social shifts had begun to occur in the Islamic lands," observes Abdul Sheriff, "and the broad ethical propositions in the Quran and the hadith [and, I would add, in Islamic legal commentaries collectively known as *fiqh*] were apparently no longer adequate to deal with new challenges, including slavery."[129]

Indeed, enslavement has never been a singular condition, a principle that undoubtedly applied during al-Khwārizmī's time. Though the distinction between "field" and "house" slave was relevant, enslaved persons under the Abbasid Empire were subject to subtler gradations of status. Children born of a concubine were considered legitimate, for example, despite the fact they remained enslaved (unless the mother were freed). The concubine would no longer be referred to as "slave," moreover, but as *umm walad*, "mother of the child." Enslaved persons could even be co-owned. Complicating matters further, it was possible for one master to offer emancipation, while the other refused to do so. In such cases, the person in question was effectively half-enslaved. Intricate rules governed sexual relations with enslaved women under such conditions, for example, during their sale to new owners, and also particularly where the timing of their menstrual periods was concerned. The rules existed to forestall uncomfortable questions about paternity. Moreover, while enslaved persons could not own other enslaved persons, they could earn capital and buy out their own slavehood by paying a "ransom" to the master, who would then be considered spiritually enriched. Even if an enslaved person managed to do so, they remained formally attached to the master's family as a "client,"[130] the closest analog to which might be domestic workers to whom the label "family" is (somewhat ambivalently) applied.[131]

With this context in mind, we can now consider some examples appearing in the *Algebra* manuscript, such as the following:

"Suppose that a man in his illness emancipate [*sic*] a slave, whose price is three hundred dirhems, but who has already paid off to his master two hundred dirhems, which the latter has spent; then the slave dies before the death of the master, leaving a daughter and three hundred dirhems." Computation: Take the property left by the slave, namely, the three hundred, and add thereto the two hundred, which the master has spent; this together makes five hundred dirhems. Subtract from this the ransom, which is three hundred less thing (since his legacy is thing [i.e., x]); there remain two hundred dirhems plus thing. The daughter receives the moiety of this, namely, one hundred dirhems plus half a thing; the other moiety, according to the laws of inheritance, returns to the heirs of the master, being likewise one hundred dirhems and half a thing. Of the three hundred dirhems less thing there remain only one hundred dirhems less thing for the heirs of the master, since two hundred are spent already.[132]

It's little wonder that al-Khwārizmī, living at the epicenter of the Abbasid Empire, would be asked by al-Mamun to compose a "useful" work addressing obligations to kith and kin from the standpoint of mathematics. These were hardly abstract concerns. If anything, they were pressing matters that pertained directly to the establishment, management, and preservation of the empire.

I'd even go as far as to claim that enslavement, and not mathematics, occasioned the writing of the *Algebra*, or at least the latter half of it. A footnote from the translator, Rosen, suggests as much:

> The solutions which the author has given of the remaining problems of this treatise, are, mathematically considered, for the most part incorrect. It is not that the problems, when once reduced into equations, are incorrectly worked out; but that in reducing them to equations, arbitrary assumptions are made, which are foreign or contradictory to the data first enounced [*sic*], for the purpose, it should seem, of forcing the solutions to accord with the established rules of inheritance, as expounded by Arabian lawyers.
>
> The object of the lawyers in their interpretations, and of the author in his solutions, seems to have been, to favour heirs and next of kin; by limiting the power of a testator, during illness, to bequeath property, or to emancipate slaves; and by requiring payment of heavy ransom for slaves whom a testator might, during illness, have directed to be emancipated.[133]

Much as the mathematical subtext of the culture and society tradition was illegible to Williams, the "cultural" (for lack of a better way of putting it) subtext of the *Algebra* was seemingly illegible to Rosen, Colebrooke, and company, despite Colebrooke's own obvious connections to the institution of slavery. Had they approached the manuscript as something other than an expression of "the culture of the sciences among the Arabs," they might have recognized some affinities between the "arbitrary assumptions" Rosen mentioned, the inheritance scenarios appearing throughout the *Algebra* text, and indeed the word *culture*. E. P. Thompson seems relevant to invoke here: "Any theory of culture must include the concept of the dialectical interaction between culture and something that is *not* culture."[134] Perhaps in this case it would be more accurate to say,

absent the word *culture*, the interactions among the spiritual-
ism of the Quran and hadith, the jurisprudence of *fiqh*, and the
mathematics of al-Khwārizmī's *Algebra* yielded practices, concepts, and expressions capable of performing roughly comparable work.

AN ALGEBRA FOR ALL OF IT

In exploring these facets of the history of mathematics, I've
endeavored to open up a broader inquiry into the relationship of
technology and culture—the focus of chapter 3. Apropos, it turns
out that technology has been the silent partner of the present
chapter, working quietly in the background as the story of *algorithm* unfolds. Verran's critique of "natural" numbers, mentioned
earlier, is instructive: she's asking us to question the purported
empirical basis of counting; she's also then asking us to think
more deliberately about what counting is, and about the means
by which it occurs.[135] The hegemony of the Indo-Arabic number
system (i.e., the "numbers of algorism") is apt to make this process more challenging for people living in the twenty-first century. It was obvious, however, to Florentine traders living seven
centuries ago. Confronted with the choice of whether to stick
with Roman numerals or to adopt the recently introduced Indo-
Arabic ones, they chose the former. Not only that, they out-
lawed the latter, owing to concerns about the ease with which
they could be altered. "The reasons for rejecting Arabic numerals," writes Patricia Cline Cohen, "show that the basic function
of written numbers in medieval and early modern commerce was
to record transactions, not to create manipulable bodies of
data."[136] This is tantamount to saying that numbers are tools for
representing and working with quantity, and that the affordances

of specific number systems allow us to perform some functions better than others. Mathematics is a technology. The computer is merely the embodiment of such technology in the form of a physical artifact.

There is, to be clear, no direct path linking the mathematics of al-Khwārizmī to algorithmic culture. The use of technology to parse kith and kin, the calculus of value and legitimacy, the dialectic of property and dispossession, the politics of allocating resources, the elusive figure of "the algorithm": *these are orienting conditions only*. In other words, it would be incorrect to conclude al-Khwārizmī's algebra was the prototype for the systems that routinely automate inequality today.

The objective of this chapter has been to extend the reach of these themes across time and space, situation and setting, but to stop short of forcing them to constellate around a totalizing figure of the West. Such is the lesson—the challenge, really—of Siraj Ahmed's critique of philological power, and of Sara Ahmed's words of warning about letting orienting conditions deteriorate into Orientalist fantasies.[137] Indeed, the risk of this chapter is that, in leaving the world of al-Khwārizmī in the past, I've ended up reproducing the very logics of media, power, and knowledge I've sought to challenge. Then again, it's important to bear in mind that Orientalism isn't strictly about form and content. It's also a process in which authoritative texts and the search for singular, definitive sources conspire to create an oversimplified version of "the East," in conjunction with a totalizing "West." Throughout this chapter, I've endeavored to dislodge originary figures, disperse authoritative documents, and displace points of origin, in an effort to amplify discursive practices and regimes of experience that are routinely silenced in more conventional accounts of "the algorithm" and its history. I hope that

I've managed to tell a more complex story than the process of Orientalism typically allows.

That desire for complexity is also the reason why, at the outset of this chapter, I urged you to question whether mathematics was best conceived in all contexts as an instance, expression, or manifestation of culture. It may be, today, that algorithms are culture.[138] Yet, it's critical to admit to a time in which *culture*'s modern senses and meanings didn't even exist, and thus to bear witness to a wider range of possible orientations for algorithms, specifically, and, for mathematics, more generally. Among *culture*'s many dangers is its tendency to assimilate all manner of human interaction, everywhere and ever since the dawn of the species *Homo sapiens*, to its decisive logics. Throughout this chapter I've tried to imagine an alternative scenario in which *algorithm*, conceived technologically, is a potential point of orientation for *culture*, and thus a figure capable of affecting the latter's own terms and conditions.

Keywords was a useful starting point, but it struggles to recognize its own mathematical subtext. More troublingly, it's ill-equipped to listen for discursive practices significantly lost to entextualization. Key-words helps us to grasp how the standard origin story for *algorithm*, in which al-Khwārizmī is the namesake, is the result of superimposing layer upon layer of textual matter atop the Khwārazmians, the anonymous "algebra people" of Persia, the early adopters of augrym stones, enslaved persons, and surely other individuals and groups whose voices echo faintly across the "enunciative gaps in the syntagmatic organization of statements," as Certeau eloquently put it.[139] Important though he may be, al-Khwārizmī exists today less as an actual person than as a proxy, one whose emergence as such occurred in and across multiple imperial formations, and one whose authority derives from their voracious textual output. He's the product, significantly, of a two-hundred-year-old "alterity script" in which, according to Bernard Dionysus Geoghegan, exoticized "intelligent" technologies are made to figure and then disavow difference.[140] Or, as Joel Dias-Porter asks in the touching poem "The Al Khwarizmi in You": "Is there an algebra for all of it?"[141] Perhaps—but only when the figure of al-Khwārizmī ceases to be the cipher.

3

CULTURE

I n February 2017, the press took a strange and sudden interest in Franz Boas. If anthropology has a patron saint, then Boas (1858–1942) is probably it. He spurned the notion that Westerners could glimpse elements of their own past in the customs of so-called "primitive" peoples. It was a forceful rebuke of the conventional wisdom of the day. All human societies deserved to be recognized as having culture, Boas insisted. Moreover, those groups ought to be interpreted on their own terms, not judged on the basis of ethnocentric standards of development. The argument became a touchstone for anthropology. Without a doubt, it helped lift the discipline from the colonial quagmire in which it had been founded in the nineteenth century. Absent Boas's intervention, anthropology might well have ended up like its kin, phrenology: another deserving entry in the Curious Catalog of Dead Disciplines.

Yet, the opening weeks of 2017 were unkind to Boas and his legacy. His standing in anthropological circles remained intact. The same couldn't be said about his reputation online. There, he and his views on culture had fallen victim to a vicious attack. Rather than the expertise of anthropologists or even the customary default *Wikipedia*, an obscure blogpost from *Smash Cultural*

Marxism, published in 2015, kept rising to the top of Google searches for "Boasian anthropology": "Judeo-Boasian Anthropology is Subversive and Psychological Racial Warfare." In leveling the cultural playing field, claimed the anonymous author, Boas had initiated a "pseudo-scientific Jewish assault on White European racial consciousness and identity." The alleged assault was predicated on the "falsehood" "that 'race was a social construct' not rooted in biology or scientific determinism."[1] Racist views, to be sure, and it's doubtful they achieved prominence on Google on their own. It's likely they ended up there thanks to someone's having planted a Google bomb: a series of dummy websites, all pointing to and thus "endorsing" some other, questionable site, that collectively trick Google's algorithms into judging the latter to be more relevant than it is, or ought to be.[2]

Order was restored by the close of February 2017, however, after Heather Van Wormer, an anthropology professor at Grand Valley State University, Michigan, discovered the incendiary search results. She promptly messaged her colleague Deana Weibel-Swanson, who in turn rallied a group of Facebook friends working in anthropology and folklore. Acting as a digital bomb squad of sorts, the group proceeded to ping Google, expressing their disgust at how a white supremacist screed could have supplanted decades of peer-reviewed, scholarly research. Essentially, they were hoping to defuse the apparent Google bomb by asking the search giant to algorithmically cancel *Smash Cultural Marxism*. Sure enough, the errant site soon received a downgrade, and the Boasian view of culture (or at least, the *Wikipedia* version of it) was back on top. A write-up on *The Verge*, an online publication for technology enthusiasts, capped off the whole affair.[3]

The Boas incident embodies the dialectic of continuity and change that is, as I noted in the introduction, characteristic of

Google

boasian anthropology   ✕ 🔍

ALL   MAPS   NEWS   SHOPPING   IMAGES

"**Boasian Anthropology** is a pseudo-scientific Jewish assault on White European racial consciousness and identity. To put it simply, the Jewish **Boasian** school of **Anthropology** suggested wrongly, that 'race was a social construct' not rooted in biology or scientific determinism." Apr 1, 2015

❬   ❭   ⬆   ▢   ⬜

FIGURE 3.1 Results of a Google search for "boasian anthropology," February 2017.

Source: Jon Bialecki's blog, https://jonbialecki.com/2017/02/27/a-pseudo-scientific-jewish-assault-on-white-european-racial-consciousness-and-identity/. Used with permission.

algorithmic culture. On the one hand, it instances the endurance of "metaculture," which Francis Mulhern defines as "discourse in which culture addresses its own generality and conditions of existence." Metaculture refers to the communicative norms, resources, and repertoires by means of which *culture* becomes a site of struggle, a locus of identification, a keyword/ key-word, etc. It doesn't refer to some abstract, second-order linguistic realm in which debates about culture transpire, while the "real" work of culture happens elsewhere. Metaculture is immanent to culture: it was constitutive of the term's rise to prominence in the nineteenth and twentieth centuries, argues Mulhern, and it continues to provide "a historically formed set of topics and procedures that both drives and regulates the utterance of the individuals who inhabit it."[4] The Boas incident also signals the degree to which metacultural discourse now includes new players, or rather, how the existing cast may be interacting in different ways. Mulhern's analysis consists of citations drawn almost entirely from printed texts, but, like Williams (see chapter 1), he says practically nothing about the "technicity," or technological entailments, of the source material. It's as if metaculture unfolded *within* media technologies rather than *depending* on them.[5] This is also what the Boas incident may prompt us to see, then: that those technologies were there all along, and maybe others too; and that they helped mold the metacultural discourse of the nineteenth and twentieth centuries no less than the writers to whom the work is attributed. The incident also demonstrates how, in our own time, technology (i.e., computers, algorithms, etc.) plays an increasingly decisive role in settling competing claims about *culture* and in mediating relations among the claimants.

This chapter, like the preceding one, is about the relationship of culture and technology. But whereas chapter 2 examined the former from the vantage point of the latter, this one alters the perspective. It is, in part, a reading of how technology has been figured *in* metacultural discourse. Where possible I'm also interested in bringing the technicity *of* metaculture back up to the surface, particularly with respect to writers from the nineteenth and twentieth centuries for whom technology was—seemingly—a source of ambivalence. Once again, I'm not searching for origins but for orienting conditions. There's no direct path leading from Matthew Arnold and F. R. Leavis, leading figures within the British culture and society tradition and the primary subjects of this chapter, to the Boas incident. Yet, in the process of reconstructing the atmospheres within which they were living, working, and in Leavis's case, suffering, critical themes manifested in the incident start to emerge: the cultural politics of race and nation; the governance of human affairs as mediated by techniques of information management; and, of course, the complex articulation of technology and culture. The central claim of this chapter is that critical elements of algorithmic culture inhere in the British culture and society tradition, but often not in the form of principal or favored texts. Instead, they manifest either in the technics of its metacultural discourse or in material that evidently had little to do with defining *culture*.

ANECDOTES

Methodologically, the challenge of the preceding chapter lay in adapting keywords, a suite of analytical tools developed in and for print culture, to a context marked by the prevalence of, and complex interactions between, manuscripts and oral discourse. While the present chapter operates well within the remit of print culture, I'm reluctant simply to apply the lessons of keywords here. They're useful in isolating intellectual-historical layers, as in *Culture and Society*, and lexical layers, as in *Keywords*. They also show us that by superimposing the two layers, an intricate story about the emergence of *culture*'s modern senses and meanings will be revealed. Keywords is highly adapted to conventional forms of metacultural discourse, but what about to other types of evidence? I raise this question bearing in mind the problems of legibility I raised in chapter 2 with respect not only to manuscripts and oral communication, but also to the mathematical subtext of the culture and society tradition. Troublingly, there are whole classes of objects and expressive forms keywords struggles to recognize, even when it's operating in its comfort zone.

Keywords is also, as I just noted, hesitant to reflect on the technicity of metacultural discourse. The words of metacultural discourse matter deeply, to be sure, but the technical entailments, both proximate and distant, have stories to tell too. In part II of the *Long Revolution* (1961), Williams considered how, in the nineteenth century, improvements in printing helped drive the expansion of the British reading public, thereby heightening concerns about the production and wellbeing of culture.[6] The connection between technology and metaculture is clear, if stratospheric; in no sense is it apparent how technology might have affected the emerging semantics of *culture* at the level of the everyday. In contrast, I'm reminded of Friedrich Kittler's curiosity about Friedrich Nietzsche's Malling Hansen writing ball, an early typewriter, on which the philosopher composed some of his later work. The writing ball wasn't simply a tool Nietzsche used to externalize his thoughts. Instead, Kittler argues, it profoundly affected his writing practices, and thus his understanding of inscription. "Writing in Nietzsche is no longer a natural extension of humans who bring forth their voice, soul, individuality through their handwriting. On the contrary: just as in the stanza on the delicate Malling Hansen, humans change their position—they turn from the agency of writing to become an inscription surface."[7]

Similarly, I'm curious about the objects that surrounded or preoccupied some of the figures associated with the culture and society tradition, and more specifically about the technologies that oriented or even frustrated their work. In a more concrete sense, I'm interested in examining metacultural discourse, albeit with a heightened sensitivity to its technical entailments and material accompaniments. Such a shift is integral to catalyzing the transformation of keywords into key-words, I contend, and to continuing to piece together the story of the emergence of algorithmic culture.

Kittler's approach is notable for many reasons, among them the way in which he finds technicity: by choosing *not* to ignore relevant scenes and settings—the sensuous worlds—within which people dwell. T. S. Eliot's use of a typewriter isn't lost on Kittler, for example, but for Williams, who devotes a chapter of *Culture and Society* to Eliot, the typewriter doesn't figure at all— this despite Eliot's own admission of how the device affected his writing and, presumably, his use of the word *culture*.[8] Thus, Kittler isolates a layer that's largely unaccounted for in keywords. It's a technical layer, in part, but the detail, intimacy, and banality also present there suggest a broader concern for everyday life.[9] Kittler accesses this layer primarily through auto-/biographical writings and archival sources, in addition to the texts for which figures like Nietzsche and Eliot are primarily known.

I don't mean to imply that Williams eschewed the everyday. I do mean to suggest that, for whatever reason, it doesn't figure as a methodological touchstone for the project of keywords—at least, for the most part. Ben Highmore calls attention to two episodes, both appearing in the introduction to *Keywords*, in which Williams briefly makes contact with the quotidian. The first I've already noted in chapter 1: Williams's encounter with Eric Hobsbawm, in which the two veterans commiserated about feeling socially and linguistically disoriented upon their demobilization from the Second World War. The second episode, which glosses Williams's "Culture is Ordinary" (1958), I address later on in this chapter: his encounter, before the war, with patrons at a teashop in Cambridge, England, who were using the word *culture* in a manner wholly unfamiliar to the young, working class Welsh émigré.[10] In neither of these episodes does Williams present the level of detail you often find in Kittler, yet the character of the writing, which Highmore characterizes as "anecdotal," is reminiscent of the prose appearing in Williams's novels and memoirs, and occasionally in his "academic" studies.[11]

Consider this passage from *Border Country* (1960), his first novel, in which Matthew "Will" Price, the main character, a university professor, travels by train from London to Wales to visit his ailing father:

> Abruptly the rhythm changed, as the wheels crossed the bridge. Matthew got up, and took his case from the rack. As he steadied the case, he looked at the rail-map, with its familiar network of arteries, held in the shape of Wales, and to the east the lines running out and elongating, into England. The shape of Wales: pigheaded Wales you say to remember to draw it. And no returns.[12]

Will realizes he's reached his destination no thanks to a placard affixed to the station wall, nor to the announcement of the conductor. Tempo and material communicate the train's arrival, and thus the entanglement of person, technology, time, and environment. Similarly, in Williams's reminiscences about F. R. Leavis, hair and hands establish connection during an interminable faculty meeting: "In one very dull patch I looked down and saw him intently examining the backs of my hands, which are covered with hair. He had spread his own hands out in front of him; the backs were quite smooth. . . . He went on staring at our hands and when he saw that I had noticed, he smiled."[13] And in the introduction to *The Country and the City* (1973), Williams finds himself living amidst a protracted struggle between natural and built environment, and between past, present, and future: "In the field with the elms and the white horse, behind my own present home, there are faint marks of a ninth-century building, and a foot below the grass there is a cobbled road, that resists the posts being driven, today, for a new wire fence."[14]

Highmore's description of this style, "anecdotal," warrants clarification. It's his name for the moments in which Williams fully embraces everyday life, both the welter and the wan, using it to demonstrate how "the semantics of keywords is a matter of social practice and social relations."[15] I assume here that "social" refers to more than just the human, and I'd downplay the degree to which Williams utilized anecdotes within the framework of keywords. Indeed, I believe they're deployed more effectively elsewhere in his work. Nevertheless, what I take from both Williams and Highmore is a sense of what key-words should aspire to do, anecdotally: situate words with respect to the interplay of bodies and their surroundings; attend to the technicity of discourse; account for objects, surfaces, tempos, and environmental conditions; situate quotidian experiences within the broader movements of history; and perhaps more.

That said, it's not as if anecdotes are without complications. *Anecdote* derives from the Greek form ἀνέκδοτος—literally, "not given out," but more generally translated as "ungiven," "unde-livered," or "unpublished." (The root $-\delta o \tau o \varsigma$, intriguingly, is the form from which the word *data* derives.)[16] This is likely the source of the "detachment" that feeds prevailing understand-ings of *anecdote*. Typically, what makes a story anecdotal is its "separat[ion], like a stray button or lost tooth, from a prior and larger whole," as Meaghan Morris puts it.[17] This also helps to explain why anecdotes have a less than stellar reputation outside of cultural studies, anthropology, and some segments of literary studies. Sure, they can liven up a cocktail party or add spark to a Rotary Club speech, but conventional wisdom says that anec-dotes are just too quirky to have relevance beyond the scene at hand. Prone to embellishment, they're anything but trustwor-thy. The *Oxford English Dictionary* describes the epistemologi-cal status of anecdotes in no uncertain terms: they're dogged by "implications of superficiality or unreliability."[18] As such, anec-dotes are often considered too flimsy, incidental, subjective, or informal to be accepted as legitimate knowledge. Their appear-ance in certain academic circles can be particularly vexing. The use of one—or worse, failing to realize you've done so—may be met with a stern calling out for having neglected to demonstrate "rigor," partake of "hard evidence," avoid "digression," question the "speaking subject," or otherwise uphold cherished norms of academic rectitude. If you really want to scuttle someone's research, summon a thinly veiled look of contempt and tell them their evidence is anecdotal.

The masculinist subtext of these objections is plain to see, as is the scriptocentrism that elevates purportedly objective accounts over ordinary experiences grounded in the spoken word.[19] Indeed, it's important to recognize how the dominant senses and mean-ings of *anecdote* don't reflect an inherent condition as much as a

notional one—a predicament of sorts.[20] There's no necessary reason why anecdotes must terminate in what Kathleen Stewart
calls "descriptive eddies."[21] You can see this predicament playing
out within the realm of scholarly communication. "Your evidence
is anecdotal" is less an empirical description than a speech act,
one whose purpose is to sever the tie, actual or potential, between
the account of an incident and official discourse. "What makes
an event 'historical' rather than 'personal' (and vice versa)?" asks
Tony Pinkney, in a study of Williams's novels. It's an apt question indeed, given Pinkney's provocative claim that Williams's
often-neglected fiction is the conceptual and evidentiary leading
edge of the author's "cultural" writings.[22] In any case, anecdotes
aren't intrinsically disconnected from larger narratives, nor are
they fundamentally lacking in broader purpose. Rather, their
detachment is a (dys)function of the discourse networks within
which they emerge and to which they're typically returned.

The sense of *anecdote* in use throughout this chapter and across
the remainder of this book is closest to a definition the *OED*
claims is obsolete: "Secret, private, or hitherto unpublished episodes or details of history. Also occasionally in singular: a work
consisting of such episodes."[23] Moreover, I follow Morris in
treating anecdotes "as a *mise en abyme*."[24] Like a play within a
play, anecdotes stage, in miniature, the "characteristic elements
of impulse, restraint, and tone"—the atmospheres—within
which they're formed.[25] Anecdotes, thus, can reveal otherwise
unobservable patterns operating at the level of the everyday and
with respect to broader regimes of experience. Morris adds that
the process of articulating anecdotes together can "initiate a
larger narration, link[ing] two or more stories and arguments
together, or enabl[ing] . . . the elaboration of another, non-
narrative discourse."[26]

The point of bringing anecdotes to the surface isn't only to put them into circulation but to ask: What buried them in the first place? The question suggests that while the *content* of any given anecdote might not tell us much, the *treatment* of anecdotes alone and in aggregate might tell us something about the norms of inclusion and exclusion operating in a given context. To that end, in the history that follows I employ anecdotes at strategic moments to re-embed metacultural discourse in the everyday. The objective is to dig deeper into the enabling conditions of this discourse, including but not limited to its technicity, in the hope of locating key elements of algorithmic culture that may lie dormant as "another, non-narrative discourse" within the British culture and society tradition. In doing so, I also hope to demonstrate the heuristic value of anecdotes for the project of key-words, particularly when it's operating within a well-established print culture whose propensity, to paraphrase Kittler, is to disavow its own hardware.[27]

FROM *CIVILIZATION* TO *CULTURE*

The year 1958 was a landmark for Williams, one that saw the publication of two of his most defining works: the book *Culture and Society*; and the essay "Culture is Ordinary," appearing in an anthology on British socialism entitled *Conviction*. The essay is among the most personal and passionate of Williams's scholarly writings. It's also an eloquent statement about the becoming-residual of a cluster of understandings that had gathered around the word *culture* throughout the nineteenth and early-twentieth centuries. The decisive moment occurs about a third of the way into the essay. There, Williams describes the passage from his hometown, Pandy, located in the mountainous terrain of southeast Wales, to the lowlands of Cambridge University, England, where, as a self-described "scholarship boy," he would pursue literary studies. The time was the late 1930s:

> I was not oppressed by the university, but by the teashop, acting as if it were one of the older and more respectable departments. . . . Here was culture, not in any sense I knew, but in a special sense: the outward and emphatically visible sign of a special kind of people. They were not, the great majority of them, learned; they practised few arts; but they had it, and they showed you they had it.

Sipping his warm, aromatic tea in between puffs on his pipe, studiously surveying the room, Williams could not but have been struck by the "extraordinary fussiness" of the patrons surrounding him.[28] I can imagine the furrow of his brow, the gentle curl of his lips, and the quiet, if puzzled, "Hmm?" he perhaps uttered upon witnessing the scene for the first time: the astonishing care they showed in smoothly stirring their tea and then quietly setting down the spoons; the painstaking handwork involved in grasping, lifting up, setting down, and releasing the delicate china teacups; the tautness of their posture; the measured volume and precise diction of their speech; and clothing not only appropriate to the season but also, of course, to the exact time of day. "Extraordinary fussiness"—a memorable turn of phrase that bespeaks the distance Williams felt from this demonstrative enactment of culture and the ordinariness to which he'd grown accustomed in Wales.

What to make of this passage? It's easy enough to read it as an account of stodgy, high-cultural snobbery, the behavior of nondescript "elites." Indeed, it is that, but to leave it there is to come away with a flattened sense of the fussy individuals about whom Williams was writing. First, the phrase "acting as if it were one of the older and more respectable departments": Williams wasn't talking about the old aristocracy—individuals whose gentility would be assured by claims to land, money, and legacy. Nor was he referring to the bourgeoisie, or, in Marxist parlance, the owners of the instruments of production. Given the security of their social standing—buttressed by property and pedigree on the one hand, command of capital on the other—neither of these groups was likely to have felt any compulsion to flaunt their respectability. Instead, Williams was referring to a class of people, not particularly "learned" or "practised" in the arts, who had nonetheless laid claim to respectability through a certain command of manners and decorum, and by leveraging their relationship, however superficial, to what you might call "high" culture—aesthetic goods purported to embody the essence of truth, beauty, and goodness, and thus to represent the highest virtues of English history. These were the members of an insurgent middle to upper-middle class whom Thorstein Veblen, writing an ocean away at the turn of the twentieth century, had dubbed the "leisure class."[29]

Next, the phrases "the outward and emphatically visible sign of a special kind of people" and "they had it [culture], and they showed you they had it." Here Williams was referring to a particular set of repertoires—dress, speech, comportment, and so forth—that were consciously externalized by the patrons of the teashop. That is, he was pointing to a version of culture that wasn't about depth or interiority, nor about moral or spiritual transformation. Instead, it was a facsimile worn outwardly on one's sleeve. This was a version of culture that had grafted itself onto an older, courtly tradition once prevalent on the European continent that proceeded under the banner of *civilization*, a term to which *culture* is sometimes opposed but that, at points in its history, it has nonetheless approached.

In *The Civilizing Process*, first published in 1939, Norbert Elias charted the political and economic conditions out of which emerged a modern, aesthetic sense of *culture*—a sense, we'll see, that differed from the one embodied by the patrons in Williams's teashop. Indeed, the aesthetic connotation of the word was something of a semantic late bloomer in Britain, also in France, where "civilization" and "civility" (*civilisation, civilité*) were the preferred terms for designating decency and refinement. The situation was different, however, in what's now present-day Germany. In contrast to Britain and France, both of which had consolidated political power after the Thirty Years War (1618–1648), Germany didn't exist as a unified state but instead as loosely-connected principalities. These were, significantly, places where French was the preferred language at court, and where courtly behavior tended to mimic that of the French monarchs.[30] "At the top of almost everywhere in Germany," wrote Elias, "were individuals or groups who spoke French and decided policy."[31] German was the vulgate—using it, a sign of one's distance from polite society and also, then, from the centers of social and political power.

All that began to change in the late-eighteenth century, when a small group of individuals began a rebellion of sorts against both the hegemony of the French language and the norms of civility that accompanied it. This wasn't a militancy, however, but a more peaceful movement whose leadership was drawn from the ranks of the emerging German middle class. These "servers of princes," as Elias called them, were erudite individuals like Johann Gottfried Herder (1744–1803), Johann Wolfgang von Goethe (1749–1832), and Alexander von Humboldt (1769–1859), who advocated for the use and respectability of the German language, and for a unified German state.[32] They were also individuals more or less lacking in formal political power, and people whose economic means, though not insignificant, were nonetheless insufficient to steer the course of German society. But they had access to something else, something that would prove a formidable resource in its own right:

> What legitimated the 18th century [German] middle-class intelligentsia to itself, what supplied the foundation of its self-image and pride, was situated beyond economics and politics. It existed . . . in books, scholarship, religion, art, philosophy, in the inner enrichment, the intellectual formation . . . of the individual primarily through the medium of books, and the personality. Accordingly, the watchwords expressing this self-image of the German intellectual class, terms such as *Bildung* [*cultivation*] and *Kultur* [*culture*], tended to draw sharp distinction between accomplishments in the areas just mentioned . . . and the political, economic, and social sphere, in complete contrast to the watchwords of the rising bourgeoisie in France and England.[33]

What we see here is *culture* emerging neither as a haughty sensibility nor as an element for preserving the status quo. If anything, it functioned as a wedge with which to pry open the German social, political, and economic structure.

What distinguished *culture* from *civilization*? The German intelligentsia of the eighteenth-century held a less than favorable view of *civilization* (*Zivilisation*), according it, in Elias's view, "a value of the second rank." The strange system of bowing and curtsying, and of rising when someone of superior rank entered a room; the elaborate rules structuring when, how, to whom, for how long, and the topics about which one should speak; the byzantine protocols governing the arrangement and use of tableware, and also bodily dispositions while dining: in contrast to *culture*, these and other aspects of civility "compris[ed] only the outer appearance of human beings, the surface of human existence."[34] Indeed, the whole system of courtesy seemed to rest on a misrecognition: the errant belief that knowing elbows-on-the-table was *verboten* somehow marked the nobility, in Germany and elsewhere, as having achieved the pinnacle of human existence. It was all just empty formality, argued their critics—a series of prefabricated repertoires designed to help aristocratic individuals navigate social situations with minimal reflection, and without challenging their own or anyone else's position in the social hierarchy.

In this, Germany's intelligentsia seemed to intuit a history of manners that Elias, writing just over a century after them, would recover. The ethos of civility, observed Elias, emerged in the wake of the collapse of feudal societies throughout Western Europe, and in the wake of the declining power and influence of the Catholic church. The gathering forces of capitalism, combined with those of the Protestant Reformation, were slowly chipping away at the edifice of social relations on the continent. Civility arrived to help fill the gap, providing individuals—especially the landed gentry—with a sense of how they might go on living and functioning at a time when the old rules no longer could be counted on to apply.

Civility was hardly an organic development, however, much less a sign that human development had reached its apotheosis. If anything, it flowed from people who offered tangible advice on how to navigate the transition from medieval to early-modern living—people who, today, might be called "life coaches" or, in a manner of speaking, "cultural intermediaries," to recall Pierre Bourdieu's phrase.[35] Among them was the humanist-theologian Erasmus of Rotterdam (c. 1466–1536 CE), whose widely circulated, translated, reprinted, and imitated book *De civilitate morum puerilium* (*On Civility in Children*), published in 1530, was something like the Emily Post of its day.[36] It counseled the nobility on how to carry themselves in a host of everyday situations: "Your goblet and knife, duly cleansed, should be on the right, your bread on the left"; "It is impolite to greet someone who is urinating or defecating"; "To blow your nose on your hat or clothing is rustic. . . . It is proper to wipe the nostrils with a handkerchief . . ."; "When you undress . . . take care not to expose to the eyes of others anything that morality and nature require to be concealed"; and so on.[37]

Virtue in early-modern courtly society was therefore a function of the degree to which one managed one's passions and conformed, both in public and private life, to a litany of exacting behaviors. On one level, this shift marked a qualitative improvement over life under medieval feudalism, at least for those fortunate enough to live as European nobility—males especially. The ethos of civilization helped to problematize some of the more flagrant acts of brutality, coercion, and abuse prevalent in and even before the feudal period, behaviors that had imbued daily life with an atmosphere of profound insecurity. (Importantly, the new attitude toward violence didn't extend beyond the borders of Europe or apply to the subjects of European colonialism, as Achille Mbembe and Dierk Walter have both shown.)[38] But the payoff in predictability wasn't without its tradeoffs, at least as far as the German middle-class intelligentsia was concerned. Elias: the "legitimation [of the intelligentsia] . . . consisted primarily in its intellectual, scientific, or artistic *accomplishments*," this in contrast to the "upper class which 'accomplished' nothing" but whose "distinctive *behaviour* was central to its self-image and self-justification."[39]

Formality may have been an effective means of social reproduction, in other words, but it seemed to produce little beyond that which fit the mold. Glossing Oswald Spengler's *The Decline of the West* (1918), A. L. Kroeber and Clyde Kluckhohn put it this way: civilization came to be seen as "merely a stage of culture—the final phase of sterile crystallization and repetition of what was earlier creative."[40] Hence, the stress placed by the partisans of culture on *Bildung*, meaning education, growth, or development, which is to say, transformational improvement of the spirit, intellect, or person. Another word often heard in this context was *cultivation*—the term poet-philosopher Samuel Taylor Coleridge (1772–1834) used to translate the arguments of his German counterparts into English. He, too, attacked what he perceived to be the vacuous conduct of the nobility, offering this memorable image in his book *On the Constitution of the Church and State* (1830): "Civilization is itself but a mixed good, if not far more a corrupting influence, the hectic of disease, not the bloom of health, and a nation so distinguished more fitly to be called a varnished than a polished people, where this civilization is not grounded in cultivation, in the harmonious development of those qualities and faculties that characterize our humanity."[41] Civilization, Coleridge claimed, was a just a glossy façade compensating for the fact that, among the nobility, there was no *there* there. Cultivation, in contrast, was a slow and deliberate process of developing an intrinsic luster, or of attempting to realize one's pre-existing potential.

Metaphors clearly abound where culture and its kin are concerned: disease and health, corruption and harmony, varnish and polish—which is to say nothing of all the agricultural overtones. It would be easy, in hindsight, to accuse Coleridge of having mixed his metaphors. But such an accusation risks imposing today's stylistic standards on the past and, more importantly, failing to appreciate how "important work on *culture* was done through the employment and development of attendant terms and concepts," as Marc Manganaro has written.[42] Indeed, I'm inclined to view Coleridge's heady brew of figurative language as a struggle to articulate new senses for *civilization* and *cultivation*, senses that were just beginning to register in English during the first decades of the nineteenth century. Such was the case with *Kultur*, *culture*, and *cultivation* as they were used by the German and British middle-class intelligentsia of the eighteenth and nineteenth centuries. All three terms analogized human becoming to the nurturance of plants and other living organisms. In this they channeled the semantics of their shared Latin root *colere* (to harvest, cultivate, worship, or wait for), but in a manner abstracted from agriculture.[43] Culture is against surfaces (a healthy-looking plant isn't necessarily a healthy plant); against stasis (a seed must grow to reach its full potential as a plant); and against strict adherence to form (growing from seed to plant means the organism must adapt and change).

Metaphors may enlarge the bandwidth of a language, but we should approach them with caution. The statements pitting *culture* (or *cultivation*) against *civilization* in the writings of Coleridge et al. shouldn't be construed as empirically descriptive. If anything, they're interested claims meant to trouble the existing order of things. Lucien Febvre, for instance, mentions "the divorce between '*culture*' and '*civilization*'" that occurred in the French language in the early nineteenth century, implying the existence of a prior semantic and conceptual union.[44] Similarly, Williams refers to the "long and still difficult interaction" between the two terms in English, as if to signal the inadequacy of any simple opposition.[45] The claim that culture is somehow superior to civilization, or that civilization is culture taken too far or become too formulaic, is, in part, an outgrowth of the taxonomies prevalent in European thought in the eighteenth and nineteenth centuries. These schemes posited developmental gradations—from savagery to barbarism to civilization— that justified European colonialism (the "civilization" of "savage" peoples) and the physical and psychological brutality on which it depended.[46]

Thus, efforts to distance *culture* from *civilization* should be taken with a grain of salt. It's doubtful that the two terms were ever fundamentally opposed. How best, then, to reckon with this discrepancy? One way would be to say that the partisans of *culture* were only pointing to tendencies, not absolutes. So, for example, although formality may not have guaranteed the reproduction of aristocratic society, it steered the society in that general direction. But this response is unsatisfying, because it explains away the opposition instead of actually explaining it. Qadri Ismail takes a different but related tack. He stresses how Edward Tylor, Franz Boas, and other foundational figures in the emerging discipline of anthropology approached *culture* and *civilization* as "homonyms, not antonyms." His position is consistent with that of Kroeber and Kluckhohn, who, in 1952, described the tension between the two terms as "a relatively minor incident which it will be expedient to dispose of."[47] But questioning the validity of the opposition doesn't absolve us of the responsibility of coming to terms with the fact of its existence. Indeed, the agnosticism of the key-words approach is critical here. Instead of feeling compelled to adjudicate among competing senses and definitions, the injunction is to account for the persistence and propagation—the effects—of particular usages in spite of contravening evidence, arguments, and understandings.

RIGHT QUESTIONS, WRONG ANSWERS

This brings us to Matthew Arnold (1822–1888 CE). Now, if you have any thoughts about Arnold, you're probably saying to yourself: elitist, racist, classist, English nationalist, conservative.

Arnold was, to greater and lesser degrees, all of these things, so why give him additional airtime?[48] Frankly, I struggle with the question. But when it comes to *culture* in the nineteenth century, you cannot go around Arnold. You must go through him. He's a pivotal figure whose life and work crystallize a complex of meanings that will prove decisive for *culture* in the twentieth and twenty-first centuries—which is to say nothing of his own century. Williams states the point succinctly. Arnold was among those "who, at the point of eruption of a qualitatively new social order[,] put many of the right questions to it but of course came out with the wrong answers."[49] It's a decisive move for cultural studies, insofar as it models an ethic of engaging—rather than dispensing—with the metacultural discourse of leading conservative figures, an ethic evident in subsequent work by Stuart Hall on Margaret Thatcher, and Lawrence Grossberg on Ronald Reagan, George W. Bush, and Donald Trump, etc.[50]

It turns out that, initially, Arnold struggled to articulate so much as a habitable response—right or wrong—to the emergence of industrial modernity in England. Writing wasn't the issue. The practice came easily to him, and he had ample time in which to hone his craft. As assistant to Lord Lansdowne, lord president of the English Privy Council, Arnold often found himself marooned in the office, unoccupied for hours on end.[51] Arriving at a satisfying answer to the "question" of modern English society, one that would inspire people to share his concerns about its character and direction—well, that was a different matter. In the early 1850s, Arnold wasn't yet the mature prose critic who's remembered today. He was a fledgling poet whose work explored a range of themes, including feelings of discomfort with the norms of English society.

And discomfort he felt, despite the respectable economic status his parents had achieved, and despite the privilege his white

flesh afforded in the period in which England was consolidat-
ing its colonies. Lumbering iron leg braces, worn throughout
early childhood, were supposed to correct a limp, possibly the
result of rickets. Instead, they exacerbated the lopsidedness of
his gait, earning young Matthew the sobriquet "Crabby." He
stuttered enough for people to notice, though eventually the condition lifted. He also suffered the effects of his authoritarian
father, Dr. Thomas Arnold, headmaster of Rugby School, who'd
not only bestowed the nickname "Crabby," but whose penchant
for beating his own and others' children was as legendary as his
insistence on both academic and physical excellence.[52] Indeed,
in contrast to his father, Matthew seemed incapable of living up
to, much less transcending, the expectations afforded him by his
circumstances at birth. A miserable showing in philology landed
the younger Arnold a second-class degree from Oxford University, thus "brand[ing] him as a shallow, lazy, silly man with a
great name, who had thrown every chance to the winds and sunk
to mediocrity."[53]

Arnold was hardly an outsider, yet in matters of physical
advantage, social standing, and self-presentation, he seemed to
fall outside the norm. Remarkably, he had sense enough to view
his questionable status as evidence of misplaced priorities, rather
than as an indication of some personal defect. Why must he or
anyone else conform to such rigid expectations? Or rather: What
to do when you're feeling out of sync with the dominant values
and dispositions of the age in which you're living? This is the
basic question of Arnold's two-act dramatic poem *Empedocles on
Etna* (1852), which he published anonymously at age twenty-
nine.[54] The consensus among Victorianists is that Empedocles
functions as "a prototype of modern man" (with all the caveats
such a categorical description entails) and, possibly, a proxy for
Arnold himself.[55] The poem also anticipates a host of concerns

evident in the social and political commentary Arnold produced upon leaving Lansdowne's office.

Set in the fifth century BCE, *Empedocles* chronicles the last, desperate hours of the eponymous pre-Socratic philosopher. The setting is colonial—Sicily was then under Greek control—although the colonial dimension is mostly submerged as Empedocles traverses the forested slopes of Mount Etna, slowly making his way to the crater. Along the way, he sings of the social, intellectual, and spiritual decay of Agrigentum, his home-town, and also then of the internal otherness he feels living in a city whose priorities have grown incommensurate with his own. Meanwhile, Pausanias, a physician of questionable intelligence, conspires with Callicles, a young musician, to buoy Empedocles with upbeat melodies played unseen and from afar. Despite their interruptions, the poem belongs overwhelmingly to Empedocles, whose despondency cedes to clarity as he ascends the volcano: "And therefore, O ye Elements, I know—/Ye know it too—it hath been granted me /Not to die wholly, not to be all enslav'd. / I feel it in this hour. The numbing cloud /Mounts off my soul: I feel it, I breathe free."[56] Empedocles has discovered the source of his troubles: in refusing to accept the norms of his compatri-ots, he's become trapped between worlds. He's alive but not liv-ing; he's socially undead. On one side lies the prospect of con-forming to values he opposes, and thus of moral and spiritual death. On the other side lies the prospect of physical death, and thus of relief from the pressure to conform. The philosopher finally understands what he must do. He alights into the fiery crater.

Culture has yet to discover Matthew Arnold. At this point, the best he can offer is a nihilistic escape fantasy—but from what, exactly, is Empedocles fleeing? The sources of his troubles are numerous, but generally, declining standards are to blame:

"The brave impetuous hand yields everywhere /To the subtle, contriving head. /Great qualities are trodden down."[57] Park Honan puts a finer point on the argument, attributing Arnold's position in *Empedocles* to the introduction of steam printing in the 1830s, and of the telegraph in the 1840s. The appearance of these new technologies precipitated a "modern information explosion," Honan suggests, casting doubt on the ability of existing regimes of value to cope with the rising tide of textual matter.[58] Through the song of Empedocles, Arnold describes the situation thus:

> We mortals are no kings
> For each of whom to sway
> A new-made world up-springs
> Meant merely for his play.
> No, we are strangers here: the world is from of old.
>
> In vain our pent wills fret
> And would the world subdue
> Limits we did not set
> Condition all we do.
> Born into life we are, and life must be our mould.
>
> Born into life: who lists
> May what is false maintain,
> And for himself make mists
> Through which to see less plain:
> The world is what it is, for all our dust and din.[59]

The "dust and din" of the present day, evidently puerile, obscures the degree to which human beings dwell within material and symbolic structures that have stood the test of time. In the language of information theory, the din is tantamount to noise, and it's drowning out the signal of tradition.

The situation threatens to deteriorate further as the "dust" continues to accumulate and the "din" grows louder. More and more, suggests Arnold, there's simply too much to know:[60]

Look, the world tempts our eye.
And we would know it all.
We map the starry sky.
We mine this earthen ball,
We measure the sea-tides, we number the sea-sands:

We scrutinize the dates
Of long-past human things,
The bounds of effac'd states,
The hues of deceas'd kings:
We search out dead men's words, and works of dead men's hands:

[. . .]

But still, as we proceed,
The mass swells more and more
Of volumes yet to read.
Of secrets yet to explore.
Our hair grows grey, our eyes are dimm'd, our heat is tam'd—

The preponderance of dust and din makes it difficult to identify what's purportedly time-honored and worthy, but, for Arnold, that's hardly the worst part of the new information ecology. Search, once a means for discovering knowledge about the world, becomes, under these conditions, an all-consuming end in itself.

Sidney Coulling is right to underscore the "pervasive melan-
choly in Arnold's poetry," particularly in *Empedocles on Etna*, in
which Arnold depicted an irredeemable world in which there
was nowhere else to go but down.[61] Little wonder critics attacked
the piece and its author, who withdrew *Empedocles* from subsequent editions of the collection in which it appeared.[62] In the
preface to the 1853 edition, from which the poem had been
excised, Arnold conceded that *Empedocles* was "poetically
faulty."[63] He also grasped for a more sustainable response to the
modern-industrial society popping up around him. Once again,
"the ancients" proved a source of inspiration:

> They wish neither to applaud nor to revile their age: they wish to
> know what it is, what it can give them, and whether this is what
> they want. *What they want, they know very well; they want to educe
> and cultivate what is best and noblest in themselves*: they know, too,
> that this is no easy task . . . and they ask themselves sincerely
> whether their age and its literature can assist them in the
> attempt.[64]

At last Arnold has landed on *cultivation*, which puts him within
semantic shouting distance of *culture*—the unspoken of *Empedocles on Etna*, I believe, and also, as far as Arnold is concerned,
the solution to information overload and other problems of the
emerging industrial age.

Here it's worth revisiting Williams's observation about "wrong
answers" in Arnold. One of them, surely, was the definition of
culture he advanced in perhaps his most famous work of prose
criticism, *Culture and Anarchy*, published in 1869. There, he
referred to *culture* as "the best which has been thought and said
[or known] in the world."[65] By this Arnold meant a canon of

outstanding artistic and literary works whose purpose was to enhance the moral, intellectual, and spiritual fiber of the people who studied them. If most of modern literature was noise, then here, at last, was signal emanating from a narrow range of sources: English, white, male, preferably Anglican, definitely not peasant or working class. Arnold's sense of "the world" was exclusive indeed—ironic too, given how elements of his views on *culture* and literary education had been anticipated in the early nineteenth century in the British colonies, particularly India, as Gauri Viswanathan has shown.[66]

If the wrong answers make it challenging to get to the right questions in Arnold, then maybe it's best to begin at the beginning, as it were: What problem did *culture* purport to solve? The answer—anarchy—seems obvious insofar as it resides in the title of his magnum opus, *Culture and Anarchy*. It's also supported by the text, where, for example, Arnold posits *culture* as "a principle of authority, to counteract the tendency to anarchy which seems to be threatening us."[67]

Nevertheless, I believe "anarchy" is a red herring. The book began life as "Culture and its Enemies," a lecture Arnold delivered in June 1867 at Oxford University, the text of which appeared the following month in *The Cornhill Magazine*. The piece, which is the basis for the introductory and first chapters of *Culture and Anarchy*, doesn't contain the word *anarchy* at all.[68] It does appear in "Anarchy and Authority," however, an early draft of the book's six remaining chapters, which Arnold published in two parts in 1868 in *Cornhill*.[69] Even then, the word *anarchy* is confined to just sixteen instances spread across eighty-eight pages of text, seven of those instances occurring on just two pages. (The word *liberal*, in comparison, appears sixty-seven times.) This bit of historical bibliography suggests that *culture* started out not as a simple, antithetical principle in Arnold's work but as a word whose purpose was to mediate multiple tensions present within British society of the 1860s.

This is something that the text of *Culture and Anarchy* says explicitly enough, but the titular pride of place given to anarchy is apt to muddle the issue. Typically, "anarchy" is understood by Arnold's interpreters to refer to the riots and demonstrations that shook London between 1865 and 1867, in which members of the white male working class demanded voting rights.[70] The book, however, opens by referring to these events only indirectly. If there's any anarchy, or confusion, in those opening pages, it surrounds the definition of *culture*. Arnold begins by quoting John Bright, then one of the leading Liberals in Parliament, from a speech in which Bright advocated for working-class suffrage.[71] But instead of keying into the issue at hand, Arnold opts to focus on Bright's use of the word *culture*, which, in the course of the speech, the MP dismissed as "a smattering of the two dead languages of Greek and Latin."[72] Arnold objects: just as civilization isn't cultivation, pretentiousness isn't culture. Forty years after Coleridge, the terms may have shifted, but Arnold still finds himself struggling to articulate what makes *culture* unique, and whether even to hold onto the word: "We will not stickle for a name, and the name of culture one might easily give up, if only those who decry the frivolous and pedantic sort of culture . . . would be careful on their part, not, in disparaging and discrediting the false culture, to unwittingly disparage and discredit . . . the true also."[73]

False culture: the idea signals Arnold's attempt to untangle *culture* from the semantic knots of *civilization*. It also epitomizes his critique of "stock notions and habits," a phrase he uses repeatedly, and negatively, throughout the latter half of *Culture and Anarchy*.[74] There, Arnold wishes to identify "enemies" of culture beyond the working class, whom he has already labeled *the*

Populace. The Barbarians, or English aristocracy, are next on his list. Instead of developing "inward virtues," Arnold claims, the aristocracy obsesses about "exterior graces and accomplishments." By overinvesting in stock notions and habits, they resemble the "barbarians" of antiquity: "All this culture (to call it by that name) of the Barbarians was an exterior culture mainly. It consisted principally in outward gifts and graces, in looks, manners, accomplishments, prowess. . . . Far within, and unawakened, lay a whole range of powers of thought and feeling to which these interesting productions of nature had . . . no access."[75] What we have here, essentially, is Coleridge's objections to *civilization* repackaged under a different label. Indeed it's no coincidence that, in a piece predating *Culture and Anarchy,* Arnold took issue with critics who'd mistaken culture for "mere varnish."[76]

But Arnold's Barbarians aren't the only, much less the most important, representatives of stock notions and habits. Arnold reserved that distinction for *the Philistines,* his name for both the rising middle class and the more peaceable segments of the working class who aspired to its ranks. Gone were the days of aristocratic rule: "If it were not for [the] purging effect wrought upon our minds by culture, the whole world, the future as well as the present, would inevitably belong to the Philistines."[77] This was true, Arnold believed, owing to the Philistines' having hitched their wagons to the forces of industrial capitalism, and more specifically to the machines out of which poured the run-of-the-mill, both literally and figuratively. "The idea of perfection as an *inward* condition of the mind and spirit is at variance with the mechanical and material civilization in esteem with us," he claimed.[78] The Philistines' relationship to contrivances and outward appearances resembled that of the Barbarians, but in the case of the Philistines, Arnold claimed, industrial machinery rather than social graces fueled the apparent conformity. It's worth mentioning that he used *machinery* figuratively too, to refer to political, religious, and other types of organizations that reinforced role and ritual at the expense of change and adaptation.[79]

This is a textbook case of how, according to Williams, "the organization of received meanings has to be made compatible with possible new meanings that are emerging," and vice versa.[80] It also goes to show how the antagonist of *Culture and Anarchy* isn't anarchy, simply, but rather a deficit of form on the one hand, and an overinvestment in it on the other. Lionel Trilling thus is right to have suggested that *Culture and Anarchy* may not be the most suitable title for the book. Yet the alternative he proposed— *Culture or Anarchy*—seems equally ill-fitting, this despite his otherwise perceptive reading of the text's complicated class dynamics.[81] The same goes for Williams, who either assimilates all classes in *Culture and Anarchy* to the cause of disorder or attributes the book's arguments to the author's antipathy toward the working class.[82] If Arnold erred in titling the book *Culture and Anarchy*, then perhaps he should have considered something along the lines of *Culture and the Antinomies of Form*.

Arnold opposed unfettered freedom as much as inflexible order. He was as suspicious of nonconformity as he was of the compulsion to conform. In the end, he was neither a romantic nor a rationalist but a proponent of what you might call, paradoxically, *managed freedom*. Such was his overarching vision for culture, which promised to dislodge entrenched interests and to develop "a finely tempered nature" among those who remained.[83] He tasked "the State" with managing this freedom, moreover, but he meant "the State" only in a manner of speaking.

Indeed, the London protests of 1865–1867 weren't the only acts of civil unrest to have caught Arnold's attention. In October 1865,

Edward John Eyre, the English colonial governor of Jamaica, brutally suppressed the Morant Bay Rebellion, in which Black Jamaicans protested impoverishment, disease, and the political disenfranchisement of formerly enslaved persons. Eyre did so by ordering the murder of more than 500 Jamaican men and women, the whipping of another 600, and the burning of 1,000 homes. According to Paul Gilroy, the violence caused a "cleavage in the Victorian intelligentsia," and should be remembered as "an instance of metropolitan, internal conflict that emanate[d] directly from an external colonial experience."[84] Indeed, reports of the brutality troubled Arnold, leading him to reference the events, albeit in passing, in a letter he published in London's *Pall Mall Gazette* a little over a year before "Culture and its Enemies." As Honan puts it, Arnold "used the Jamaican occasion to strike to the heart of conventional belief in political liberty. The murdered Black Jamaicans had not been especially 'free'; and perhaps, by equating freedom with 'political liberty,' Englishmen had blinded themselves to humane lessons they might learn from nations less democratic than their own."[85] Put differently, "free" elections and other, ostensibly democratic processes and institutions were insufficient to guarantee the physical, psychological, and spiritual wellbeing of the subjects who were governed. Plus, and more to the point, the peoples of colonized nations who may have appeared less "democratic" to British imperialists when they were first encountered, nevertheless held important clues about how to govern human affairs more inclusively and, indeed, less violently compared to "civilized" European nations.

The Morant Bay Rebellion marked a shift for Arnold, or rather anticipated a turn he'd make in earnest toward the end of his life. An early version of "Culture and its Enemies" finds him advocating for swift and repressive government action against protesters—although he saw fit to excise the passages from later versions, and from *Culture and Anarchy*.[86] By the time of his four-month lecture tour of the United States and Canada, from 1883–1884, his position on politicians, protest, and state violence had aligned with his response to Jamaica. The change is most apparent in "Numbers," one of three presentations he delivered while on the circuit in North America. As before, Arnold looked to the English colonies as a gauge for what the state, left to politicians, was capable of. What he saw distressed him: "Every one [*sic*] knows that there has been conquest and confiscation in Ireland. So there as elsewhere. Every one knows that the conquest and the confiscation have been attended with cupidity, oppression, and ill-usage. So they have everywhere." The relationship of England to Ireland, and to its colonies more generally, "will not become solid by means of the contrivances of the mere politician."[87] It's not that politicians were inherently bad people. Instead, Arnold believed the "contrivances"—the form—of political parties and platforms disposed politicians to act domineeringly on behalf of the state.

But if not the politicians, then who? If not a government traditionally conceived, then what? "To reform the State in order to save it, to preserve it by changing it, a body of workers is needed as well as a leader—a considerable body of workers, placed at many points, and operating in many directions."[88] Quoting Plato and the prophet Isaiah, Arnold dubbed this group "the remnant": the portion of the population left over once you've subtracted the Populace, Philistines, Barbarians, and politicians (who, in Arnold's judgment, were tantamount to Philistines). A numerical minority, the unfortunately named "remnant" would be tasked with spreading the word about "things true, things elevated, things just, things pure, things amiable, things of good report"—that is, about culture.[89]

Here's another of Arnold's notorious wrong answers: the view that culture and, indeed, the state were best administered by a small group of unelected officials—people who were uniquely disposed to recognizing what was "elevated" and "pure." The answer was also self-serving insofar as Arnold, a state-school examiner for thirty-five years, was imagining how to secure positions of authority for civil servants like himself. The elitism is impossible to ignore—and yet, it's neither simple nor straightforward. He was proposing a state in which a *body of workers* would serve in lieu of, or perhaps alongside, the existing political caste. The cultural administrators would be expected to interact regularly and directly with the English citizenry, from whose ranks they'd be drawn, ostensibly to narrow the gap between governor and governed. And while it's doubtful that the members of this body would hail from the working class, at least initially, it's worth noting that Arnold—his bank accounts serially overdrawn, his debts unreliably repaid—was no admirer of the English class structure. He viewed it as another mechanical form imposed on society and hence an impediment to change.[90] A corollary was that this "considerable" body of cultural workers would be placed at many points, thereby dispersing power and authority throughout English society.[91]

Did Arnold really wish "to preserve the State by changing it?" Maybe—although it seems more plausible that he wished to displace many of the state's administrative functions into the realm of culture, thereby pursuing politics by other means. A little over a century later, Tony Bennett would rediscover this thread in defining *culture* as a "reformer's science," although he saw fit to jettison Arnold's fixation on goodness and purity, adopting instead a more agnostic view of culture as "a means of acting on the social." Particularly important for Bennett were libraries, museums, theaters, and related institutions whose purpose, in part, was to "induct their visitors into new ways of acting on and shaping the self." Provocatively, he dubbed these institutions "cultural technologies."[92] Arnold, for his part, may have defined *culture* as "the best that has been thought and said in the world," but equally important for him was the notion that it should serve as a locus of human governance. It was a way of redressing what he considered to be the failures and excesses of the state form, both at home in England and abroad in the colonies. Today you might say that Arnold was proposing to reboot the state with a new operating system, culture, having witnessed the old software, politics, crash one too many times.

I'm getting ahead of myself, clearly. The point is that Arnold was more than the priggish aesthete he's often made out to be. As book historian Bill Bell has shown, a skewed portrait of Arnold started to emerge in the decades following his death in 1888. Though Arnold had been accused in his lifetime of endorsing patrician interests, it was largely posthumously that critics and editors began emphasizing *high culture*. This wasn't because it was the sine qua non of Arnold's work, but "because it conveniently served to legitimize the function of the reviewing establishment."[93] Bell goes on to suggest that another—more popular—Arnold exists, one whose range, reach, and positions persist but tend to be overshadowed by the elite view. By 1900, Arnold's books had sold more than 200,000 copies in Britain alone. Several editions remained in print well into the twentieth century, selling tens-of-thousands more copies.[94] An estimated 40,000 people attended his lectures in North America, including figures ranging from Andrew Carnegie to P. T. Barnum, and from Ulysses S. Grant to Mark Twain—not to mention a personal audience with U.S. President Chester A. Arthur.[95] Moreover, as Honan notes, Arnold's career as an itinerant school inspector brought him into regular contact with individuals throughout England, from all walks of life. He "spoke to more schoolchildren, teachers, and petty officials than any other man of letters" and did so by making extensive use of the country's burgeoning train system—a quintessentially modern technology, if ever there was one.[96]

The problem with the "Arnold-as-aesthete" narrative is that it leads to an erroneous set of conclusions about *culture*'s encounter with this fraught figure and, equally important, about the social, political, and technological conditions in which he lived. Instead of exploring how the semantics of *culture* expanded in relationship to the moment of Matthew Arnold, the meaning of the word tends to contract into "selective tradition."[97] As such, it becomes difficult to apprehend the degree to which Arnold and, surely, other observers at the time were struggling to articulate three emergent senses of the word: (1) *culture* as a means for mitigating the "dust and din" of human expression, or what will later come to be understood as the processing of information; (2) *culture* as a mediating principle, or rather, a means for attenuating excesses of anarchy and formality, of disorder and order, of entropy and negentropy; and (3) *culture* as a political technology, or as a flexible set of techniques for managing human affairs in lieu of or alongside established political forms.[98]

RUNNING MAN

Scholars are rarely remembered for their extraordinary physical prowess. Frank Raymond (F. R.) Leavis is an exception. After Leavis's death, Williams reminisced about how "everybody, it seemed, had a Leavis story."[99] That they did—a surprising number of them involving episodes in which Leavis was moving rapidly. He was known to put in "quasi-Olympic times" running ten-mile stretches along the highway between Ely and Cambridge, the city where he spent most of his life.[100] Downtime consisted of bicycle expeditions, canoe trips, and walks so grueling that his spouse Queenie Dorothy (Q. D.) Leavis, née Roth, a formidable intellectual and physical presence in her own right, described them as "exhausting."[101] Even simple errands, like a trip to the post office or bank, were apt to be undertaken at full throttle. Frank's complexion was often tan, even in the dead of winter, owing to his refusal to yield to adverse weather conditions. Michael Black, an editor at Cambridge University Press and, earlier, one of Leavis's Cambridge undergraduates, suggested his former literature professor "seemed to live mostly on sunlight."[102] Or as Queenie put it, her husband "had so much energy he could never get enough physical exercise."[103]

It had long been that way. Even as a young man, Frank seemed almost compelled to move—fast, far, and outdoors. He excelled at cross-country running, his times outstanding for an amateur. Once, as an eighteen-year-old, Leavis won a seven-mile race averaging well under five minutes per mile. He reportedly won another contest so decisively that, after waiting . . . and waiting . . . and waiting for the runner-up to complete the course, he decided to call it a day and go home.[104] This surplus of energy persisted throughout his adult life. But by his mid-twenties, the underlying reasons for the activity started to change. True, he still needed to put all that energy somewhere, yet he no longer moved simply for the sake of physical release. In some sense, his body no longer fully belonged to him. His war service, which had interrupted his undergraduate education, had seen to that.

Leavis was fortunate on some level. Of the undergraduates with whom he began studies at Emmanuel College, Cambridge, in autumn 1914, mere months after Britain had declared war on Germany, one in ten was killed. Leavis not only came back alive from what was then known as the Great War but promptly returned to Cambridge University in January 1919, dropping his earlier course of study, history, for English, after a lackluster showing on the first qualifying exam, or Tripos. He served as a non-combatant, moreover, working primarily on a hospital train. Not quite twenty years old and anticipating conscription, Leavis opted to withdraw from Cambridge, joining the Quaker-run Peace Service upon completing his freshman year. The Friends' Society, which provided non-military support for Britain and its allies, helped secure Leavis's status as a conscientious objector.[105]

But luck is relative in war. Leavis may not have been compelled to carry a rifle, but he was hardly sheltered during his four-year tour of duty. The first seven months were somewhat low-key, first training and later working as a hospital orderly in Britain. Nevertheless, Leavis developed digestive difficulties during this period, which continued to affect him long after he was demobilized. And that was just the start of his troubles. He was shipped off to France in the summer of 1916, where, after a short stint as a cook, he began working on the hospital train.[106] The ensuing five months of fighting, known as the Somme Offensive, came to epitomize the First World War: "The whistle summoning men 'over the top' of their trenches to be slain instantly by machine-gun fire; mass slaughter for pitiful gains of ground; indifferent and incompetent officers refusing to acknowledge that their plans had gone desperately wrong. And then there was the mud."[107] Another future Oxbridge professor, Lieutenant John Tolkien, who was entrenched for four months along the Somme, would later recast those horrors in composing the battle scenes for his epic trilogy *The Lord of the Rings*.[108]

As the offensive wore on, British casualties topped 400,000. The next summer, at Ypres, roughly another quarter-million was added to the tally. Consequently, Leavis and his co-workers languished through impossibly long days. When they weren't caring for the sick, wounded, and dying, they spent hours cleaning and restocking the train. Night brought little respite, the killed and injured usually loaded under cover of darkness. And the train itself, though a medical facility, was hardly a safe haven. It was subject to attack, bitter cold in wintertime, infested with lice, and, owing to its itinerancy, effectively cut off from communication back home. Worse still was the poisonous gas. Personnel aboard the train were subject to second-hand exposure due to the toxins having absorbed into the patients' clothing.[109]

After the war, some observers attributed Leavis's penchant for wearing open-collar shirts to his repeated exposure to gas residue, although Leavis himself disputed the claim that he needed additional room to breathe.[110] So-called peace service had nonetheless taken a toll, both physically and psychologically. He returned to Cambridge at age twenty-three with impaired speech, insomnia, and the persistent indigestion that had manifested shortly after induction. Only his speech returned to normal, though even then it's unclear if the issue had resolved itself, or if Leavis had figured out a work-around. His frame was muscular, but gaunt. Having lost his appetite, he spent the rest of his life looking as if he'd inherited a wardrobe from a considerably larger older brother. Running remained a constant, but now, on doctor's orders, it was also a way of tempering the insomnia that dogged him. Another one of his undergraduates, John Harvey, recalled that Leavis "returned from the war severely shell-shocked." Today, we'd say his symptoms were consistent with Post-Traumatic Stress Disorder, or PTSD.[111] Whatever the diagnosis, the war had effectively dispossessed him of his own body.[112]

Leavis may have worn the effects of war literally on his sleeve, yet he said little, publicly, about the experience. On the subject

FIGURE 3.2 F. R. Leavis during his war service (*left*) and, later in life, as a Cambridge professor (*right*). Note the physical and sartorial transformations after the war.

of war, Ian MacKillop describes Leavis as "controlled"—a word echoed by G. Singh—this in contrast to the "massive detonations" about literary-critical matters for which Leavis would become notorious among friends and colleagues.[113] Raymond Williams also found him to be guarded about such matters, and about his personal life more generally, stating that "as I got to know him [I] knew that I was not getting to know him."[114] Leavis was not entirely reticent about the war, however, occasionally sharing recollections in letters exchanged with his inner circle of friends and family. Moreover, much as Tolkien turned to fiction writing to reflect on the conflict, Leavis developed his own indirect discourse. "Throughout his whole career, Leavis attempted to compensate for this silence about the war through a consistent denunciation of the modern civilisation which had produced it," argues Carl Krockel.[115] While it would be wrong to suggest Leavis's oeuvre must be read in the singular light of his war experience, it would be equally wrong to underestimate the degree to which those experiences affected his relationship to watchwords such as *culture* and *criticism.*

Leavis borrowed these terms from Matthew Arnold, whom he treated as something of a patron saint. It's no coincidence that Leavis opened *Mass Civilization and Minority Culture*, published in 1930 and one his most widely-read works, with an epigraph from *Culture and Anarchy*, nor that he quoted Arnold repeatedly throughout the small volume, and indeed elsewhere in his writing.[116] Williams put it succinctly: "The process which Arnold began, where he virtually equated 'culture' and 'criticism,' is completed by Leavis."[117] But the characterization isn't entirely accurate. The intellectual and semantic through-line Williams saw running from Arnold to Leavis was less direct than he realized: the trajectory having been altered by the consensus view, established in the 1890s, of Arnold-as-aesthete; the angle made more acute by virtue of Leavis's experiences at war.

Like Arnold, Leavis did little to help himself seeming like a prig. His argument—the wellbeing of a society should be entrusted to "a very small [read: white, mostly male] minority" whose judgments amounted to "the consciousness of the race (or of a branch of it)"—smacks of elitism.[118] But what does it mean, really, to call Leavis "elite," or to describe his position as such? He likely would have scoffed at the label. His PhD in English, awarded in 1924, conferred some status on him, but not entirely of the preferred kind. True, it was a high-level credential from Cambridge, one of the oldest and most venerable universities in the world. But in the 1920s, 1930s, and 1940s the degree was apt to seem "distinctively modern"—appropriate for scientists, maybe, but still somewhat vulgar for their counterparts in the humanities.[119] Also, the PhD was generally pursued by students who, like Leavis, had sought academic careers but were not the cream of the crop at the baccalaureate level. For the latter, the path to a professorship would be paved in prizes, fellowships, and other plum recognitions. A PhD, on the other hand, was a way of announcing your path had started out bumpy, and that you needed to clear a substantial, additional hurdle to prove your readiness for the professoriate.[120] Stefan Collini describes the credential thus: "He was always referred to as 'Dr. Leavis,' a title which could, in the delicately layered nuances of social interchange in mid twentieth-century Britain, be made to carry connotations of abstruse academicism or even the lack of a desirable kind of effortless *sprezzatura*."[121]

Leavis went on to teach at Cambridge, in English, but as contingent faculty in what, in the late 1920s, was still a new and relatively unproven department. Only in 1945, at age fifty, did he secure a full-time faculty position, and only in 1952 did he finally achieve the rank of full lecturer. Frank's employment status belied his popularity among students, groups of whom gathered weekly at his home to discuss literature, culture, and criticism. They were intimate gatherings but, as Mulhern has noted, they also literalized Leavis's symbolic distance from the center of "Cambridge English."[122] Queenie, for her part, never pursued regular academic employment, despite having received a PhD in English from Cambridge in 1931, and despite an impressive publication record including *Fiction and the Reading Public*.[123] It's worth mentioning that she published the volume owing to its intellectual merits but hastened to do so out of financial expediency. With Frank temporarily unemployed, someone needed to put "butter on the family bread."[124] But even when Frank was working, the family's meager income left them consistently "hard up" for cash.[125] Neither one had much of a safety net. Queenie's immediate family had rejected her for having married Frank, eleven years her senior, and a non-Jew. Reconciling was out of the question: a German air raid having seen to her mother and sister in 1940, her father having passed away shortly thereafter.[126] Harry, Frank's father, a piano dealer, managed to achieve a level of respectability in part because he traded in middle-class trappings. But a motorcycle accident in 1921 cut short his life. Otherwise, Frank was only a couple of generations removed from ancestors who'd made a living weaving baskets in the rural East Anglian fenlands. The family had emigrated from France to Britain, incidentally, hoping to escape Protestant persecution at the hands of the Catholic majority.[127]

All that to say, we should be wary of reading F. R. Leavis's writings on culture as an effort to consolidate wealth, power, and privilege. They were composed by an outsider looking into that world—someone who felt as though significant aspects of daily life were beyond his control, and indeed beyond that of most people. Call it a crisis of faith: "What especially wore [Leavis] down, added to direct suffering, was vicarious suffering—the need to witness, without possibility of protest, agonised deaths attributable to stupidity-in-office," observed Raymond O'Malley, who, even in the late 1920s, could not help but notice how the war had affected his teacher, with whom he shared weekly one-on-one meetings during his studies at Cambridge.[128] More to the point, O'Malley articulated how Leavis must have felt as masses of sick, wounded, and dying passed day after day, year after year, through the hospital train: the anger at military and government officials for having allowed these poor souls to end up there; the frustration at anointed leaders who were unable or unwilling to contain the slaughter; and the sense of ineffectualness at being unable to intervene much beyond dressing the wounds of the injured and comforting the doomed.

The war was many things for Leavis. Among them, it was a referendum on a world that politics, traditionally conceived, had played a major part in producing. He found that world unacceptable. "The need for political action few will be inclined to deny," wrote Leavis in the second issue of *Scrutiny*, the journal he co-edited, and where he developed his critical program. "But," he added, "it seems pertinent to inquire [into] the worth of political action or theory that is not directed towards realizing some idea of satisfactory living."[129] The statement, appearing in 1932, displays Leavis's pragmatic approach to politics. It's not that he opposed politics—the art, science, and practice of allocating resources and managing human affairs—per se. Nor was he so cynical as to believe politicians were ill-intentioned on the whole. Rather, he objected to how elected and unelected officials, acting through government institutions, had failed to deliver a reasonable degree of peace, prosperity, and fulfillment. The war and its aftermath were Leavis's yardsticks for determining "satisfactory living." How he felt and what he saw around him hardly measured up. If he—a non-combatant, and ostensibly one of the lucky ones—could return so damaged from the war, then clearly he lived in a society that had acquiesced to low standards. Worse, it had granted leadership to officials who mistook unsatisfactory living for its opposite.

In 1934, the editors of *Scrutiny* (then D. W. Harding, L. C. Knights, Denys Thompson, and, of course, Leavis) referred to this state of affairs as "the social and cultural disintegration that has accompanied the development of the vast modern machine."[130] It's an open question whether social and cultural life rapidly deteriorated in the early twentieth century, or whether Leavis et al. lacked perspective. Either way, their patience had worn thin. The tools of politics must have been in the wrong hands, or else they were the wrong tools with which to ensure living meant *living* instead of trauma, injury, or death. "Without an intelligent, educated and morally responsible public, political programmes can do nothing to arrest the process of disintegration—though they can do something to hasten it," wrote Leavis and his colleagues. The argument appears within the context of a discussion of the "emulators of Hitler and his accomplices," whose political insurgency they already found deeply troubling.[131]

For Leavis and his co-editors, the system of checks and balances internal to the political sphere was no longer sufficient to contain it. Perhaps it had never been. Accordingly, they imagined a group of people existing outside the halls of government, whose role would be "to forestall or check" the politicians.[132] This is indeed the public sphere Jürgen Habermas would rediscover in 1962—at least, some version of it. Habermas treated discussions of literature and aesthetics (i.e., cultural affairs) as "precursor[s]" to the substantive work of the public sphere: namely, debates about political and economic affairs.[133] For Leavis, on the other hand, cultural affairs were not only *not* a stepping stone to more substantive topics; they were the substance by means of which to begin recalibrating the standards of satisfactory living.

It's not as if Leavis wanted people to appreciate beauty in the abstract. Nor did he want them simply to fetishize good literature and condemn the bad (though he did a fair amount of that himself). Rather, he wanted a public capable of recognizing a raw deal when it got one. This meant, first, rejecting crude indicators such as the "standard of living." In Leavis's view, this was an abstract benchmark, one that allowed politicians, economists, and intellectuals to fixate on ways and means instead of asking difficult questions about "the ends of life," or about "what kind of life is desirable."[134] It also meant cultivating discernment. By this Leavis referred to a specific type of critical awareness, one that would help people come to terms with the fact that they'd accepted unacceptable conditions or, more to the point, that their ability to recognize those conditions as such had diminished compared to previous generations. The argument, which he developed in 1933 with Denys Thompson in *Culture and Environment*, follows a fairly complex logic. They begin by discussing artisanship, which, they assert,

> involved a subtle training of hand, eye and body in co-ordination. . . . [S]enses were trained to discriminate extreme delicacies of difference. [Craftspeople] had to be masters of a very wide range of varied knowledge concerning the way to do things, their material, the environment it came from, and the environment which their products had to serve. Their work trained them aesthetically and morally.[135]

Industrial production, in contrast, enforced such a rigid division of labor that only specialists, like engineers, were encouraged to scrutinize processes and materials—but even then they remained at a significant remove from the contexts of production and use. The result, argued Leavis and Thompson, was "a habit of cheerfulness based on a refusal (which amounts in the long run to inability) to see things as they are."[136]

Leavis and Thompson developed the argument in conversation with George Sturt, whose *The Wheelwright's Shop* (1923), a sensuous account of wagon wheel production in nineteenth-century England, they quoted extensively. Sturt held that handicraft encouraged a deeply embodied relationship to tools and, thus, a capacity to adduce otherwise unobserved or unobservable qualities in their application to the material world: "Under the plane (it is little used now) or under the axe (it is all but obsolete) timber disclosed qualities hardly to be found otherwise. My own eyes know because my own hands have felt, but I cannot teach an outsider the differences between ash that is 'frow as a carrot,' or 'doaty,' or 'biscuity.' "[137] Leavis, for his part, seems to have taken the view to heart in opting to use a scythe to trim the yard at 6 Chesterton Hall Crescent, where he and Queenie lived with Ralph and Kate, their two children. It was also a way of channeling some of his excess energy—at least until his eightieth birthday, when, his health deteriorating, he finally gave in and purchased a hand-powered lawnmower.[138]

It's easy to mistake Leavis and Thompson's account (and Leavis's own relationship to tools) for simple nostalgia—a defiant exaltation of *human* industry in the face of a violent and dehumanizing modernity.[139] Yet, the position is scarcely so simple. "There can be no mere going back," wrote Leavis and Thompson. "It is useless to think of . . . scrapping the machine in the hope of restoring the old order."[140] Leavis reinforced the point thirty years later: "I am not preaching that we should defy, or try to reverse, the accelerating movement of external civilization . . . that is determined by advancing technology."[141] The problem wasn't large-scale industry per se, despite what Leavis may have claimed in *Mass Civilization and Minority Culture*.[142] With Thompson, and also on his own, he seemed to accept the givenness of modern machinery, albeit begrudgingly. But this presented a dilemma: If the tools and practices of handicraft had become outmoded, and if those tools had once helped nurture a discerning attitude among those who'd used them, then how could he reignite the capacity to differentiate good from bad, right from wrong—living from dying? That is, how could he compensate for the emergence of a mode of production that positioned quality control as separable from and subordinate to the act of producing?

The answer, for Leavis, lay not in the *specific* relationship between artisan, implement, and material under handicraft, but rather in their *abstract* relation: the latter consisting of a heightened sensitivity to and scrutiny of one's surrounds, material or otherwise. High-quality craftwork depended, in essence, on a type of close reading mediated by technical artifacts. More important, the critical repertoires rehearsed in the artisan's workshop might then be applied to other aspects of daily life. Leavis, having identified the general pattern, sought to reconstitute it in a different context—literature—where the analog for biscuity wood might be, say, the unique structures of irony present in the writings of Jonathan Swift.[143] And as in the artisan's workshop, so too in literature: Swift and his literary devices weren't the ultimate goal. Rather, the goal was to better attune people to the moral character of their milieux. Literary study was the cultivation of discernment by other means. As Leavis put it: "Literary study, so far from producing the 'literary mind,' . . . should be the best possible training for intelligence—for free, unspecialized, general intelligence, which there has never at any time been enough of, and which we are peculiarly in need of to-day." Or, as Mulhern puts it in his study of Leavis and *Scrutiny*: "Literary criticism possessed a special heuristic capacity that was essential to contemporary intellectual life in general."[144]

Given Leavis's fixation on the minutiae of literary works, he's still apt to come across as a bourgeois aesthete. Stuart Hall once called him a "conservative liberal."[145] But Leavis's politics are more difficult to define, owing to his habit of keeping politics in abeyance until a clear strategy emerged. "One does not necessarily take one's social and political responsibilities the less seriously because one is not quick to see salvation in a formula or in any simple creed," he wrote in 1932, as if to echo Arnold's concerns about "stock notions and habits."[146] Among the culprits was Marxism, whose laws of historical necessity he believed "obliterate[ed] difficulties" in the analysis of social and economic relations. As such, it mimicked the logic of modern industrial society, its intellectual tools routinizing analysis and thus obviating the need "for elementary discriminations."[147] Thus the Marxists, in Leavis's view, were more or less Philistines in disguise. He rejected their calls for revolutionary violence, moreover, a move likely stemming from the trauma he'd experienced at war.[148]

Little wonder Leavis fiercely rejected the label "Luddite," not only for himself but for colleagues whose disposition might have resembled his own.[149] Culture and technology, art and industry, the humanities and the sciences—they weren't antitheses per se, despite what his foe, Sir Charles (C. P.) Snow, had suggested in his famous 1959 lecture on the "two cultures." *Culture* implied neither a denunciation nor a denial of technology—a fundamentalist "literarism," to recall Aldous Huxley's disparaging term— but a way of asking much more it, and of the surrounding society.[150] Leavis's own experiences embodied this ethic, given how trains, tools, and books (the latter so quaint, they're easily overlooked as technologies) are touchstones in his biography, and in his encounter with *culture*. That is, he approached these and other technologies not as objects of alienation but as resources for *living critically*—for refusing to accept the conceit that "not simply not dying" was equivalent to flourishing.[151] In this regard, *culture* inched quietly away from the aesthetic view, which tended to oppose culture and technology, at the same time that it slipped almost imperceptibly from the anthropological view, which tended to subsume technology under the rubric of culture.

TWO SHIPS PASSING

The Boas incident—the opening anecdote for this chapter—is startling for many reasons. Among them is the relative ease with which a white-nationalist blogpost could become the leading source of information on the web about the late anthropologist and his views on culture, even if temporarily. Also startling, perhaps, is Google's authority in presiding over which view of culture would achieve prominence on the site, and the part its algorithms presumably played in making that determination. As I noted earlier in this book, much has been written about algorithms and their role in contemporary cultural politics. What the Boas controversy also shows is the critical role algorithms are playing in *meta*cultural politics—that is, in prioritizing among competing definitions and interpretations of *culture*, and thus in sketching the contours of culture's very existence. This is a somewhat recent development in the sense that computational technologies now seem to be settling these claims in a prominent, public setting. But, as this chapter has shown, technology isn't newly applied to metacultural discourse. It's long been there in the form of hand tools, weapons of war, and modern conveyances, and in a more general concern for information overload, instanced by the industrialization of printing and the implementation of the telegraph system. Technology may not have been adjudicating among competing definitions of *culture* in the nineteenth and early twentieth centuries but, even then, it had something important to do with how the term came to be defined in Arnold and Leavis, and eventually Williams, in the thick of the British culture and society tradition.

This is hardly *algorithmic culture*. Nevertheless, the methodology of key-words shows how senses and meanings pertinent to the phrase began to coalesce at least a century before Silicon Valley. Anecdotes are powerful tools for accessing these latent senses and meanings. In broadening the frame beyond intellectual history and historical semantics, they've aided us in identifying the entailments—both proximate and distant, intrinsic and extrinsic, technical and otherwise—of metacultural discourse. With this, they've enlarged the bandwidth of keywords, and helped reboot the project under the heading of key-words. Meta-cultural discourse remains a significant object of study, to be sure, but equally significant for key-words are metacultural discourse *networks*: the patchwork "of technologies and institutions that allow a given culture to select, store, and process relevant data"—in this case, data about *culture*.[152] I should add that, in this chapter, anecdotes have received only preliminary treatment: a few each for Williams and Arnold, and several for Leavis. They will accumulate more rapidly, and with greater density, in chapter 4, as the narrative shifts from Cambridge, England, to Cambridge, Massachusetts, and as the First World War gives way to the Second and, eventually, to the Cold War. There, crit-ical themes we've encountered throughout this book will come together, setting the stage for the emergence of algorithmic cul-ture in the final quarter of the twentieth century. These include culture-as-governance, computation, state politics, war, impe-rialism/colonialism, race, gender, sexuality, family, normativity, and totalitarianism.

Nevertheless, in 1853, terms closely related to *algorithm* and *culture* had a near miss, if you will, in the work of Matthew Arnold. This was the year *cultivation* finally found him, reveal-ing itself as preferable to the fiery abyss when it came to respond-ing to information overload. This was also the year Arnold pub-lished one of his most admired dramatic poems, *Sohrab and Rustum*.[153] A retelling of a famous episode from the *Shāhnāmeh*, a Persian epic penned by Abu'l-Qasim Firdausi in the tenth century CE/fourth century AH, Arnold's poem is a blatant instance of cultural appropriation. It's also notable for having been set on the banks of the Amu Darya (Oxus) River near Khiva, amid the "the hush'd Chorasmian waste," an area also known as Khwarizm. That Arnold happened upon *cultivation* and al-Khwārizmī's ancestral homeland—his namesake—in exactly the same year is nothing short of astonishing. By the same token, Khwarizm didn't land in Arnold's poetry by accident. As Kate Teltscher and Reza Taher-Kermani have separately noted, the Amu Darya and surrounding region were of strategic importance to the British Empire, acting as a buffer against Russian incursions into the northernmost reaches of colonial India. As such, it was a favored topic among English scholars, journalists, writers, and administrators of the colonial era.[154] The resulting "river of texts," as Teltscher puts it, evidences the importance of Central Asia in the English colonial imagination.[155] In the case of Arnold's texts from 1853, something else is apparent too: the words *algorithm* and *culture* drifting forth as if two ships passing in the night, the one vessel flying the Chorasmian flag, the other the flag of *cultivation*.

4

ALGORITHMIC CULTURE

Algorithmic culture," I'm told, "is a historical process that is used to organize human culture by means of computational process." The source of the definition is a UK-based term paper writing service, UKEssays.com.[1] I'm directed there after "waking" Amazon's personal digital assistant, by calling out the name *Alexa* to the app residing on my mobile phone, and then asking for a definition of algorithmic culture. Initially, I'm overwhelmed by the circularity of the results. I've asked a device, one that uses natural language processing algorithms, to define algorithmic culture, only then to be directed to a paper mill that quotes back to me a distorted version of myself defining the term. (My research is mentioned, but not cited, in the paper for sale on the site.) I wonder why Alexa's search algorithms determined *this* was the authoritative site from which to pull the definition—whereupon my mind races to consider the cultural and economic implications of paywalls for scholarly research.

But then I take a step back from the scene and, as I do, I start to grasp a different—if related—set of dynamics playing out before me. I observe that I'm at home, working, and that I've asked the dutifully listening Alexa to act as my research assistant. I've long thought it predictable that Alexa's default voice is coded as female, as is the name, only now I connect those attributes directly to my own identity as a white, middle-class, heterosexual, cis-gender male. My thoughts turn immediately to Thao Phan's outstanding article "Amazon Echo and the Aesthetics of Whiteness."[2] Phan reminds us of what Alexa, an algorithmically-enabled digital artifact, embodies: a history of heterosexual middle class families securing their economic status in part by hiring women, who were less financially well off than themselves, to perform domestic labor. In asking the device to define "algorithmic culture," I've implicated myself in a legacy social script, one rife with hierarchies of gender, sexuality, and class. Phan further reminds us that, historically, Black women and women of color have served disproportionately in the role of "domestics," and that the families that employed them have tended to be white. The bitter irony is that Alexa's voice, "underwritten by ideals of whiteness," as Phan puts it, effaces the racial dimension of this history while reinforcing dated stereotypes about gendered labor.[3] Suddenly, I come to understand that my concerns about Alexa's algorithms, justified though they may be, are nonetheless embedded in a troubling history of white heterosexual middle class families complaining about "the help."[4]

Those complaints often stemmed from perceptions of the quality of the work, but, as Phan observes, they were also derived from anxieties about domestic laborers eavesdropping on private conversations and, thus, potentially exposing the secrets of the "polite" families for whom they were working.[5] It also worked the other way around, albeit asymmetrically, with white employers listening in on the communications of servants who may have wished for, but had little expectation of, privacy in what for them was a workplace. As I think about these complex dynamics of interaction, I start to appreciate the delicate

FIGURE 4.1 Alexa, imagined as the Victorian-era maidservant "Alessa," in the "Before Alexa" advertisement (Amazon, 2020).

relationship between capitalism, domesticity, information, and privacy. According to Williams, the word *private* "is a record of the legitimation of a bourgeois view of life: the ultimate generalized privilege . . . of seclusion and protection from others (*the public*); of lack of accountability to 'them'."[6] Perhaps it goes without saying that, historically, that privilege has tended to insulate dominant groups from accountability far more than subordinate ones. Nevertheless, that privacy is a privilege means that it's potentially revocable for everyone.

Little wonder that, today, local and federal law enforcement are clamoring to obtain transcripts and recordings of Alexa conversations from Amazon, hoping the data will aid in criminal prosecutions, especially ones occurring at home.[7] Amazon may have started life as an online bookseller, but increasingly it's an information technology company, one whose capacity for remote sensing—surveillance, eavesdropping—extends into the most public and intimate of spaces, at scale. And that capacity, significantly, is aided and abetted by a repertoire of algorithms that seeks to transform the data deluge into actionable intelligence. That may sound creepy, and on some level, it is. That may also sound cutting-edge, and on some level, it's that, too. Yet, we'd do well to appreciate the degree to which Alexa participates in a long-established pattern whereby the relationship between capitalism and the state is mediated, significantly but not exhaustively, by figures of family and home.

That is to say: Alexa offers a fitting parable for the consequences of connecting *algorithm* and *culture*. This chapter is about how, in the mid-twentieth century at Harvard University, *culture* came to be understood through a metaphorics of computation, setting the stage for the pre-emergence of algorithmic culture, both semantically and technologically. Maybe surprisingly, this fusion occurred neither in mathematics nor in engineering, where advances in computer science are typically thought to originate, but in the social sciences. And it occurred within the paranoid atmosphere of the McCarthy-era "witch hunts" that sought to expose alleged communist infiltration into U.S. government agencies, educational institutions, the media, and civic organizations. The central claim of this chapter is that the construct *algorithmic culture* coalesced in relationship to the Cold War-era emphasis on family and, more specifically, the pressure to abide by highly circumscribed norms of gender, sexuality, race, class, and national belonging.

KEY-WORDS AFTER DARK

As with the preceding two chapters, this one begins with a reflection on methodology. By now it should be obvious that it's nearly impossible to tell the story of algorithmic culture using only the tools of keywords. The specific challenge presented in this chapter is how to reckon with anecdotes and other forms of evidence that aren't, for the most part, matters of public record. To that end, let me begin with an anecdote that *is* a matter of public record, albeit one that points to provisional documents and other types of textual matter hiding out in the recesses of print culture.

Raymond Williams often had far more to say in his books than his publishers would allow. *Culture and Society* was no exception. As I discussed in chapter 1, he intended to include some preliminary keyword entries as an appendix to the manuscript, but his publisher balked. Concerned about its unwieldiness, Chatto & Windus insisted he excise the additional section. "I had little effective choice," Williams recollected. "I agreed, reluctantly. I put in a note promising this material as a separate paper. But the file of the appendix stayed on my shelf" until it appeared, almost twenty years later, in the form of *Keywords*.[8]

I mention this bit of textual history to mark some idiosyncrasies in Williams's approach to keywords. It overwhelmingly favored terms appearing in the published writings of men of European descent—an effect, in part, of Williams's having absorbed some of the bad habits of both intellectual history and historical semantics. Of the forty figures discussed in *Culture and Society*, only one—Elizabeth Gaskell—is female, and she is also of European descent. The imbalance raises questions about the legibility of race, gender, and sexuality—all themes from the preceding chapters—to the methodology of keywords.[9] It also raises questions about the classes of objects and experiences keywords has tended to privilege. Imagine, for a moment, that the appendix Williams drafted for *Culture and Society* had remained in the file on his shelf, untouched. The only public evidence of the work would have been an odd footnote tucked into the margins of *Culture and Society*. It's doubtful these paratexts would have registered for someone working in the vein of keywords, given the fixation on authoritative public statements manifested in the form of principal text.[10] Williams's occasional references to postal correspondence demonstrate this tendency as well, given his proclivity to forego the archive in favor of published (i.e., curated and sanctioned) anthologies of authors' letters.[11] One useful point, then, is to recognize that salient statements exist in places that often pass under the radar of keywords, and that these statements can infuse public discourse in ways Williams likely would have found difficult to recognize.

Like the preceding chapters, the story of this chapter develops through a process of questioning major moves and assumptions embedded in Williams's own body of work. We would do well in this regard to recognize keywords not as *a* method but as a set of contextually-bound methodological principles requiring adaptation depending on time, setting, mediality, subject matter, and circumstance.[12] We'd also do well to recognize the degree to which keywords—and, indeed, key-words—is a gendered (and raced, and classed, and sexualized . . .) project through and through. Beyond *Culture and Society*, consider the clumsy treatment of explicitly gendered terminology in *Keywords*. The 110-entry first edition of the book (1976) includes words such as *family*, *humanity*, and *man* (*career* might qualify, too).[13] Williams denies *woman* a stand-alone entry, the word appearing twice under the entry for *man*, specifically as an episode in the term's "sexual specialization."[14] The absence of *feminism* from the entry on *-isms* is another glaring omission, one he never bothered to correct. Surely Williams must have been aware of the significant traction women's movements had achieved by the mid-1970s. *Feminism* was hardly a new word for that matter, having appeared in the English language at least a century earlier.[15] The revised edition of *Keywords* (1983) saw Williams add *generation* and *sex* (along with 19 other entries) to the mix, with the entry for *sex* providing the most sustained exploration of gendered words and themes in *Keywords* and, likely, his *oeuvre*. But there, again, no unique entry for *woman*, let alone any number of other gendered identities, practices, and dispositions that were coming to public awareness in the late 1970s and early 1980s.[16]

Despite more recent efforts to address these and other awkward silences surrounding gender and identity in *Keywords*, there's been little reflection on how those silences may have affected the methodology, and not just the content, of Williams's project.[17] As Dorothy Smith observed in 1990: "It is not enough to supplement an established sociology by addressing ourselves to what has been left out or overlooked, or by making women's issues into sociological issues. That does not change the standpoint built into existing sociological procedures, but merely makes the sociology of women an addendum to the body of objectified knowledge."[18] Put differently, adding terms to Williams's vocabulary of culture and society may help to manifest a broader range of experiences. Yet, there may be objects, individuals, and more that are unintelligible to keywords, owing to the "conceptual practices of power," as Smith called them, that enabled the development of Williams's approach in the first place.[19]

Smith's argument may seem dated, given the move away from feminist standpoint theory over serious concerns about its propensity to universalize and essentialize: that is, to generalize from the experiences of white, straight, able-bodied women living in the Global North, at the cost of a more intersectional approach.[20] We should nonetheless bear in mind that Smith was attempting to describe gendered relations of power, authority, and knowledge production prevalent in the Western academy in exactly the period in which Williams, and indeed all of the figures discussed in this chapter, were operating: the second half of the twentieth century. More specifically, her research explored the institutional and interpersonal arrangements whereby the sociology of knowledge, a kindred spirit of keywords, papered over the "actualities" of human experience by favoring public documents produced under formal conditions of work, typically outside the home. Smith argued that a fixation on artifacts endemic to the everyday world "subsumed" much of what went on after hours or out of view of the public eye, in what she dubbed the "everynight world."[21]

Consider, for instance, Williams's keyword entry for *family*, which traverses the Judeo-Christian bible, the *Oxford English Dictionary*, and the work of James Mill (father of the British utilitarian philosopher John Stuart Mill). There, Williams charted the term's association with the concept of familiarity, its application to both broad and narrow definitions of kinship, and its inflection by capitalism in the nineteenth century. It was in this period, Williams argued, that a "distinction between man's *work* and his family" emerged: "He works to support a family; the family is supported by his work."[22] Now, contrast this oddly circular account with that of Smith in the essay "Women, the Family, and Corporate Capitalism," published the same year as the first edition of *Keywords*. While not addressing Williams directly, Smith observed that a distinction such as the one he'd drawn "separates women from the locus of 'where history is made to happen'."[23] Her purpose, then, was to show how partners and children (and, I would add, domestic workers, maintenance people, and . . .) acted as "sub-contractual" labor under capitalist relations of production, insofar as they engaged in material and symbolic work, often after so-called "business hours," critical not only to processes of *re*production but indeed to production itself.[24] But there was more. The trouble with *family*, she added, was that "you can use the concept . . . to carve up the real world, and it doesn't matter if nothing in the real world corresponds to your system of carving." With that, a "virtual reality vested in texts" comes to stand in for the specificity of actual relations.[25] Williams's work thus was indicative of how patriarchal working conditions in the academy reinforced masculinist accounts of the relationship between culture, society, and language, and, by extension, allowed critical methodological questions to go unanswered.[26] *Family* looks a certain way, and comes to be researched as such, depending on where, when, and among whom one goes looking for definitions.

All that to say, a fixation on "definitive" public statements isn't strictly an archival question but also one with any number of implications along axes of identity, including gender. And that question hinges on a methodological maneuver whereby statements are situated by their handlers in abstract "textual time," a scholarly chronotope that, according to Smith, authorizes researchers to interpret texts in a manner divorced from the conditions under which they were produced.[27] Thus, moving forward, key-words faces a challenge: How to re-embed language in the actualities of the everyday/everynight world, so as to provide context for the twisting and turning of relevant semantic figures?

In the remainder of this chapter, I respond to this challenge by surfacing "grey literature" and "hidden transcripts"—powerful resources for auditing publications that tend to transact in textual time. By "grey literature" I refer to a class of documents, often ephemeral, whose authority and aesthetics are generally considered inferior to those of texts published through conventional, accredited channels. Examples include reports, newsletters, memos, internal studies, working papers, self-published materials, and the like.[28] "Hidden transcripts," a term I borrow from James C. Scott, refers to an even broader class of discourse consisting of statements, often "fugitive," manifested in the "backstage" of public and professional life— a realm that overlaps substantially with Smith's everynight world. Hidden transcripts aren't private communications per se. Instead, they're discourses that demand a heightened sense of discretion on the part of social actors, owing to the ways in which those discourses challenge dominant repertoires and established social scripts. Because hidden transcripts "cannot," under most circumstances, "be openly avowed," people risk shame, humiliation, loss of status, ostracism, retribution, violence, and other disastrous consequences in invoking them— including people vested with power. On the other hand, sharing in hidden transcripts may also reinforce a sense of trust and solidarity among social actors who maintain a common disposition toward the "public transcript of power relations."[29]

This isn't an argument for excluding traditionally credentialed publications from the endeavor of key-words. It *is* an invitation to further expand the object domain by embracing the complexities of life after dark, particularly as those complexities played out in the United States throughout the third quarter of the twentieth century. The goal is to refuse entry "into a universe of texts in which personal matters have no place," without, at the same time, simply reifying the speaking subject and its agency.[30] The challenges are almost identical to those of the preceding chapters: account for the agents and agencies that print culture has tended to paper over; do so in a manner that's sensitive to the intersections of identity, mediality, and institutional context; and, meanwhile, tell a story about the relationships among language, experience, and processes of social and technological change leading to *algorithmic culture*'s pre-emergence.

MARGINS

Despite twenty years working at the Center, her traces exist mostly in the margins. One of her notes, scrawled in pencil below the signature line of Clyde Kluckhohn, famed anthropologist and director of Harvard University's Russian Research Center, says: "Telephoned[–] HP 12/17/48." The letters "HP" are the initials of Helen Parsons (1902–1993), née Helen Bancroft Walker, secretary to Kluckhohn and wife of Talcott Parsons, titan of sociology and chair of Harvard's path-breaking if controversial Department of Social Relations, launched in January 1946. The note appears on a typewritten letter Kluckhohn had sent to her husband, inviting him to attend a 2 p.m. seminar and "small dinner" on January 7, 1949, with Margaret Mead, who, at age forty-seven, had already established herself as grand dame of anthropology—Ruth Benedict having passed away in September 1948. Mead would be travelling to Cambridge, Massachusetts, to share some of her research on the Soviet Union, which she had recently begun under the auspices of the U.S. military-funded RAND Corporation. Helen, having confirmed her husband's availability for the 7th, conveyed the news to Kluckhohn, who then proceeded to jot down the final arrangements: "OK– for dinner. Probably not– 2 PM."[31]

The letter is almost unremarkable in its genericness: a piece of inter-office mail, sent from one university colleague to another, inviting the recipient to an upcoming event. Today, such a message hardly would have survived the ruination of email. Even in its day, it's surprising the document escaped the circular file. And

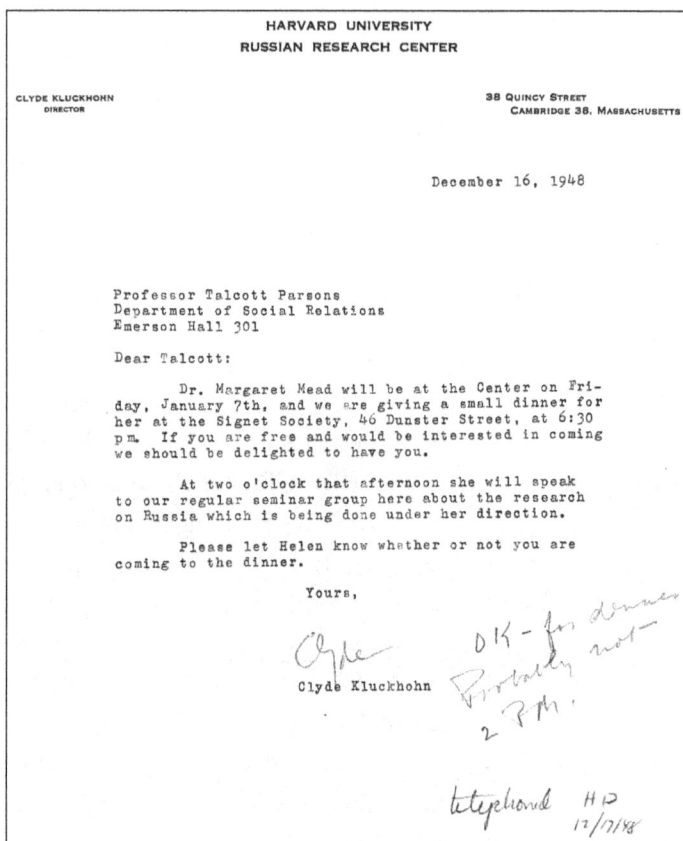

FIGURE 4.2 Letter from Clyde Kluckhohn to Talcott Parsons, December 16, 1948. Note the annotation by "HP," Helen Parsons.

Source: Harvard University Archives. Used with permission.

yet, the letter is significant precisely because of its ordinariness. It's indicative of the conditions out of which algorithmic culture—first the term, and eventually its materialization in the form of technologies, corporations, etc.—would emerge: a context beset by the new postwar geopolitics, the term "Cold War" having been coined by presidential advisor Bernard Baruch only the year before, in 1947, also the year George F. Kennan first proposed the doctrine of "containment"; a moment rife with concern about communist infiltration of the United States government and government-sponsored agencies; a period in which the guardians of liberalism puzzled incessantly over the appeal of totalitarianism; and a time when a historically specific articulation of gender, sexuality, and family emerged in the United States as a "bulwark" against Soviet expansionism.[32]

One can only wonder if Helen was included in the "small dinner" honoring Mead, a plus-one despite some impressive credentials of her own: a 1920 graduate of Abbot Academy, an elite, East Coast prep school for girls (later absorbed by Phillips Academy Andover); an AB from Bryn Mawr, in 1924, followed by a year of graduate work at the London School of Economics (where she met Talcott); and a master's degree in economics from Radcliffe College, in 1928. Indeed, Helen's intellect was one of her defining attributes. In addition to chronicling regular appearances on the Abbot Academy honor roll and two terms as class treasurer, the writeup appearing in "HP"'s senior class yearbook noted: "[Helen's] latest achievement is to demonstrate the quality of her brains by serenely going seven full points ahead of the rest of the school in our recent psychological examination." So memorable was Helen's performance, in fact, that it was recounted twenty years later in the Abbot Academy alumnae bulletin: "Helen has proved beyond doubt that those intelligence tests which Dr. Fuess gave us at Abbot and in which she led the entire school were certainly correctly interpreted."[33]

The obituaries for Helen Parsons, published upon her death in April 1993 at age 90, do little to affirm her intellect, much less the extent of her professional imprint. The obituary appearing in *The Boston Globe*, a scant two column-inches or so, states that she was wife of the late Talcott Parsons, mother of three, and grandmother of four—little else. *The Boston Herald* manages to list her academic credentials and notes twenty-one years of employment as "administrative assistant of the Russian Research Center at Harvard University."[34] Both newspapers neglect Helen's run of professional activities preceding and postdating her time at the Center.

Her career began as an industrial secretary with the YWCA of Worcester, Massachusetts, where she was engaged in educational outreach with female factory workers. In the U.S. South of the 1920s, work of this kind often morphed into labor organizing—sometimes radical—benefitting white women factory workers and, to some degree, Black women seeking factory employment. In the North, where Helen was stationed, the work tended to have more moderate aims: "general educational work on industrial problems" combined with efforts to "extend acquaintance between the industrial membership and women of different experiences in order that they may understand each other's point of view."[35] Later, Helen moved on to a post as secretary and research assistant to Edwin Francis Gay, professor of economic history and founding dean of the Harvard Business School, working closely with him for eight years. The Parsons' three children—Anne, Charles, and Susan—were all born during that time (1930, 1933, and 1936, respectively). Helen then became research assistant to Dr. Douglas Brown, of Harvard Medical School, upon Gay's departure from the university in 1936. The work tapped her background in economics, applying it specifically to healthcare. The renowned Harvard political scientist Carl J. Friedrich hired her two years later to be his secretary and editorial assistant. She makes a brief appearance in the acknowledgments to the 1941 edition of Friedrich's *Constitutional Government and Democracy* for having "rendered great assistance in preparing the new manuscript and bringing the bibliography up to date." Even in retirement she remained active as a volunteer for Medicine in the Public Interest, a healthcare think tank focusing on "nutrition, delivery of medical care, [and] professional standards."[36]

The point isn't simply to note Helen's presence at the side of prestigious male faculty members, but to underscore the different standards of legibility for scholarly production throughout the period in which she lived. As Allison L. Rowland and Peter Simonson have shown, the "founding mothers" of the communication discipline consisted largely of "research assistants, interviewers, and secretaries"—women whose substantive contributions either passed under the radar or, when publicly avowed, tended to be remanded to acknowledgments, footnotes, and other instances of paratext. This pattern, however, wasn't unique to any field or discipline. If anything, it was generic: "In scholarly works where men relate to women in a sentence of preface mention, that sentence may carry as much intellectual weight in terms of substantiating the inequities of the female/male social order as the 500 to 700 pages of manuscript that follow add to the discipline of the scholar," observes Marilyn Hoder-Salmon. Or, as Karen Lee Ashcraft and Peter Simonson put it: "It becomes difficult to deny that the world of intellectual production is *premised on* the gender relation and, particularly, on a reverence for masculinity."[37] In a similar vein, it was challenging for women in the United States, Helen included, to resist the assimilation of their professional accomplishments to the realm of domesticity.[38] Consider this update, which appeared in the *Bryn Mawr Alumnae Bulletin* of 1928: "Helen Walker Parsons is living in Cambridge and studying economics with her husband at Harvard. Besides getting her MA she is cooking and keeping house and in her odd moments wishing that everyone would pay the money they have pledged to Goodhart Hall."[39] The statement is a textbook example illustrating how "married women [were] in many ways asymmetrically drawn into the 'social person' of their husbands."[40]

While we must always be wary of invoking types, Helen Parsons's life certainly displays characteristics consistent with the concept of a "faculty wife."[41] This category refers to women who occupied positions, both formal and informal, within and beyond the universities where their husbands were employed as professors. Faculty wives were mainstays of university life throughout much of the twentieth century, providing care work, extracurricular programming, social engagement, logistical and administrative support, research and teaching assistance, editorial guidance, authorship (often uncredited), and more. They not only bolstered their husbands' careers but helped colleges and universities keep pace with the extraordinary expansion of higher education happening in North America, Europe, and elsewhere.[42] One account, focusing on Dalhousie University in Nova Scotia, Canada, found that "during the middle decades of the twentieth century, the number of professors' wives who taught or did other significant work for their husbands' university for little or no salary was legion." Although it's difficult to determine exactly how prevalent was this corps of "surrogate professors" in colleges and universities writ large, it seems reasonable to surmise that Helen Parsons and "administrative assistants" like her engaged in work far exceeding what their titles would have implied and, thus, that they were critical to advancing the mission of higher education throughout much of the last century.[43]

Furthermore, it's important to appreciate the range of occupations that once fell under the rubric of "administrative" labor. It wasn't only traditional secretarial work of the type Helen Parsons was engaged in. As Nathan Ensmenger, Janet Abbate,

Margot Lee Shetterly, Marie Hicks, and other historians have observed, computation and programming were also identified as such from the mid-1930s until the early 1960s. Shetterly uses the word "sub-professional" in *Hidden Figures*, a history of Black female "computers" in U.S. aerospace, to describe where this type of work tended to fall within the occupational hierarchies of the time. And indeed it fell, more often than not, to women, since it was thought to squander the talents and training of the (predominately white) men for whom hardware comprised "the real business of computing," as Ensmenger puts it.[44] The irony is that these women found themselves as primary users of some of the most powerful devices of the burgeoning information age, a relationship that in principle might have destabilized masculine control of the public sphere. As Kathleen McConnell writes of midcentury office workers: "In possessing the means of communication, female typists only compounded problems by threatening to dispossess men of their ability to create and control discourse." The same was true of female switchboard operators, who occupied a comparable position within the telephone system.[45] The threat to male dominance was ultimately attenuated, however, in part through an ideological process whereby women were figured as mere extensions of the machines they were working on, the men they were working for, or both. Male scientists, for instance, tended to imagine the work of female programmers as nothing more than the "mechanical translation or rote transcription" of their instructions for a particular machine. In refusing to acknowledge the creativity, passion, and intellection programmers brought to their work, these scientists figured it in much the same terms as secretarial labor, which was often considered to be unimaginative, passive, and automatic.[46]

All that is to say: Helen Parsons's work in and beyond the Russian Research Center may be history-of-computing adjacent, but in critical respects it belongs to a broader history of gendered labor that encompasses that history of computing. That is, it points to how the category "faculty wife" emerged in relationship to a division of labor that was hardly unique to academe, let alone any profession. Rather, the "sub-contractual" arrangement discussed by Smith was indicative of the larger trend by means of which wives, and to some degree, children, were "incorporated" into the professional responsibilities of husbands/fathers during the middle decades of the twentieth century—particularly in the postwar period.[47] Hicks refers to this pattern as the "nearly compulsory form of midcentury heteronormativity [that] stranded most women with limited career prospects," which in turn instanced how "sexuality, the organization of labor markets, and the functioning of the economy as a whole [had become] inextricably interlinked."[48]

It also depended on a historically specific configuration of family in which social and geopolitical strife would be managed significantly at home. According to Elaine Tyler May, the United States underwent a period of retrenchment in the years and decades following the Second World War. Women who had joined the public workforce during the depression and war years were often compelled to return to the role of homemaker or, if they already occupied the role, to double down on it as "family fever swept the nation."[49] Those who remained at work tended to experience low wages and limited career options. Administrative posts like the ones Helen occupied were not uncommon, especially for educated white women who sought employment. Women of color typically found themselves channeled into more "menial and subordinate" jobs, where those jobs existed.[50] The arrangement wasn't simply a function of male GIs returning en masse from the war and displacing female workers, as the story conventionally goes. Rather, it embodied an emergent ideology in which the effects of family stability were thought to scale up to the rest of U.S. society, creating an atmosphere of peace and prosperity that would neutralize the allure of communism, and of political activism more generally. As May has shown, this ideology served as the domestic counterpart to the doctrine of containment, not only in the sense that it indirectly targeted the spread of communism, but also in the sense that it encouraged men, women, and children to assume excruciatingly narrow role definitions as breadwinner, housewife, and "well-adjusted" offspring, respectively. At the heart of the arrangement lay a sexual contract in which the ideal couple was imagined to be procreative and, above all, heterosexual, lest any corner of society be perceived as "soft" and thus insufficiently hardened against radical influence.[51] In the postwar years, social and professional status frequently depended on just how well one inhabited these roles.

The word "conformity" is often used to describe the culture of postwar America, especially that of the white suburban middle class. Yet, the term is inadequate to account for the complex and diffuse set of pressures prevalent in this period. Helen, for her part, would have been doubly affected. As a faculty wife, she participated in a gendered division of labor whose outcome, ideally, was containment on the home front; as administrative assistant to the Harvard Russian Research Center, whose staff routinely consulted with the U.S. State Department on high-level Soviet affairs, she helped further the cause of containment abroad. And yet, her traces are few and far between: some initials, scrawled on a memo—and on rare occasions, a memo written under her own name, often addressed to her husband (and likely preserved for that reason); life events, sporadically recorded in memorabilia; a generic acknowledgment; etc.[52] It's telling that the Federal Bureau of Investigation (FBI) maintained detailed files on Clyde Kluckhohn, Talcott Parsons, the Russian Research Center, and many of its affiliates, but no unique file for Helen—despite the fact she was likely to have come in contact with or been in close proximity to classified documents, which the Center routinely handled. She makes a cameo appearance in the Center's FBI file, but only long enough to be dismissed as a potential informant: "Mrs. Helen W. PARSONS – Administrative Assistant. This individual is the wife of Professor TALCOTT PARSONS, mentioned below. ND BOS 540 has advised Special Agent THOMAS F. McLAUGHLIN, JR. that Mrs. PARSONS holds liberal views with respect to political and social matters and would probably not be a desirable contact in seeking information relating to the Russian Research Center."[53] The report is dated May 5, 1949. Just a year into the Center's existence, and already a powerful federal agency determined that a member of the Parsons family had violated the terms of containment.

SPY GAMES

It probably began with an unexpected knock at the door. Startled, he gathered his papers, arranged them neatly on one side of the writing table, and arose to see who was there. As he strode across the room buttoning his shirt, he pondered who might be the source of the interruption. Anyone close to him knew he always wrote during that time of the day, and they would know he didn't like to be disturbed. No, it must be a stranger—maybe someone from the local bank asking him to buy war bonds, or perhaps an emissary from one of the nearby churches, wondering if he'd found Jesus. Whoever it was, he was always "happiest, more relaxed, and in his best form" when conducting ethnographic fieldwork in New Mexico and Arizona among the Diné (also known, then especially, as the Navajo), whom he had first encountered during a period of convalescence when he was seventeen years old, in 1922.[54] He was in about as good a frame of mind now as anyone would find him, even with the intrusion into his workday. But by the time he arrived at the door, his mind had already drifted back to his writing. Instead of peeking out the window to see who was there, he grasped the knob instinctively, turned it, and felt a blast of parched afternoon air as he swung open the door.

"Good afternoon, sir, and sorry to bother you. I'm an investigator working with the Navajo Indian Agency out of Shiprock, New Mexico. Are you Professor Clyde Kluckhohn of Harvard University?"

"Uh, yes—yes I am," Kluckhohn responded. Confused, his mind raced to assemble the jigsaw puzzle that suddenly lay before him: "investigator," "Navajo," "Shiprock," "Harvard" . . .

"Would you mind if I came in and asked you some questions?" the investigator queried.

As the picture started to form in Kluckhohn's mind, a gnawing sensation began swelling in his stomach. "May I ask what this is about?" Kluckhohn replied, steadily.

"It would be better if we talked about this *inside*, sir," said the investigator.

Kluckhohn exhaled. "Of course—please come in," he said, waving for the investigator to enter.

While the men exchanged handshakes, Kluckhohn wondered whether the perspiration he felt on his hands was from the heat of the day, or if he'd suddenly gone clammy.

He plucked a chair from the corner of the room, brought it over to the writing table, and invited the investigator to sit down. He returned to his own seat on the opposite side of the table.

The physical arrangement reminded him of office hours at Harvard. Only this time, he knew he wouldn't be steering the conversation.

"What would you like to talk about?" Kluckhohn inquired. Glancing down at his notes and then up at the investigator, envisaging all that he had accomplished and had yet to achieve, he pretended not to know the answer to his own question.

The dialog and details of the scene are imaginary, admittedly. No one knows for sure where the conversation took place, nor when, exactly. Based on information appearing in the FBI files for Kluckhohn and the Russian Research Center, the meeting likely transpired in late June 1943. Most of the names included in the report, dated November 17, 1943, have been redacted, including that of the investigator, who identifies himself only as a "former newspaperman." The document consists of twelve single-spaced pages and appears in a section of the Kluckhohn file labeled "obscene."[55]

The designation refers to sodomy allegations brought by a twenty-year-old Diné man with whom Kluckhohn had been working. On June 11, 1943, the unnamed individual reported to Diné authorities having had multiple sexual encounters with Kluckhohn between late May and early June, and the following morning he swore out a complaint in which he detailed the incidents, some of which allegedly involved monetary exchanges the anthropologist was said to have claimed were "gifts." The accusations stemmed from the complainant's ambivalence about the purported encounters and, more urgently, from a sense that he couldn't escape "Mr. Clyde's" advances. He reports telling a friend that Kluckhohn was "not good to be with" and "a bad man" after concocting an excuse to get away from the professor for a few days, only to have Kluckhohn insist the man return to him as soon as the trip was over. The complainant adds that he'd grown uncomfortable with the degree to which Kluckhohn "hovered over me," stating that the anthropologist had even advanced him five dollars to secure his services in the future.[56]

Kluckhohn, for his part, offered "a vigorous deniel [*sic*]" to the investigator and, when pressed about who might have made such an allegation, identified the complainant by name. The report states that Kluckhohn went on to describe the man as "an obvious paranoiac" who had become embittered once Kluckhohn refused to let the man accompany him back to the East Coast, the trip scheduled for early July. Kluckhohn states the man grew hostile when asked to share sacred Diné songs and legends, and again when Kluckhohn offered wine to white guests while entertaining, but not to him. Moreover, we learn from the report that Kluckhohn produced a series of letters from his wife Florence, "because he thought their contents would demonstrate a normal, happy married life, a life which might preclude homosexual practices such as charged."[57] He also furnished, at the investigator's request, a list of local contacts who could vouch for his character. Under the guise of conducting a routine background check on researchers working on Diné affairs, the investigator interviewed two persons who were acquainted with Kluckhohn, both of whom offered "good reports" on the anthropologist (where "good" was understood to mean *not disposed to homosexuality*). One of the references was another Diné man— "one of the highest type of Navajos, a young man of character, dependability and honesty"—whose testimony the investigator found so compelling as to effectively exonerate Kluckhohn.[58] Ultimately, the U.S. attorney declined to prosecute the case.

Despite being the subject of the complaint, Kluckhohn figures comparatively little in the investigator's report. Instead, the author casts disproportionate attention on the psychological and emotional stability of the Diné man, who, notwithstanding his

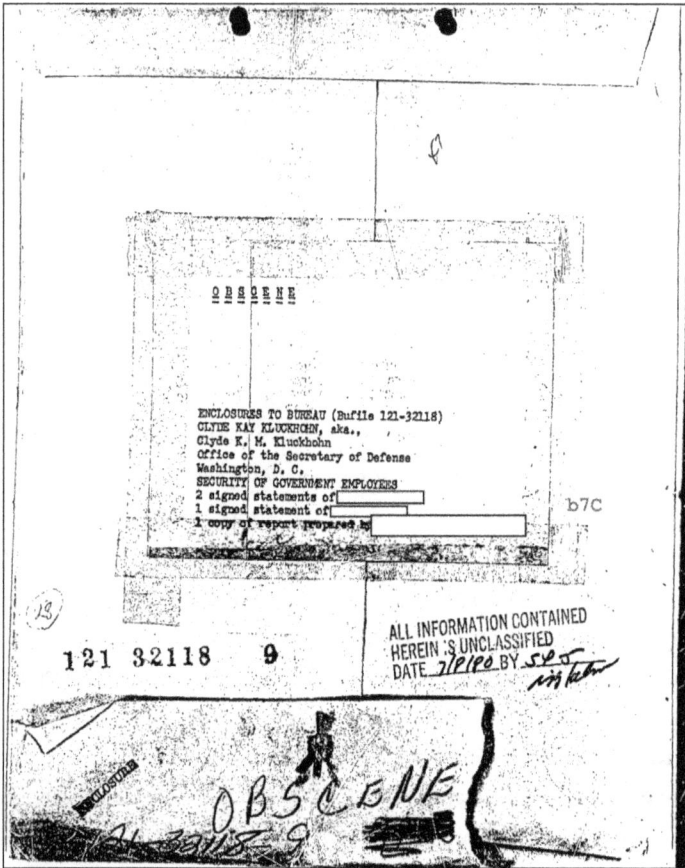

FIGURE 4.3 Photocopy of the envelope containing documents labeled "obscene."

Source: FBI file of Clyde Kluckhohn (Bureau File 121–32118), December 1953.

age, is referred to as a "boy" at nearly every turn. The investigator seems to assume the man is pathologically unstable, and that his identity—Indigenous, seemingly poor, and possibly queer—is incidental, perhaps even irrelevant, to the state in which he's encountered him. The document ends with the investigator wondering whether the complainant should receive "adjustive" treatment so as "to bring about a cure of any ailment that exists." It's telling, indeed, that he doubts the allegations against Kluck-hohn yet seems to have no question as to the complainant's sexuality. Inasmuch as this former journalist professes to "have endeavored to be at once objective, discreet and thorough," the account is suffused with the politics of race and sexuality, and with the legacies of settler colonialism.[59] And while Kluckhohn himself may not be directly responsible for the investigator's choices, he's undoubtedly implicated in the tenor of the result-ing narrative. Ironically, within days of meeting with the inves-tigator, Kluckhohn gave a speech before the Rotary Club of Gal-lup, New Mexico, in which he reflected on the corrosive effects of racist thinking: "We are fighting a war, one of whose aims, ostensibly, is to crush the theory of the superiority of certain racial grounds and to establish the equality of all men. Certainly in a democracy such as ours, it is intolerable to encourage dis-crimination against any group of people on the mere ground of race and we must do some serious thinking along these lines."[60]

I don't enter into this story lightly. Above all, the point isn't to scandalize Kluckhohn's sexuality—but nor is it to retreat from it. As Ann Cvetkovich observes: "That gay and lesbian history even exists has been a contested fact, and the struggle to record and preserve it is exacerbated by the invisibility that often surrounds intimate life, especially sexuality."[61] Similarly, as Charles E. Morris III has argued, material, symbolic, and insti-tutional barriers are often constructed around archives, queer or otherwise, in an effort to "protect" the reputations of the people addressed in archival materials. Though perhaps well-intentioned, such efforts tend "to deflect queer inquiry" by enforcing implicit—typically conservative—standards of moral-ity where questions of sex and sexuality are concerned.[62] Morris further notes the challenges confronting queer historiography when the "standards of daylight" are strictly observed. By this he's referring to an evidentiary benchmark, often assumed, at or above which historians are understood to have presented a thoroughly supported, and thus a "proven," case. Yet, the "daylight" standard tends to work against queer historiography, Morris contends, in that the silences, invisibilities, and intimations endemic to queer archives rarely lend themselves to the amassing of incontrovertible evidence. Even worse, he writes, is the tendency among seemingly "benevolent colleagues who, smelling blood, ratchet up the professional standards that constitute our distinctive burden of proof." They're motivated to do so, apparently, for much the same reason as the archivists for whom the mere topics of sex and sexuality equate to shame and humiliation, prompting a series of defensive maneuvers to resist "tarnishing" someone's legacy.[63]

The ethical questions surrounding Kluckhohn's life are complicated, clearly, but at the end of the day they're not simply about whether he was queer, or about who he "really" was (or might have been). The intimate details of Kluckhohn's personal life belong to him, but in important respects they're also bigger than him. As Jacob Gaboury argues in his "Queer History of Computing":

> If we consider queerness simply in terms of sexual preference or as an alternative formation within an established set of desiring modes, then describing any form of computing as "queer" may seem absurd. If instead we understand queerness as a process of self-shattering rather than self-fashioning, then we begin to align it with . . . exceptional objects and practices that exist beyond the limits of a system such as computation.[64]

The language of "self-shattering" could not be more apt in this case. Clifford Geertz, who worked closely with Kluckhohn while in graduate school, described his former professor as "tortured," "deeply conflicted," and a "haunted man"—instances, perhaps, of what David K. Johnson has characterized as the tendency to use innuendo when speaking publicly about homosexuality in the twentieth century. There's also scattered evidence, mostly anecdotal, suggesting that Kluckhohn did indeed live a double life.[65] If so, then we begin to glimpse the degree to which he was subject to the heteronormative pressures—the "family fever"—prevalent in the United States at midcentury. The more difficult question pertains to Kluckhohn's guilt or innocence as someone whom we would now describe as suspected of both sexual harassment and sexual assault or, at minimum, as someone who possibly overstepped ethical bounds with one of his informants.[66] But the purpose of this story is neither to absolve Kluckhohn nor to condemn him, nor is it to cast him strictly as perpetrator or victim.[67] Rather, the point is to consider how the allegations of 1943 were enfolded into the larger social and geopolitical tapestry of the Cold War-era United States, and how those allegations were leveraged through Kluckhohn's role as director of the Harvard Russian Research Center.

Even Kluckhohn's closest colleagues had to admit that he, as someone lacking expertise in Soviet affairs, "raised many eyebrows" with his appointment in 1947. They countered by touting his aptitude as a social science generalist which, they claimed, enabled him to see the big picture, where specialists could not.[68] This was also the year the American Anthropological Association elected him president. At forty-two years old, Kluckhohn's career was on a major upswing—success fueled, in part, by his war service. A heart condition may have disqualified him from military duty, but from 1944–1945 he worked alongside Ruth Benedict and Margaret Mead at the Office of War Information, where they carried out in-depth studies of Japanese morale.

According to David C. Engerman, "Kluckhohn took important lessons from . . . wartime service: the need to relax disciplinary boundaries; the value of collaborative work, often on a large scale; and the importance of applied projects."[69] He took away other things from the experience too, including ties to influential private foundations, a top-secret security clearance, and connections to high-level officials in the United States government and military. Geertz would later say that Kluckhohn "knew his way around the corridors of power in . . . Washington"—and certainly beyond them.[70]

Harvard's Russian Research Center opened on February 1, 1948, and for a decade was underwritten by grants from the Carnegie Corporation, totaling $875,000. It never was a purely academic endeavor. In fact, the Center was a Carnegie-initiated project that landed at Harvard thanks mostly to Talcott Parsons's lobbying efforts. Moreover, it was but one asset in a portfolio of Carnegie-backed area studies centers, programs, and institutes that cropped up throughout the United States after the Second World War, some of which had their genesis in specific wartime projects and the innovative, interdisciplinary ways of working they'd encouraged.[71] The overarching goal at Carnegie was to "fund . . . efforts that would support a strong Cold War posture for the United States," which would in turn bolster the interests of the Corporation's backers and board members, most of whom hailed from the commanding heights of business and finance.[72] The Center also worked closely with and in some cases received funding from the U.S. State Department, the Department of Defense, the Office of Naval Research, Air Force intelligence, and the Central Intelligence Agency.[73]

And here we must pause, for it may be tempting to overestimate the nature of "the arrangement" (to use Sigmund Diamond's phrase) between the Russian Research Center and these high-level institutions.[74] Declassified FBI records make it clear that such arrangements existed and were, to some degree, actively pursued by parties on both sides. Yet, the records also indicate frustration on the part of the Center's partners with respect to the low yield of actionable research, at least in its early years. An FBI memorandum dated March 17, 1949, indicates the U.S. State Department "place[s] a very, very low evaluation" on the usefulness of the papers and publications sent along by contacts at the Russian Research Center. Similarly, in a letter dated May 11, 1949, FBI Director J. Edgar Hoover instructed the agency's Boston field office to discontinue "contact[ing] the President of Harvard University, James B. Conant, to secure further material," given that "it appears that the work of the Russian Research Center is not of primary interest to this Bureau." The memorandum from March also raises doubts about the objectivity of the studies carried out under the Center's auspices and raises concerns about the researchers' possible "pro-communist leanings."[75]

Kluckhohn and the Russian Research Center participated in Cold War-era spy games, in other words, but the level at which they were playing was probably closer to checkers than chess. But while we must be cautious about overestimating the impact of the Center's work on U.S. government policy, we must be equally cautious about underestimating the degree to which the Center's backers and partners steered its agenda. According to Martin Oppenheimer, "Carnegie, not Harvard, determined overall research priorities, and even named the personnel who would operate the HRRC. Carnegie vetted the center's scholars who then pursued a research agenda largely funded and determined by government agencies, utilizing sources, the access to which was also provided by intelligence agencies."[76] FBI records show that Kluckhohn was directly implicated in these covert exchanges:

One of the jobs of KLUCKHOHN is to obtain pertinent information requested by government departments and, within limits, shape the research program of the Center to the needs of the United States. He [Kluckhohn] cited as an instance of this application the State Department would communicate with him to suggest they were short in certain aspects of Soviet activity. KLUCKHOHN would then suggest to a graduate fellow at the School that he might do a thesis on this particular problem, making no mention to him of the fact that the State Department was also interested. Subsequently the results of the individual research could be brought to the attention of the State Department, and in this and other matters KLUCKHOHN advised that the Center maintains a very considerable contact on a non-classified basis with the Departments of State and Commerce and all three of the Armed Services.[77]

The passage appears in a memorandum dated August 17, 1951—eight years after the sodomy allegation at Shiprock, and seven years after the FBI first caught wind of it.[78] But this isn't the only time the passage has seen the light of day. David H. Price quotes it in *Cold War Anthropology*, making no mention of the complaint, despite the fact that he references Diamond who, in 1982, was probably the first author to grasp Kluckhohn's predicament. Diamond writes: "That Kluckhohn may have felt under pressure to cooperate with the F.B.I. is suggested by an . . . F.B.I. memorandum . . . in which the F.B.I. claimed to have information that, if leaked, could have subjected Kluckhohn to humiliation."[79] Diamond doesn't delve into detail, however, perhaps hoping to avoid outing Kluckhohn, who'd suffered a fatal heart attack in 1960. Within the limits of my own research, there's no indication of a federal agency using knowledge of the sodomy allegation to *directly* coerce Kluckhohn. That said, the

FBI was keenly interested in the possibility that Kluckhohn was "a degenerate," and in how lingering questions about his sexuality might affect his loyalty to the United States.[80]

Effectively, it didn't matter whether Kluckhohn was queer, or not. What mattered was the existence of the sodomy allegation, and how it raised any doubt whatsoever about his professed heterosexuality. Kluckhohn's career would be ruined if it (or he) ever came out, and surely he understood that. In the 1920s, Harvard had convened a secret disciplinary tribunal in a successful effort to purge gay students and faculty, and in the 1940s, the Universities of Texas, Wisconsin, and Missouri followed suit, albeit openly.[81] Such actions were consistent with broader efforts occurring at the federal level, in response to what Johnson has dubbed the "lavender scare." The phrase refers to a moral panic lasting from approximately 1947 to 1970, in which federal officials convinced themselves of the rampant infiltration of gay men into government agencies. The U.S. State Department, to which the Russian Research Center was attached, was of particular concern, perhaps owing to stereotypes of sexual permissiveness associated with foreign service.[82] "The logic," writes May, "went as follows: National strength depended upon the ability of strong, manly men to stand up against communist threats. It was not simply a matter of general weakness leading to a soft foreign policy; rather, sexual excesses and degeneracy would make individuals easy prey for communist tactics."[83] Countless men lost government employment during the lavender scare, often on the basis of little more than insinuations of a homosexual encounter.[84]

Also concerning were the "eggheads": professors, policy wonks, and civil servants whose expanding role in postwar federal agencies threatened to erode Congressional power and authority. Much like the geeks and nerds of the 1980s and 1990s, eggheads were often portrayed in popular media of the 1940s and 1950s as weedy and frail. In the eyes of critics, their passion for intellectualism was a function of their substandard physical constitution, even effeminacy—qualities that cast doubt upon their capacity to uphold heteronormative masculinity and thus adequately safeguard the nation.[85] Harvard's leadership was keenly aware of these associations, and of how the presence or even perception of too many eggheads on campus could damage the university's reputation. As Jerome Karabel has written: "The threat of excessive intellectualism was also intertwined with the image of Harvard as a haven for 'pansies' and 'communists.' . . . In the minds of Harvard's many critics, 'communism,' 'homosexuality,' 'intellectualism,' and 'neuroticism' [code for Judaism] constituted an interrelated syndrome that cut Harvard off from mainstream America." Consequently, the university began an overhaul of its admissions process starting in 1952, a primary objective of which was to screen more effectively for—and thus, to screen out—homosexual applicants. University officials were open about their reasons for implementing these changes, at least internally, further adding to the homophobic atmosphere within which Kluckhohn was working.[86]

Meanwhile, as far as the FBI was concerned, Kluckhohn checked all the boxes of a potential security risk: a brainiac whose weak heart had gotten him excused from the front lines; a suspected "degenerate" with close ties to the State Department; and the director of a research center, some of whose staff had neglected to toe the hard line against communism. Surely, it also didn't help that he belonged to the American Civil Liberties Union, an organization flagged by both the California Committee on Un-American Activities and the FBI as "heavily infiltrated with Communists and fellow travelers."[87] The irony is that while there's no record of Kluckhohn's having succumbed to subversive influence, it's highly likely that he bowed to pressure, direct or indirect, to align the Russian Research Center's program with that of the Carnegie Corporation, the United States government, and its military—an alignment that would have direct repercussions on the work of Clifford Geertz, particularly the material in which he would draw together culture and computation. Kluckhohn avoided the purges, in other words, but in the process became a domestic intelligence asset by virtue of exactly the type of coercive techniques government officials purportedly feared.

REDS

During the McCarthy years, there was never a good time to be accused of being a communist. There were worse times, however, and Talcott Parsons found himself in the midst of one. It was February 1954. Parsons was midway through a yearlong visiting professorship at the University of Cambridge, England, when a colleague from the United States, Samuel Stouffer, contacted him with the news. Both men were faculty in Harvard's Department of Social Relations, which Parsons chaired from 1946 to 1956. Stouffer had been seeking access to classified documents as part of an ongoing research project but was unexpectedly turned down by the Eastern Industrial Security Board. Among the reasons for the denial was his association with Parsons, who'd been under investigation for two years by the FBI owing to accusations he was a communist. Stouffer wrote to Parsons: "It will shock you, I'm afraid, to report that the statement of reasons why I should be called a security risk said that I have been a 'close and sympathetic associate' of members of organizations cited by the Attorney General of the United States

as subversive, and that the list given included some of our colleagues. Unhappily it also included you."[88]

A complaint to the FBI by an unidentified former student of
Parsons seems to have prompted the investigation.[89] The student
in turn referred the bureau to a member of the Social Relations
faculty who became the principal informant in the case. According to FBI records, the faculty member agreed to be interviewed after a wealthy, conservative student twice flunked out
of the program. The dismissal, claimed the colleague, had nothing to do with the individual's performance, who'd earned
straight As across all other subjects. Instead, the student's "theory of Government and sociology did not coincide with that of
the leaders of the Social Relations Department"—namely, Parsons, Kluckhohn, and psychologists Henry A. Murray and Gordon W. Allport.[90] It's unclear from the records if the student in
question was the one who'd initiated the complaint. The faculty
member's name is redacted throughout Parsons's FBI file, albeit
haphazardly enough that contextual clues and cross-referencing
point directly to Carle C. Zimmerman—rural sociologist and
author of the tome, much beloved (even today) by Christian con-
servatives, *Family and Civilization* (1947). Zimmerman repre-
sented the old guard of the department, having aligned himself
with the former chair of sociology, Pitirim A. Sorokin, who was
ousted by Parsons upon the creation of Soc-Rel, as the new
department was colloquially known.[91]

Zimmerman's distress over the student's dismissal was just the
tip of the iceberg. Parsons, he claimed, was the clandestine leader
of a communist party cell at Harvard, one with close ties to
Columbia University's Robert K. Merton and possibly to faculty
at other leading universities throughout the United States. He
was also accused of secretly coordinating the defense in the Alger
Hiss trial, of condemning the faculty loyalty oath recently

have been a "close and sympathetic associate" of members of organizations cited by the Attorney General of the United States as
subversive, and that the list given included some of our colleagues.
Unhappily it also included you. Specifically, the following was
stated: "Subject listed as a character reference, Talcott Parsons,
who is reported to be a member of the Communist Party and of the
American Committee for Spanish Freedom. These organizations have
been cited by the Attorney General of the United States as coming
within the purvue of Executive Order 9835."

     While, of course, the charge concerning Communist member-
ship is a slanderous libel, I do not know the facts as to your
membership on the Committee for Spanish Freedom, but I assume that
if you were a member it was at a time when there was no reason for
supposition that the committee had improper connotations.

     Arthur Sutherland advises me, since I wish to make a
complete and candid statement in all respects before the appeals
board to the end that the records may be clear regardless of the
ultimate disposition of the case, that I should obtain from you an
affidavit which lists and explains every membership or connection
with any kind of an organization that may be on the Attorney
General's list. He has been good enough to prepare a very rough
draft of an affidavit. I am enclosing it. He suggests that you
revise it any way you choose, fill in the blanks, and send it back
to me as a draft. He and I would like to go over it again and
then send it back to you for final execution before a notary.
Because the hearing comes on March 1, 1954, there is obviously very
little time. We will have to move fast.

     I'm terribly sorry to bother you about this matter,
Talcott, but it obviously is somewhat critical in the life of our
Department, and it could be of the University as a whole.

                 Sincerely yours,

                 Samuel A. Stouffer

FIGURE 4.4 Detail of letter from Samuel A. Stouffer to
Talcott Parsons, February 5, 1954, alerting Parsons to the secret
investigation into his loyalty to the United States.

Source: Harvard University Archives. Used with permission.

adopted by the University of California system, sporting pro-communist paraphernalia, and more. The most bizarre claim, also mentioned by the student-informant, was that Parsons's adolescent son, Charles, had "recited the communist manifesto [*sic*] from memory at a cocktail party," having joined a gathering hosted at the Parsons's Belmont, Massachusetts, home in 1948, "for a few minutes." The FBI's own investigation further revealed that Parsons once served as faculty advisor to Harvard's John Reed Club, named for the left-wing journalist and political agitator whose book *Ten Days That Shook the World* (1919) chronicled, sympathetically and from the inside, the Bolshevik revolution in Russia.[92]

Zimmerman clearly had a bone to pick, so much so that Special Agent James T. Sullivan, lead investigator on the case, described the professor as "rambling," and even asked him if the allegations were motivated by academic "sour grapes."[93] An FBI memo authorizing further investigation similarly affirmed:

> During each of the investigations the possibility should be constantly borne in mind that Professor [redacted, presumably Zimmerman's] allegations concerning Allport, Parsons and Stouffer as well as the Russian Research Center were motivated to a degree by pique and resentment toward the current administration of the Department of Social Relations at Harvard University.[94]

Despite these doubts, the Bureau appears to have proceeded largely on the basis of Parsons's proximity to the Russian Research Center and, thus, to the sensitive information to which he could gain access. It wasn't only that he served on the executive committee, nor that he and Kluckhohn were close colleagues. The student-informant and Zimmerman separately stressed the suspicious circumstances under which Helen

Parsons had secured her secretarial job at the Center. Both men characterized the appointment as "nepotism," the former student even going as far as to suggest the existence of "a cover up." As such, they implied, Helen was in an ideal position to funnel state secrets to her husband, who could in turn pass them on to his nationwide network of communist conspirators.[95]

It's doubtful either Talcott or Helen was fully aware of the scope of the inquiry. Federal agents never knocked at their door, nor does the couple appear to have had any clue about an investigation proceeding behind their backs. By the time it concluded in September 1955, it had involved FBI offices in thirteen states plus the District of Columbia, the U.S. State Department, and the CIA.[96] Wrote Special Agent Sullivan: "Since investigation has failed to develop proof of the allegations made against him [Parsons], Boston feels that active investigation in this case should be concluded and that the case should be closed." It was, although Parsons's FBI file remained active until February 1968.[97]

The loyalty drama implicated Talcott's professional life, clearly. The Bureau's express concern about getting roped into adjudicating a possible instance of academic infighting attests to this. So, too, do the letters Parsons and McGeorge Bundy, then the dean of arts and sciences at Harvard, traded back and forth throughout spring semester 1954. As Parsons wrote on February 24: "I am of course aware that, according to the declared policy of the Harvard Corporation, if this allegation is true I should be dismissed from my professorship in the faculty. I am naturally ready to cooperate fully in any investigation the University may wish to make of the facts and am extremely anxious to be cleared of this charge."[98]

What's also evident from FBI records and other archival sources is the degree to which suspicion extended beyond the office to Talcott's immediate family. In effect, the FBI was asking: How well was the Parsons family upholding the subcontractual arrangement, and were they, in their respective roles, adequately fortifying the United States against communism? In a handwritten letter to Talcott dated May 21, 1954, Stouffer underscored this dynamic: "When a guest in one's home, identity unknown, can inform the secret police that the 15[-]year-old son of the host is familiar with the *Communist Manifesto*, and such information is produced to deny the country of the host's services—this is terrifying."[99] Parsons would go on to address the episode in a lengthy interrogatory addressed to the International Organizations Employees Loyalty Board: "That my son's alleged interest in Marx could be construed as evidence of my own acceptance of Marxism, which he allegedly got from me, is completely out of the question because I have always been in radical disagreement with Marx'[s] theories."[100] Similarly, in a letter to Stouffer sent in February, Talcott discussed the "vulnerability" his eldest daughter, Anne, presented to his loyalty case, even though FBI informants hadn't made any allegations against her: "As you probably know in her Swarthmore days Anne played around some with the radical student groups there. So far as I know, however, she did not 'join' any communist-front group, and I am sure as I can be that she has not lately been involved in anything of the sort."[101]

The irony here is that one of the foremost sociologists in the world hadn't fully grasped the sociological entailments of his own denials, particularly as they related to gender and sexuality. It wasn't enough to assert that he hadn't commanded his children to pursue leftwing radicalism. Equally disturbing was the prospect that Charles or Anne might have sought that out on their own, thus proving they were maladjusted. If Talcott and Helen were this "soft" on their own kids at home, how could they possibly harden Soc-Rel and the Russian Research Center against communist influence? Or, as Smith put it: "Simply because they have not yet been fully or adequately trained, or *because their training has been imperfectly done* . . . children are likely to present constant problems and difficulties with respect to the imaged order of the home."[102] Helen likely experienced this pressure twofold, as U.S. mothers of the 1940s, 1950s, and 1960s had to walk an impossibly fine line between under- and over-parenting. Raise your children with insufficient boundaries, and at best they'll end up as juvenile delinquents; at worst, they'll remind your martini-sipping house guests that they have nothing to lose but their chains. But the opposite was true too: smother your children, and they'll never develop the resiliency and individualism expected of capitalist subjects. Their weakness and dependency will in turn prime them to accept communism. These pressures were heightened in the case of male children, for whom a "smother-mother" was seen by psychologists, government officials, and even popular media as inclining their sons toward homosexuality—and, thus, to communism.[103]

The Parsons loyalty investigation underscores the logics of gender and sexuality that at once threatened and sustained white professional masculinity at midcentury.[104] After nearly twenty years of synthesizing Durkheim and Weber *against* Marx, whose work he considered to be more political religion than political theory, Parsons was positively dismayed at how anyone could imagine him to be a mustache-twisting communist ideologue.[105] And, no doubt, he must have been deeply alarmed by the possibility of unemployment, irreparable damage to his professional reputation, public humiliation, and loss of status at home.[106] It didn't help that he was thousands of miles from Massachusetts and thus vulnerable to deportation, cancellation of his passport, or any number of other dreadful consequences, never mind the fact that any personal files that might help his case were all but inaccessible to him.

Less than three weeks after receiving Stouffer's initial communique, Parsons dispatched a sworn affidavit through the American embassy in London, in which he affirmed his loyalty to the United States and refuted the more outlandish charges, calling them "preposterous."[107] But the tone of the document wasn't simply defensive. Despite the delicacy of Parsons's situation, he devoted significant space to extolling the virtues of liberalism, which he contrasted with totalitarianism "of the left or of the right":

> It could not fail to be evident to one of my profession that freedom for the scientific study of social problems was drastically curtailed under any totalitarian system. Experience as a student in Pre-Nazi Germany made me particularly sensitive to this feature of the Nazi regime, and I have been highly conscious that essentially the same kind of conditions if not worse prevailed in Soviet Russia.

He offered more or less the same rationale in explaining his advisorship of the John Reed Club, claiming that he viewed his support as an "endorsement of the principle of free speech" but not "of the views of the group."[108]

Despite the focus on Nazi Germany, it's difficult to imagine that Parsons's critique of totalitarianism had nothing to do with the U.S. government's secret investigation of him, nor the threat that it posed to his status and reputation. The evidence here is inferential, but intriguing. It includes an essay he published in *The Yale Review* in 1954 on McCarthyism, a phenomenon he attributed to the tensions resulting from increased state intervention into the economy, social welfare, and broader aspects of daily life; and his involvement throughout the late 1950s with the American Association of University Professors, where he served on committees addressing academic freedom and tenure and, most saliently, loyalty-security cases like his own.[109] Indeed the critique of totalitarianism is a motif running throughout the first half of Parsons's career, including a series of articles he penned in the late 1930s and early 1940s on Nazism and academic freedom.[110] From the early 1940s, moreover, the word *culture* enjoyed pride of place in this critique, acting as a foil to domineering forms of government.

Nowhere is this more apparent than in a white paper justifying a short-lived interdepartmental program at Harvard that would, after the war, reinvent itself as Soc-Rel. The piece, penned in 1941, is entitled "Toward a Common Language for the Area of Social Science."[111] Professors John. T. Dunlop, Myron P. Gilmore, and Overton H. Taylor are listed as coauthors alongside Kluckhohn and Parsons, although the latter two figures—Parsons, especially—appear to have written the bulk of the document.[112] Soc-Rel emerged from much the same crucible as the Russian Research Center, wherein disciplinary boundaries were understood as impediments to addressing complex questions about human interaction at scale. Parsons et al. sought an integrative approach in bringing together faculty from sociology, social anthropology, clinical psychology, and social psychology, and in developing a "common language" or shared conceptual vocabulary by means of which to effect this synthesis at the level of research and teaching.

It's doubtful that Soc-Rel ever fully achieved the unity its founders had hoped for. After Parsons's decadelong term as chair expired in 1956, internal tensions and personal acrimony began to overtake the department, and it disbanded in the early 1970s. It didn't help that Soc-Rel faculty members Timothy Leary and

Richard Alpert (later known as Ram Dass) had begun administering psychedelic drugs to Harvard undergraduates in one of
Alpert's off-campus homes, as part of their research into the psychological effects of hallucinogens. The resulting scandal not
only damaged the department's reputation, but resulted in Leary
and Alpert's dismissal from Harvard in 1963. Alpert went first,
prompted by whispers that he was gay.[113] Soc-Rel's first decade
was something of a heyday, however, and in that relatively short
period of time it attracted approximately 1,000 undergraduate
majors and more than 300 graduate-degree seeking students,
many of whom would go on to become leaders in the social sciences and related professions.[114] Significantly, "Toward a Common Language for the Area of Social Science" wasn't only an
administrative document. It was also the centerpiece of a yearlong graduate-level proseminar, often led by Parsons, that a
former student once described as "a kind of collective baptis-
mal ceremony designed to certify us as members of a common
congregation."[115]

After setting forth the need for synthesis in the social sciences
and then proposing specific areas for investigation, the authors
of "Toward a Common Language" discussed the main theoretical tenet binding this new endeavor. The phrase Parsons and his
colleagues landed on was "the ethos of a culture," which they
defined as the "totality" of "patterns of basic value-orientation"
prevalent within a society. The ethos, they added, gave "a distinctive 'style' or 'configuration' to all the activities of all its
members and to its cultural products in thought, in art, even in
utilitarian artifacts."[116] The ethos of a culture was culture writ
large—culture taken as a whole, in all its complexity. But this
wasn't just a social, aesthetic, or even psychological theory of culture. Much as Matthew Arnold had sought to reimagine culture as a domain for human governance, one that compensated

for the subtle and brutal excesses of state power, so too did Parsons and his colleagues. Culture, they contended, "supplement[ed] the work of 'government'," for it provided a means by which to manage human affairs independent of the state, at least in principle.[117] This was especially true—even urgent—in places where totalitarianism prevailed:

> The conception of government by naked, overwhelming power alone . . . is of course the conception of tyranny or despotism. . . . A stable and effective yet 'tempered,' non-tyrannous government is possible only where a strong, coherent, prevailing ethos [i.e., culture], embodied in a written or/and unwritten 'constitution,' firmly orients the organization, pursuit, and exercise of power.

Parsons and his colleagues further contended that culture ought to come *first* as a system of governance, "so that actual coercion [by law, the state, etc.] is required and sanctioned only when individuals or groups transgress the standards implicit in the ethos."[118]

This was something of an odd undertaking, given the close ties members of the Soc-Rel faculty shared with the U.S. government during and after the Second World War: Parsons, to the Foreign Economic Administration; Kluckhohn, to the Office of War Information, etc.; Stouffer, to the Education and Information Division of the War Department; Murray, to the Office of Strategic Services (precursor to the CIA); George C. Homans, to the U.S. Navy; and surely more. So why, then, the theoretical and institutional effort to diminish state power by way of culture? On the one hand, Parsons and his colleagues were keenly aware of the dangers of totalitarian governments, having devoted their war service to defeating Nazi Germany, fascist Italy, and imperial Japan. Culture, they suggested, could be a means for preventing future totalitarian states from emerging, by holding in check the desire to govern excessively through formal political structures. On the other hand, it seems reasonable to surmise that a sense of betrayal at the hands of the United States government factored in as well, given Kluckhohn's "arrangement" with the State Department, enforced under possible threat of his outing, and the Parsons loyalty investigation, in which he experienced government overreach into his personal and professional affairs. That is, Kluckhohn and Parsons were painfully aware of how authoritarian tendencies inhered even in purportedly democratic political systems, and as such they sought a vocabulary for governing otherwise.

Parsons's encounter with the entomologist Alfred E. Emerson, in 1953, is all the more significant in this regard. Parsons met Emerson at the Conference on Systems Theory, an exclusive, biannual gathering in Chicago of researchers from the natural and behavioral sciences, whose charge was to produce a unified theory of human behavior. There, Parsons responded to Emerson's presentation on "Homeostasis and Comparison of Systems," and engaged with him further about the relationship of biological and cultural evolution on the heels of Lawrence K. Frank's talk on "Social Systems and Culture."[119] Emerson advanced a provocative thesis about species evolution as driven by culture, the basis for which was the transmission and mutation of symbols (words, images, numbers, etc.), as opposed to hereditary traits. Almost two decades later Parsons would say: "Among the several participants whose ideas were important to me, the social insect biologist Alfred Emerson stands out." Parsons added that he was "particularly influenced" by Emerson, whose work would indeed go on to become a touchstone for his thinking about culture until the end of his career.[120]

Parsons also picked up on the problem of governance in Emerson's writings.[121] Parsons was especially taken with the word *control*, which Emerson used to refer to the "broad social understanding and skill" through which cultural systems achieved stability, or homeostasis. In Emerson's view, control "[did] not imply force by a dictator or dictatorial clique, often with false concepts."[122] Rather, it was a framework for managing human affairs indirectly, even spontaneously—one that in principle eschewed the traditional mainstays of political authority: violence, coercion, and ideology.

Parsons would later say that "clarification of the problem of control" occurred "at a most strategic time for me." What exactly he meant by "a most strategic time" is suggestive, if unclear, although the timing relative to the loyalty investigation is worth noting. What's clear is that Emerson's words helped bring Parsons to a turning point in the definition of *culture*, and in understanding culture's relationship to other so-called "action systems"—systems (including the organism, personality, and the social) whose purpose is to coordinate functions necessary to the production and maintenance of society: "It could now be plausibly argued that the basic form of control in action systems was of the cybernetic type and not primarily, as had been generally argued, the analogy of coercive-compulsive aspects of these processes in which political power is involved," Parsons observed.[123] Culture had a dual—even tautological—purpose, that is to say: it served as a rubric from which to derive a theory of human governance, whose main point of contrast was the totalitarian state; and it served as a privileged domain in which to operationalize that theory. Moreover, Parsons had come to view society (i.e., institutions, structures of kinship and filiation) and technology (i.e., know-how and technique) as "corollaries" to culture, or as

214 ℴ ALGORITHMIC CULTURE

systems whose purpose was to materialize cultural patterns and transmit them in the form of symbols to future generations.[124]

Like Emerson, and indeed any number of communication theorists, Parsons saw symbols and symbol use as essential to cultural process. But what if we *Homo sapiens* aren't unique in our ability to produce and manipulate symbols? What might that do to the idea of culture and the prospect of governing through it?

FOOTPRINTS

Literary novelist. Such was twenty-year-old Clifford Geertz's ambition upon his discharge from the U.S. Navy in 1946, having served for almost three years in the Pacific theater during the war. He'd aced the Navy's V-12 exam, which helped land him a position repairing radar equipment aboard the USS *St. Paul*. A future classmate, David E. Apter, would later say that the naval exam may have been the first time Geertz "discovered how bright he was," having grown up in foster care in rural northern California in the throes of the Great Depression. Geertz's biographer Fred Inglis suggested that the exam "probably saved his life" in keeping him off the front lines. Whatever the case, his talents had already been recognized by others, including an English teacher who first planted in Geertz's mind the seed about writing—the same individual who would later encourage him to take advantage of the GI Bill and apply to Antioch College, the institution from which Geertz received his AB, in 1950. There he became somewhat disillusioned with writing, however, finding his anticipated major—English—too "constraining." An internship with the *New York Post* disabused him of becoming a journalist. He eventually settled on philosophy, owing less to the intellectual discipline than to the fact that it allowed him to take whatever classes he wanted.[125]

If the first twenty years of Geertz's life were like pages out of a Steinbeck novel, then the next decade would open up a new story. A plum graduate fellowship from the American Council of Learned Societies landed him at Harvard's Department of Social Relations, where, on the advice of George Geiger, one of his philosophy professors from Antioch, he took up anthropology.[126] Geertz naturally gravitated to Kluckhohn, who suggested that he explore fieldwork possibilities in Modjokuto, Indonesia, beginning in 1952. According to David H. Price, the work there would "fill a gap in the ethnographic record," but it's unlikely Modjokuto was chosen strictly on the basis of scholarly interest. The Indonesian Communist Party, or PKI, was active throughout the area in the 1950s. Price's insinuation is that the CIA may have been behind the Modjokuto Project, as the broader endeavor was known, and that Kluckhohn funneled Geertz and other Soc-Rel students to it owing to "the arrangement."[127] Geertz received his doctoral degree from Soc-Rel in the area of social anthropology in 1956, submitting a thesis entitled *Religion in Modjokuto: A Study of Ritual and Belief in a Complex Society*, which was a basis for several scholarly publications that followed in the 1960s. He'd later say that Kluckhohn "launched [his] career" and "fixed its direction," even though, curiously, the renowned anthropologist didn't serve on his doctoral committee.[128]

Kluckhohn provided Geertz with resources, infrastructure, and a methodology, but in terms of a definition of *culture* it was Parsons who may have left the deepest impression. Interpersonally, Geertz considered Parsons to be a "bunny"—a stark contrast to Kluckhohn, whom he considered to be "very, very hard to deal with."[129] Intellectually, Geertz and Parsons shared a somewhat vexed relationship—a result of Parsons's penchant for abstract theoreticism colliding with Geertz's captivation with the welter of social life. Never, as far as I can determine, did Geertz pay Parsons his highest compliment—to praise the quality of his writing—as he had Kluckhohn's.[130] And yet, despite their obvious differences, Parsons's intellectual footprints are all over Geertz's work, particularly the material he published in the 1960s and early 1970s. Geertz never tried to hide these footprints. Toward the end of his life, Geertz noted that his graduate training had, as its overarching goal, the construction of "A Common Language for the Social Sciences."[131] And from time to time he was known to quip "We are all parsnips now," invoking what in all likelihood had been a graduate student's sobriquet for the towering scholarly figure he saw in Parsons, who, along with Cora Du Bois and Evon Z. Vogt, served on his doctoral committee.[132]

In terms of definitions of *culture*, Geertz is probably best known for the one appearing in the general introduction to his collection of essays *The Interpretation of Cultures*. There, in the famous chapter in which he outlined the practice of "thick description," he referred to the "webs of significance" we human beings spin for ourselves, and within which we live out our individual and collective lives. "I take culture to be those webs," wrote Geertz, "and the analysis of it to be therefore not an experimental science in search of law but an interpretive one in search of meaning."[133] Written at the behest of his editor at Basic Books, Geertz's intention was to summarize the whole of a theoretical and interpretive project he'd spent more than fifteen years developing.[134] "Webs of significance," thus, was less a definition of *culture* than a capsule containing many, but not all, of the essential elements.

The real work of defining *culture* begins in the subsequent chapter, "The Impact of the Concept of Culture on the Concept of Man," published originally in 1966. Geertz argued that anthropology had become stuck in a "halfway house between the eighteenth and twentieth centuries," the result of an outmoded understanding of the key term of the discipline. He called this understanding the *consensus gentium*—the notion that there exist patterns of thought, conduct, and expression universal to all human beings, and that the purpose of anthropology was to engage in comparative studies aimed at discovering those patterns. It was, essentially, philology by other means. Kluckhohn's work was "perhaps the most persuasive" exemplar of this view in yoking the word *culture* to *civilization*, the latter term referring to the unique, non-biological attributes that, some observers determined, set human beings apart from—and arguably above—other species.[135] According to Geertz the *consensus gentium* resulted in misdirection: "Rather than moving toward the essentials of the human situation it moves away from them," he claimed. At best it could produce only a "cartoon" sketch of cultural life, since it encouraged anthropologists to distill complex variations in thought and practice into indistinct "uniformities"—a conception of property, for instance, or of kinship.[136]

The turn Geertz then makes there and in the chapter on "Religion as a Cultural System," also published in 1966, follows closely in the footsteps of Parsons—and Emerson, whom he disguises as the philosopher Kenneth Burke.[137] I won't belabor the point other than to note, first, that Geertz situated his understanding of culture within the program of developing an integrative language for the social sciences, quoting directly from the white paper authored by Parsons and Kluckhohn, et al.[138] Second, Geertz emphasized the symbolic dimensions of culture, describing its patterns as "complexes of symbols" whose function was analogous to DNA: "It is precisely because of the fact that genetically programmed processes are so highly generalized in men, as compared with lower animals, that culturally programmed ones are so important."[139] Finally, like Emerson and Parsons, he understood culture as a predominately regulative system: "Culture is best seen not as complexes of concrete behavior patterns—customs, usages, traditions, habit clusters—as has, by and large, been the case up to now, but as a set of control mechanisms . . . for the governing of behavior."[140]

Geertz didn't, however, frame the matter within the explicit problematic of the totalitarian state. As an anthropologist he was disinclined to generalize from "the extreme pathologies of ideological thought."[141] On one level he appears to have done so anyway, in failing to acknowledge the complex dynamics of gender, sexuality, family, and political economy out which had emerged the culture-as-control view. But footprints are always subject to distortion, depending on the type of surface in which the feet leave an impression. Apropos, Geertz seems to have been less interested in reinforcing the state's role as culture's foil than he was in pointing out some affinities between culture and technology. One of Geertz's most significant theoretical contributions lay in shifting the register of the conversation about culture from a political to a technological one. In Geertz's work of the mid-1960s, what we today call computer software would become an operative metaphor through which to articulate a nascent set of understandings about what culture meant, and how it worked.

Symbols yoked these terms together. Like Emerson, Geertz viewed symbols as bearers of information—not in the general sense of the term, but rather in the specific sense handed down from information theory, where it denoted a small pocket of orderliness within an otherwise chaotic system. "We live, as one writer neatly put it, in an 'information gap'," wrote Geertz.

"Between what our body tells us and what we have to know in order function, there is a vacuum we must fill ourselves, and we fill it with information (or misinformation) provided by our culture."[142] Geertz didn't conceive of culture as if it were an etiquette book, however, ready at hand should the need arise. Symbols took a more active role in the shaping of human affairs. For Geertz they resembled "plans, recipes, rules, instructions (what computer engineers call 'programs')." These "cultural programs," Geertz added, were integral to the "ordering of [human] behavior."[143]

Geertz didn't end up a literary novelist, but clearly he was no stranger to metaphors. In his work from the mid-1960s, he figured *culture* not only through the language of computation but also through accompanying terms like "plans," "instructions," and "recipes," all noted above, as well as "flow charts," "blueprints," and "templates."[144] It was quite a cocktail, to be sure; collectively, the value of these terms lay in how they honed the computational metaphor. It wasn't only that complexes of symbols were akin to cultural software. Rather, they more resembled a specific type of procedural decision-making that could be executed in code—*algorithms*. To wit: in *Nine Algorithms That Changed the Future*, computer scientist John MacCormick defines *algorithm* using identical terminology, calling it "a precise *recipe* that specifies the exact sequence of steps required to solve a problem."[145] In mixing so many metaphors, Geertz seems to have been grasping for a term whose sense was palpable—on the tip of his tongue—but at the time not yet fully accessible within the English language.

Intriguingly, Geertz began moving away from this nascent sense of "algorithmic culture" almost as soon as he'd happened upon it. In the late 1960s and early 1970s he started distancing his work from that of Parsons, his teacher, particularly with respect to the metaphorics of symbol processing, and from that of other anthropologists who'd similarly conceived of culture. In making this shift, however, Geertz came as close as he ever would to uttering *algorithmic culture* out loud. The first instance occurs in a review of Claude Lévi-Strauss's *The Savage Mind*, published in 1967. According to Geertz, Lévi-Strauss's copious footnotes to cybernetics and information theory provided cover for the author's having attempted to smuggle Enlightenment-era universalism in through the metaphysical backdoor. "The philosophical conclusions which for Lévi-Strauss follow from this postulate—that savages can only be understood by reenacting their thought processes with the debris of their cultures—add up, in turn, to a technically reconditioned version of Rousseauian moralism." As such, Geertz concluded, "Lévi-Strauss has made for himself . . . an infernal culture machine."[146] It wasn't exactly "algorithmic culture," yet it's clear Geertz had put a finger on the impulse to reinterpret *culture* through cybernetics, information theory, and the figure of the machine.

The second instance occurred in 1971, in an essay on nationalism in which Geertz walks back the language of computing, attributing it not to himself, but to Parsons. "There is a sense in which a computer's program is an outcome of prior developments in the technology of computing . . . and a recipe of a long series of successful and unsuccessful cakes," Geertz observed. "But the simple fact that the information elements in these cases are materially separable from the processual . . . makes them less useful as models for the interaction of cultural patterns and social processes."[147] Instead of an algorithmic understanding of culture, Geertz advocated for a position in which established cultural repertoires were understood to coevolve with emergent cultural practices. Finally, in 1973, he shifted his attention from Parsons's theoretical system to cognitive anthropology. According to

Geertz, cognitive anthropologists premised their work on an untenable, solid-state definition of culture, conceiving of it as "systematic rules" purportedly internalized by human beings. Moreover, in imagining culture as the psychological cause of, rather than a public context for, human affairs, cognitive anthropologists stripped ethnography of its art, subtlety, and play.[148] In their hands, argued Geertz, it was akin to watching an athletic event, writing down the rulebook, and then claiming to have provided a comprehensive account of the sport. But ethnography for Geertz was never so simple as running culture in reverse. There was no "ethnographic algorithm," he insisted.[149] But neither then, apparently, was there an algorithmic culture—still unspoken—to which that ethnographic algorithm could be applied.

NEVERTHELESS

As home to both the Massachusetts Institute of Technology (MIT) and Harvard University, the city of Cambridge, Massachusetts, is renowned for having helped to usher in the information age. Among the standout figures at MIT were mathematician Norbert Wiener and engineer Claude Shannon, faculty at the university from 1919–1960 and 1956–1978, respectively, both of whom laid the foundations for information theory.[150] Harvard, for its part, usually gets credit for Bill Gates, of Microsoft, and Mark Zuckerberg, of Facebook (now Meta), even though their respective business ventures preempted completion of their studies. Comparatively unacknowledged, however, is Harvard's earlier role in providing a decisive institutional context for the articulation of an algorithmic understanding of culture. There, in the middle decades of the twentieth century, the experiences of figures constellated in and around the social sciences helped provoke a semantic fusion whereby culture came to be understood in terms of computation. This fusion had something to do with the power and allure of computers which, in helping to decipher Nazi codes and calculate ballistic trajectories throughout the Second World War, had proven themselves invaluable tools for preserving democracy, acting impartially and according to predictable rules. But the fusion had equally as much—if not more—to do with the paranoid atmosphere of the Cold War-era United States, an atmosphere in which homophobia, anti-communism, patriarchal masculinity, and whiteness combined to reinvigorate doubts about whether the state could govern without destroying its people—bodily, spiritually, or reputationally. No one associated with Soc-Rel ever uttered the phrase *algorithmic culture* out loud, admittedly. Nevertheless, Geertz's struggle to articulate just such an understanding, combined with his yearslong effort to contest it, suggest algorithmic culture was *virtually* available by 1975, the same year Bill Gates headed west, having abandoned his studies at Harvard.[151]

It would take several more books to show how this understanding later materialized in the form of Amazon, Google, Facebook, LinkedIn, Netflix, Spotify, TikTok, Tinder, Twitter, and other corporate embodiments of algorithmic culture. Those books would need to explore how algorithmic culture jumped species, if you will, moving out of the realm of literary studies and social science and into computer science, where it was implemented in code. Williams, for his part, glimpsed the beginnings of this process in his work from the early 1980s, although the future he foresaw consisted of information infrastructures as public goods in public hands, performing public services. In *The Sociology of Culture*, published in 1981, he noted how "information processes . . . have become a qualitative part of economic organization" and how, in turn, "a major part of the whole modern labour process must be defined in terms which are not easily theoretically separable from the traditional 'cultural' activities."[152] Two years later, in the essay "Culture and Technology," he took a further step in identifying a class of objects with which those processes were associated: what he referred to as "the new cultural and information technologies."[153] While the phrase didn't exactly hit the note of *algorithmic culture*, it's clear Williams was beginning to come to terms with the semantic, functional, and existential proximity of culture and computation.[154]

Williams also reflected on the potential databases held "for a greatly expanded system of public inquiry and reference."[155] Prophetically, he imagined "a library or backlist [television] network, serviced by an electronic catalogue from material now owned or stored by a wide range of producer companies."[156] Williams further noted the existence of "a body of already stored but now largely inaccessible information, in public hands, about the real and comparative qualities of various goods and services. This is the public information system," he observed, "which could steadily replace advertising."[157] A few decades later, he might as well have said "Netflix," "Google," or "Amazon"—but surely, had he lived to witness them, he would have been aghast at their acquisitive disposition toward the public.

It would be easy enough to attribute Williams's attention to computers, databases, and information systems, however uneven, to the spread of digital technology in the 1970s and 1980s. He became aware of them and began reflecting on their significance because suddenly and undeniably they were *there*—in homes, businesses, banks, educational institutions, government facilities, popular culture, and more. While there's surely truth to this explanation, to accept it fully would be to commit the error of technological determinism against which Williams (and so many others) vociferously argued: "The moment of any new technology is a moment of choice," he insisted.[158] Instead, we should appreciate the degree to which Williams's interest in the relationship between culture and computation may have emerged not only from digital technology's heightened presence in daily life but also, critically, from semantic work undertaken within the context of the Cold War, to say nothing of earlier.

EPILOGUE

Coming to Terms

This book has cut a perpendicular pathway through the culture and society tradition. Along the way I've homed in on terms that, taken together, comprise the first entries in a vocabulary of algorithmic culture: *capitalism, computation, civilization, class, colonialism, communism, containment, criticism, dispossession, disruption, enslavement, family, form, gender, government, Islam, key-word, philology, liberal, mathematics, Orientalism, race, sexuality, technology, totalitarianism, translation, violence, war*, and, of course, *algorithm* and *culture*. It's not an accident that some of these terms overlap with the ones appearing in Williams's vocabulary of culture and society, and it's also not an accident that many of the terms are newly added. Collectively, they bear witness to the endurance and transformation of *culture*'s dominant (i.e., modern) usage. They also provide a bit of context for Mario Vargas Llosa's claims about the "death" of culture, which I mentioned in the introduction.[1] Culture isn't dead—far from it! Instead, the word *culture* is doing exactly what it's been doing for the last couple of centuries: shifting semantically as it encounters new technologies and other emergent aspects of reality. It baffles me why anyone would expect one of the most complicated words in the

English language to cease being so complicated, and yet that's precisely what critics who declaim the "death" of culture seem to be assuming.

For all his prescience, even Williams didn't quite read the room. He may have borne witness to the growing association of culture and computation, and elsewhere to the insurgency of reactionary political interests.[2] Nevertheless, he failed to grasp the extent to which this union had emerged, significantly, in relationship to the machinations of political partisanship and the excesses of state power, which realized themselves in the forms of colonization, war, genocide, totalitarian rule, and so many more patterns of violence, oppression, and inequality. While it wasn't named as such until roughly 2006, algorithmic culture was supposed to have been a solution to these and other intractable problems, relieving us imperfect human beings of the burden of governing ourselves, playing politics, finding our way, making choices, seeking knowledge, connecting with one another, and managing routine affairs. But it was mostly just a fantasy, observes Sarah Sharma, a fantasy in which "social justice is no longer demanded because all of the seemingly malfunctioning parts (non-conforming subjects) can be discarded and replaced" by digital technology. Sharma challenges us to question just how well algorithmic culture is actually working and, assuming it's not working as well as it could (or should), to seek political and technological inspiration from the margins of apparent "malfunction."[3]

Indeed it wasn't so long ago, was it, that writers, confident in the ability of algorithms to parse canyonsful of data into perfectly optimized outcomes, heralded the arrival of "collective intelligence," "smart mobs," "wise crowds," and other, decentralized forms of computationally assisted mass collaboration?[4] Today, the exemplary instance of online interaction might well be Gamergate (c. 2014–2015), a harassment campaign in which right-wing trolls systematically bullied, doxed, threatened, and inflicted other harms on minoritized populations, women especially, aided and abetted by algorithms that "objectively" amplified—and along the way, helped Twitter et al. to monetize—hate.[5] While it's true that social media is more than a forum for vitriol, who can deny the atmosphere of "normalize[d] public viciousness," as Lawrence Grossberg calls it, whose lingering odor you smell, even if only the faintest whiff, whenever you go online?[6] Without diminishing the ways in which algorithmic culture assists us in the day to day, it seems reasonable to conclude that, in some fundamental respects, the solution has become the problem.

I'm not suggesting that algorithmic culture, as proposition or practice, necessarily terminates in a political, economic, or technological cul-de-sac. A protracted journey through history shouldn't maroon you in the past, nor leave you feeling hemmed in in the present. That is, however, one of the potential downsides of keywords, an approach whose fixation on the "community between past and present," as Williams once put it, could leave you wondering: *Where do I go from here? What if I don't want to belong to this community?*[7] Over the years, friends and colleagues have encouraged me to write about contemporary algorithmic culture. I've heard them—and still I've opted to focus primarily on conditions of possibility. It's not that I'm not aware of the crises today; it's just that there's been a voice in my head telling me that a preoccupation with "now" might just miss how we ended up here, and therefore miss some important diagnostic clues about how to improve the current situation.

Apropos, Raphael Samuel once likened the perspective of keywords to a journey on "a backward-moving escalator."[8] There's no better image to describe it, nor is there a better one for addressing the question of what cultural studies wants from history.[9] Imagine stepping onto an up-escalator, not at the bottom where the journey typically begins, but at the top. You're facing forward, as you normally would, but instead of traveling up, the motor shifts into reverse, and you travel down. As your point of departure recedes, you start to discover what precedes and surrounds it, and gradually you grasp the broader context within which your starting point—your present—exists. You linger for a while at the bottom. Key-words reminds you to return to the top once you've taken it all in, and to ask yourself a series of questions. Now that you're back where you started, what are you aware of that you weren't aware of before? Is the atmosphere the same, or does the energy feel a little different? Is the surrounding context as habitable as it might have initially appeared? What seems to be working, and what would you change—assuming you could? Based on what you've witnessed, what would you expect to encounter at the top of the next escalator, and the next? What should be added to, removed from, or revised in your present context for those expectations to be realized?

There is, in other words, a concourse (rather than a community) between past, present, and future. History isn't a destination, but a detour.[10] And the history of algorithmic culture matters insofar as the future is at stake. The preceding chapters are meant to remind us that "whatever we construct we do so in the midst of a populated space of structures, objects, rubble, and wastelands," as design theorist Tony Fry puts it.[11] Add to the list, key-words: "When you take a word in your mouth," observes Hans-Georg Gadamer, "you have not taken up some arbitrary tool that can be thrown in a corner if it doesn't do the job, but you are committed to a line of thought that comes from afar and reaches beyond you."[12] Indeed, the words *algorithm*, *culture*, *algorithmic culture*, and accompanying vocabulary may delimit an object domain, but more important is the historical baggage they carry with them. They're touchstones by means of which to assess the terms and conditions of the technological age in which we're living, and of the future(s) whose contours are just now starting to emerge. Their history helps us to grasp that the present isn't fleeting, that it abounds in remnants from the past, and that as we begin thinking about the future of algorithmic culture, perhaps we'll be more aware of those remnants and the extent to which it's prudent to build with, around, on top, or in spite of them.

It's time, then, to glide back up the escalator. In these closing pages I want to say a few words about the "predicament" of algorithmic culture today, bearing in mind the many floors of historical context you've just traversed.[13] The objective is to inventory operative definitions of *algorithmic culture* and, judging by their historical entailments and present-day articulations, to determine the degree to which they're capable of sustaining us into the future. I'll do so by focusing initially, albeit briefly, on the Cambridge Analytica scandal of 2018. I'm interested in what it can tell us about how *culture* has been and continues to be defined within the framework of algorithmic decision-making. The point, however, isn't to accept senses and meanings of *algorithmic culture* at face value. As I suggest later in this epilogue, the point is to invite you to reclaim definitional agency: by recognizing that building a better algorithmic culture isn't strictly a technical challenge, but a definitional one too; by questioning the seemingly monumental status of words and their definitions; and by reminding you that *you* are a part of the collective endeavor whereby new and better meanings "are offered, felt for, tested, confirmed, asserted, qualified, and changed."[14]

CULTURE IS EXTRAORDINARY

Gamergate should have been a learning opportunity for progressives, giving pause to reflect on how to disrupt an increasingly organized and aggressive—if considerably decentralized—right wing. And surely it was a learning opportunity, although the lessons seem to have been absorbed primarily by the perpetrators, and by persons sympathetic to their racist, misogynistic, and homophobic agendas. In March 2018, major news organizations in the U.S. and UK revealed that Cambridge Analytica, a subsidiary of the London-based political consulting firm SCL Group, had in 2014 misappropriated the data of approximately eighty-seven million Facebook users, many of whom had had their profiles and private messages scraped by virtue of a single friend's having consented to take an online personality quiz. Later, analysts at Cambridge Analytica used sophisticated machine learning algorithms to create granular psychological profiles of voters in both countries, which became the basis for micro-targeted political ads aimed at swaying the outcomes of two pivotal votes occurring in 2016: the UK referendum to leave the European Union (i.e., "Brexit,"), and the U.S. Presidential election.[15] By now it's well established that Steve Bannon masterminded Cambridge Analytica, in between stints serving as executive chairman of Breitbart, a leading far-right news syndicate, and as chief political advisor to former U.S. president Donald Trump. As Christopher Wylie recounts in *Mindfuck*, a memoir of his tenure as a data scientist with SCL, where he worked closely with Bannon: "Gamergate was not instigated by Breitbart, but it was a sign to Bannon, who saw that angry, lonely white men could become incredibly mobilized when they felt that their way of life was threatened."[16]

Since 2018, Cambridge Analytica has been the subject of countless news stories, at least two tell-all books by company insiders, and a feature-length Netflix documentary entitled *The Great Hack*.[17] While it's clear from this outpouring that Cambridge Analytica represents one of the more significant political-technological touchstones of the preceding decade, it's also proven to be something of a cliché. Too often the conclusion seems to be about the subtle and irresistible effects of algorithmic power, whose decisive nudges are apparently enough to bring sovereign nations to the brink of internecine conflict.[18] For the better part of fifty years, scholars from a range of humanities and social science disciplines have challenged this type of "decontextualized technological determinism," as Grossberg calls it, in which media and technology become the causes of, and thus the scapegoats for, the totality of a society's problems.[19] It's important to hold fast to the critique, at the same time as we acknowledge the imbrication of technology and the "forms of life," or cultures, we inhabit.[20] As Tara McPherson puts it, "Computation responds to culture as much as it controls it."[21] Beyond the clichés, this relationship seems to me the critical stake of the whole Cambridge Analytica affair, and why the incident is worth revisiting here at the end of this book: not because it's a parable for the overwhelming power of contemporary technology, but because the relationship of culture and computation has everything to do with our capacity to build the technological future we deserve.

I don't wish to overindulge the example beyond noting the central role *culture* plays throughout Wylie's memoir, which sets it apart from most other accounts of Cambridge Analytica. What's striking is that, inasmuch as Wylie saw himself as a data scientist, he also recognized his role as a cultural worker; or rather, data science and cultural work were essentially one and the same for him: "In September 2013, I distinctly remember thinking, *How cool is this?* I get to work in culture, but not just for someone's branding campaign. I get to work in culture for the defense of our democracy."[22] (Only later would he come to appreciate the naïveté of what he believed he was doing.) It's also worth noting that while Wylie was working at SCL, he was also pursuing a graduate degree in fashion at University of the Arts London. The algorithmic tools and data analysis techniques he developed for SCL? It turns out, he'd piloted them in his doctoral studies: "When I started my research into cultural information for SCL's counter-extremism work, I drew upon similar concepts, approaches, and tools to those I was exploring in fashion forecasting—adoption cycles, diffusion rates, network homophily, etc."[23] Finally, Wylie's memoir reveals how coming to terms with *culture*'s emergent senses and meanings was a critical element of the work that transpired at Cambridge Analytica. "When Bannon said he was interested in changing culture, I asked him how he defined culture. There was a long pause. I told him that if you can't define something, you can't measure it, and if you can't measure it, you can't know if you're changing it."[24] That Bannon apparently couldn't define *culture* is perplexing given the Breitbart doctrine, "Politics is downstream from culture." On the other hand, that Wylie would later define it in terms of "personality," "metrics," "distribution curves," "data," "information," and "algorithms" is telling.[25] Collectively, these words map how older senses and meanings attached to *culture* have taken up residence in a newer, computationally-intensive technological environment (i.e., "personality" as "ways of life," "distribution curves" as "patterns," "data" as "webs of significance," etc.). As such, they help us to appreciate the degree to which the category—indeed, the very existence—of culture is paradoxically the same *and* different today.

If Cambridge Analytica was in fact the "great hack" it's purported to be, then we should stop to ask: What exactly was hacked? Western democracy? Perhaps—although it's difficult to ascertain the degree to which Cambridge Analytica's strategies actually swayed the outcomes of the elections in which it meddled. Notwithstanding legitimate concerns about the vulnerability of election systems, there's a case to be made for how the company hyped its results in an effort to bolster its reputation and attract new clients, as *The Verge* has reported.[26] Was Facebook hacked? No—the user data acquired by Cambridge Analytica had been harvested according to the company's own policies, demonstrating for the umpteenth time how "the problem with Facebook is Facebook," as Siva Vaidhyanathan has so memorably put it.[27] By the same token, we need to recognize the extent to which "the problem with Facebook" is irreducible to the affordances of the platform, or to lax company policies. It's a function of the broader milieu—algorithmic culture—in which Facebook exists. Ironically, the calls to #DeleteFacebook, which began trending on Twitter shortly after news broke of the Cambridge Analytica affair, reinforced the very logics that Facebook depends on; so did the Netflix algorithm that recommended *The Great Hack* to me.[28] With or without Facebook, the cycle repeats. At the end of the day, it seems to me that if Cambridge Analytica hacked anything at all, then it hacked algorithmic culture.

Indeed, the cycle repeats—and not just the immediate cycles by means of which algorithmic culture reproduces itself in the present day, but also the longer patterns, the orienting conditions, that pointed the way to the contemporary conjuncture. Is it a coincidence that Trinidad and Tobago, a former British colony, was in 2010 the location for one of SCL's initial forays into using algorithms and big data to exacerbate cultural tensions for purposes of electioneering? There, the company sought to exploit the longstanding "mutual antipathy" between the country's two primary ethnic groups: the one of West African ancestry, mostly the descendants of enslaved persons brought to the island nation to work the sugar plantations; the second of South Asian ancestry, mostly the descendants of indentured laborers brought from India after Trinidad and Tobago abolished slavery in 1838.[29] As Jerome Teelucksingh has noted, British colonial authorities actively pitted the two groups against each other throughout the second half of the nineteenth century, in an effort to quash their demands for political power and economic justice.[30] Their doing so, as Wendy Hui Kyong Chun explains, was in keeping with the etymological entailments of *culture*:

> "Culture" is not simply a noun, but also a verb. To culture is to cultivate: "to propagate, grow, or develop . . . under artificial conditions or in a nutrient medium." "Culture," "colony," and "colonization" are all derived from the Latin *colere*, "to cultivate or worship." A *colonus* was a settler: a Roman soldier-farmer, who was posted in foreign or hostile territory and who seized land by enclosing or settling on it. Cultures are and depend on invasive separations.[31]

Similarly, in calling the techniques SCL used in Trinidad and Tobago "digital colonialism," Wylie underscores the embeddedness of contemporary algorithmic culture in a complex history that crisscrosses multiple continents and involves multiple technological modalities.[32]

Moreover, it's critical to recognize that Cambridge Analytica became a scandal only after digitally domineering practices from the Global North returned home, as it were, having been honed in the Global South, where their uses and effects were mostly ignored by Western media. Aimé Césaire identified this vicious, narcissistic circle back in 1955, powerfully connecting Nazi Germany's crimes against humanity to the brutalities that had been and continued to be exacted in Europe's colonies: "What he [Westerners] cannot forgive Hitler for is not *the crime in itself*, *the crime against man*, it is not *the humiliation of man as such*, it is the crime against the white man, the humiliation of the white man, and the fact that he applied to Europe colonialist procedures which until then had been reserved exclusively for" colonial subjects.[33]

SCL's involvement in Trinidad and Tobago, and the pathways leading from the Caribbean back to Britain and the United States, underscore the importance of Raka Shome's recent argument about the theoretics of culture as viewed from the Global South. Shome is interested in how human displacement resulting from environmental and political catastrophes disrupts the interpersonal and institutional dynamics whereby cultural knowledge is otherwise transmitted and preserved. That is, Shome is interested in what culture "is" when it ceases to be "ordinary," as Williams insisted it was. "Is culture always ordinary and nonexceptional," Shome asks, "when we consider the numerous travails and terrors of dispossession in the Global South?"[34] SCL didn't foment any such catastrophe in Trinidad and Tobago, admittedly, although it did take advantage of legal and political-economic conditions that—in principle, anyway— would have been considered exceptional or extraordinary throughout much of the Global North. "The team anticipated vast swaths of data," Wylie recounts, "because senior Trinidad government contacts were offering SCL access to unredacted, de-anonymized census [information]—in the developing world, privacy is a concern usually reserved for the rich. Essentially the Trinidadian government was violating the privacy of its citizens in one swoop."[35] To the extent that SCL was able to relieve people of their data on an even larger scale in the Global North, we must admit that the "exception" the company exploited in Trinidad and Tobago isn't specific to the Global South—it is endemic to algorithmic culture. It manifests as willful indifference to law, right, custom, and propriety (i.e., "disruption"), and it simultaneously propagates and normalizes the experience of (digital) dispossession across the globe. Prosaic though it may seem, algorithmic culture is extraordinary.

Accordingly, we'd do well to reject the argument that our present reality, in which culture and computation have become so grossly entangled, is somehow "unprecedented," as Shoshana Zuboff claims throughout *The Age of Surveillance Capitalism*.[36] I'm puzzled by the argument, frankly, and also by the comparison Zuboff draws between our present situation and the allegedly "unprecedented" experience of midcentury totalitarianism, whose antecedents Césaire and, more recently, Achille Mbembe, have laid out in no uncertain terms. Or, as Nick Couldry and Ulises A. Mejias explain: "The exploitation of human life through data is the climax of five centuries' worth of attempts to know, exploit, and rule the world from particular centers of power. We are entering the age not so much of a new capitalism as of a new interlocking of capitalism's and colonialism's twinned histories, and the interlocking force is data."[37] I assume Couldry and Mejias are using "data" here as a synecdoche, one that would encompass computer hardware and software, algorithms included. In any case, the point is to recognize how the "costs of connection" (the title of their book) are borne unevenly with respect to algorithmic culture, and that both the roots and the routes of this unevenness were established centuries, rather than mere decades, ago.[38]

Historical amnesia is an appalling side effect of the cult of the new that so often surrounds digital technology, but Big Tech isn't uniquely to blame. In a fascinating study of the origins of the UNIX operating system, McPherson urges us to consider how the forces that shaped the development of computation in the United States at midcentury spilled over into a globalizing academy, producing methodologies that were inadequately attentive to race and other forms of cultural difference: "Might we argue that the very structures of digital computation develop at least in part to cordon off race and to contain it? Further, might we come to understand that our own critical methodologies are the heirs to this epistemological shift?"[39] Hence my interest in history, and also my commitment to revising and updating the methodology of keywords. Of course, Britain isn't the United States. Yet, as I've shown throughout this book, keywords struggles to identify and come to terms with difference, owing to the ways in which social and technological arrangements, prevalent at midcentury, imprinted themselves on its norms, rules, and procedures. My hope is that the methodology of key-words helps us to grasp how algorithmic culture is neither unprecedented nor inevitable; how its ontogenesis is long and fragmentary; and how algorithmic injustice is as much a terminological problem as it is a technological, sociological, regulatory, and economic one.

TOPPLING MONUMENTS

Oscar H. Gandy Jr.'s *Panoptic Sort*, published in 1993, was among the very first texts to discuss how "searching algorithms" and other forms of computer-assisted decision-making both reflected and reinforced patterns of racial discrimination.[40] Since then, numerous writers have extended Gandy's thesis. In a meticulous study of race and gender in online search, Safiya Umoja Noble found that Google's algorithms were disposed to "technological redlining," or to repeated instances of discrimination, segregation, and stereotype whose cumulative effect recalls the United States' racist housing policies of the twentieth century. Similarly, Ruha Benjamin has documented the emergence of "the New Jim Code" whereby laws, policies, and social customs that long promoted white supremacy in the United States—the Jim Crow laws in particular—are given a new lease on life in the form of digital technology.[41] In June 2020, the *New York Times* reported on Robert Julian-Borchak Williams, a Black man living in Detroit, Michigan, who was arrested for grand larceny after having been incorrectly identified by a facial recognition algorithm. This humiliating incident, which occurred just five months prior to the brutal murder of George Floyd at the hands of Minneapolis police officers, is a textbook example of Benjamin's thesis, and also a clear indication of how so-called "standard algorithms" can enshrine some of the most pernicious and enduring patterns of social injustice, as Simone Browne has argued.[42]

The issue runs deeper still. As we saw in chapter 2, the word *algorithm* itself is a monument to imperialism and white supremacy, at least as that term exists today in the English language. *Algorithm* may not have started out that way, and of course it followed multiple pathways into the lexicon, but the Orientalist discourse network through which the term passed in the nineteenth century was decisive with respect to present-day understandings, imaginings, and implementations of the word. People like Henry Thomas Colebrooke and Friedrich Rosen were among the first figures to have engineered *algorithm* for the modern English language, transforming the *Algebra*—a multi-faceted moral drama about life, death, morbidity, bondage, family, and legacy—into little more than a math book whose significance lay primarily in its status as a West Asian antiquity. That they could all but ignore this drama is telling. My colleague Nabil Echchaibi refers to their ability to do so as "a relentless disease called the privilege of forgetting"—a habit that endures among contemporary monument preservationists.[43] Moreover, that Colebrooke and Rosen failed to grasp the *Algebra*'s broader intellectual contributions is unsurprising given the ethnocentric frameworks that guided their translations and interpretations of the text. In saying this, I don't mean to imply that etymology is destiny. Yet, if the history of *algorithm* teaches us anything, then it teaches that words are freighted with historical traces for which, and even despite the endeavors of the key-words project, there may be no adequate inventory.

Culture is another one of those monuments—but that's hardly news. Scholars from a range of disciplines have been making that argument for decades.[44] The details may differ, but the crux of the matter generally comes down to how *culture*'s modern usage empowered white Europeans and North Americans to conceive of themselves, their values, and their aesthetic objects as embodying the highest principles of humanity. In turn, the word authorized them to imagine peoples from what today would be known as the Global South as "primitive" or "savage," which is to say, culturally deficient and thus belonging to an inferior class of humanity—if they were considered human at all. But if *culture* was the problem, then its champions also understood it to be the solution. The cure for such "backwardness" would consist of compulsory immersion in the objects, customs, and thought styles of white Europeans and North Americans, delivered as part of any number of colonial projects and backed up by force of arms.

Yet, for all this, *culture* remains a term of ambivalence insofar as it also provides a set of resources—practical, imaginative, institutional—by means of which disenfranchised groups have sought recognition, access to goods and services, and political redress.[45] I mention this because the story of algorithmic culture is similarly fraught with ambivalence. While I was writing this book, I couldn't help but be struck by how much optimism the figures appearing in chapters 3 and 4 invested in *culture*, and how that optimism was dashed time and again. In Matthew Arnold's work, there emerges the semantics of culture-as-governance— and what a heady articulation of *culture* it is. It would be the anti- dote to form, especially in politics where form manifested *in extremis* as state-sanctioned violence against marginalized peo- ples including the English working class, the Irish, Black Jamai- cans, and surely more. With F. R. Leavis, *culture* is drawn into the orbit of tools and technology. The result, semantically, is a more sensuous (i.e., critical) relationship to the minute aspects of one's physical and social environment, and thus a heightened perspective on a life worth living. For Helen Parsons, Talcott Par- sons, Clyde Kluckhohn, and the curriculum of Social Relations, *culture* becomes the semantic figure by means of which to estab- lish first principles of governance—principles that might prevent an overinvestment in the state, and thus forestall future totalitari- anisms. The position is reminiscent of Arnold, at least in the broad strokes, although we should bear in mind how "family fever" and Cold War-era government surveillance uniquely inflected *culture* in and around Soc-Rel. In Geertz's writings, *algorithmic culture* comes together, albeit in incipient form, in a union of sorts between culture-as-governance and culture-as-technology.

That Geertz ultimately resisted this inchoate understanding of culture is telling. If nothing else, his having done so should give us pause to revisit the provisional definition of algorithmic culture appearing in the introduction, a definition that concretizes senses and meanings very close to ones Geertz had intuited: *the use of computational processes to sort, classify, and prioritize people, places, objects, and ideas; and the repertoires of thought, conduct, expression, and feeling that flow from and back into those processes.* It's descriptive enough, but is it the definition we need right now? I ask because, if the "solution" of algorithmic culture is now the problem, then it would make sense not to surrender the future to this particular framework. Across the pages of this book we've encountered instances of people feeling as if their lives have become too constrained, too unlivable, to continue as they are, and that the terms and conditions must change, even if subtly, to enhance possibilities for living. We find ourselves at a similar crossroads today, where we cannot but register the inadequacies of algorithmic culture, both experientially and definitionally. It's up to us to let those feelings in, and to let them move us to redefine the terms of our lives, collectively.

The prospect of doing so may be daunting, I know. For instance, I'm struck by the hesitancy of my students to define terms without simply quoting authoritative sources, especially dictionaries. Almost without exception they balk at my requests to do so, as if to say: *Who am I to define a word?* That hint of imposter syndrome has everything to do with the commercialization of lexicography, a field of language study that sells dictionaries in part by trading on the notion that defining terms is an art best practiced by professionals, and that lay people are presumptuous when we imagine ourselves as stewards of sense and meaning. "Dictionary companies had no problem setting themselves up as an authority on life, the universe, and everything throughout most of their history, because doing so ultimately *sold books*," observes lexicographer Kory Stamper, in a memoir of her time at Merriam-Webster.[46] "Amateur" lexicography exists, of course, but that it's labeled as such should tell you something about the hold commercial lexicography has over official practices of defining. But the issue isn't strictly commercial; it's tonal as well. Williams once described the *Oxford English Dictionary* as having an "air of massive impersonality"—a description that seems equally applicable, for whatever it's worth, to the placards affixed to most physical monuments. Or, as Stamper puts it: "The majority of people give no thought to the dictionary they use; it merely *is*, like the universe."[47] How could you ever hope to redefine a word when definitions, and the volumes in which they're collected, seem preternaturally given?

At stake here, ultimately, is definitional agency—that is, the degree to which we're empowered to explicate the terms of our lives, both individually and collectively. I hope this book has shown that we have more power to do so than we might realize. And I say this acknowledging the point I made earlier, about how remnants from the past populate the present and persist into the future. Words aren't redefined by fiat; you cannot wish history away. You can, however, try amplifying some of its more compelling aspects, with the objective—in this case—of pushing back against the worst tendencies of algorithmic culture, and perhaps then of getting on good terms with a more equitable and inclusive version of it. A better definition of algorithmic culture isn't mine to offer, however; or rather, it's not mine to offer *alone*. Williams's publisher, at his request, appended six blank pages to the end of *Keywords*, "not only for the convenience of making notes, but as a sign that the inquiry remains open."[48] Unfortunately, I don't have the luxury of additional pages—and besides,

I have misgivings about the resources they'd consume. Nevertheless, I embrace the spirit of Williams's gesture. Because words and language are irreducibly social, any effort to redefine algorithmic culture must proceed accordingly.

Doing so shouldn't preclude technical solutions, regulation, social justice activism, or other types of intervention. Politics must be multiply pronged. And for that reason I'm encouraged, but still somewhat ambivalent, about Instagram's decision in 2021 to adjust its algorithm, in response to concerns about the platform's algorithmic suppression of pro-Palestinian content, which the company claims was unintentional.[49] To the extent that incidents such as this keep reoccurring (remember, from the introduction, the #AmazonFail incident of 2009?), it should be clear by now that tweaking the algorithm may be a necessary response, but it will never be a panacea. Redefining the phrase *algorithmic culture* is another crucial step, and maybe even the first step for inspiring other ways of fomenting change in and beyond the realm of digital technology. To that end, and building on the historical material from preceding chapters, here are a few *tentative* principles for redefining *algorithmic culture*. I invite you to add, subtract, revise, and compile based on your own encounter with this book, in addition to your own research and experience. You'll find a few blank lines as further encouragement to join in this important work.

1. Culture and computation are deeply entangled, yet they're irreducible to one another.
2. Algorithms and culture underwrite oppression, but they have the potential to do otherwise.
3. Care and nurturance ("cultivation") should be core values of algorithmic culture, against an overinvestment in class structure, the state, and other impositions of form.

4. Algorithmic culture should inculcate practices of discernment, specifically—but not exclusively—with respect to the quality of our conditions of existence.
5. When algorithmic culture ceases to be ordinary, it's time for a course correction.
6. Since key-words don't exist in isolation, efforts to redefine *algorithmic culture* must account for the broader vocabulary to which the phrase belongs, or could possibly belong.
7.
8.
9.
10.
11.
12.

Because the core chapters of this book only go as far as 1975, the broader vocabulary of algorithmic culture isn't as up-to-date as it could be. Fortunately, a slew of books and articles has been published over the last fifteen or twenty years, many of them dealing with themes germane to this book, and many of them, intriguingly, featuring one-word titles. Perhaps they too are seeking to make sense of some aspect of our new technological reality, by zooming in on key-words. And perhaps, then, some or all of those terms might appear in a more up-to-date vocabulary of algorithmic culture: *access, amplify, analog, anonymous, app, artificial, assistant, authentic, bully, cancel, cloud, code, comment, computer, connection, cookie, copy, curation, data, delete, design, digital, engagement, exploit, fake, file, free, friend, game, Google, graph, hack, hashtag, influence, information, intelligence, interface, learning, like, love, machine, meme, memory, message, mine, mobile, moderation, neighbor, network, news, password, phone, pirate, platform, post, privacy, profile, reality, reputation, save, screen, search, security, server, share, social, source, spam, status, story, trend, troll, tweet, user, viral, virus, wearable, web.*[50] This is, however, just a provisional list—nowhere near complete. As before, you should add, subtract, revise, and compile as you see fit.

This book has been an exercise in listening to words, but it's equally a book about politics. I see these aspects as one and the same, or at least closely related. And on that note, I want to underscore that the narrative of *Algorithmic Culture Before the Internet* isn't without hope, despite the many ways in which the political fortunes of *algorithm* and *culture* have been bankrupted time and again. By turning to moments from the past, we're reminded that algorithmic power is not all-encompassing. It's a process born of particular conditions, which continue to be as contested as culture itself. Moreover, key facets of human action, expression, and feeling still exceed capture by the new algorithmic authorities. They may listen in, but still they don't hear everything. Such is our task, then: to become the better listeners, and to come to terms with how we come to terms.

NOTES

INTRODUCTION: WELCOME TO THE MACHINE

1. For more mature viewers, the joke might also have something to do with former Vice-President Al Gore's claim to have invented the internet.

2. Ted Striphas, "Algorithms," in *Information: A Historical Companion*, ed. Ann Blair et al. (Princeton, NJ: Princeton University Press, 2021), 298.

3. Blake Hallinan, "Like! Feelings and Friendship in the Age of Algorithms" (PhD diss., University of Colorado, Boulder, 2019), 300; see also Tania Bucher, *If . . . Then: Algorithmic Power and Politics* (New York: Oxford University Press, 2018), 150.

4. Joseph Weizenbaum, *Computer Power and Human Reason: From Judgment to Calculation* (New York: W. H. Freeman & Co, 1976), 46.

5. Karl M. Fant, "A Critical Review of the Notion of the Algorithm in Computer Science," *Proceedings of the 1993 ACM Conference on Computer Science*, March 1993, 3; for corroboration of the timing, see "Algorithm," Google Books Ngram Viewer, accessed May 27, 2022, https://books .google.com/ngrams/graph?content=algorithm&year_start=1800 &year_end=2019&corpus=26&smoothing=3&direct_url=t1%3B% 2Calgorithm%3B%2Cc0; thanks to Ben Peters for confirming the Russian title of Markov's book.

6. Carolyn Kellogg, "'Culture' Is Merriam-Webster's Word of the Year for 2014," *Los Angeles Times*, December 15, 2014, https://www.latimes

.com/books/jacketcopy/la-et-jc-culture-word-of-the-year-20141215
-story.html.

7. On "cultural intermediaries," see Pierre Bourdieu, *Distinction: A Social Critique of the Judgment of Taste*, trans. Richard Nice (Cambridge, MA: Harvard University Press, 1984), 91; on "automatic critics and censors," see Vilém Flusser, *Into the Universe of Technical Images*, trans. Nancy Ann Roth (Minneapolis: University of Minnesota Press, 2011), 117.

8. Max Horkheimer and Theodor Adorno, "The Culture Industry: Enlightenment as Mass Deception," in *Dialectic of Enlightenment*, trans. John Cumming (New York: Continuum, 1997), 120–67; David M. Berry, *Critical Theory and the Digital* (London: Bloomsbury Academic, 2015), 23–51.

9. Alexander R. Galloway, *Gaming: Essays on Algorithmic Culture* (Minneapolis: University of Minnesota Press, 2006). The term appears in the subtitle of Galloway's book but, curiously, he never defines it.

10. Blake Hallinan and Ted Striphas, "Recommended for You: The Netflix Prize and the Production of Algorithmic Culture," *New Media & Society* 18, no. 1 (January 2016): 117–37, doi:10.1177/1461444814538646.

11. Tarleton Gillespie, "The Relevance of Algorithms," in *Media Technologies: Essays on Communication, Materiality, and Society*, ed. Tarleton Gillespie, Pablo J. Boczkowski, and Kirsten A. Foot (Cambridge, MA: MIT Press, 2014), 184; on vernacular understandings of how algorithms work, see Bucher, *If . . . Then*, 150; Taina Bucher, "The Algorithmic Imaginary: Exploring the Affects of Facebook Algorithms," *Information, Communication & Society* 20, no. 1 (2017): 30–44, https://doi.org/10.1080/1369118X.2016.1154086.

12. Karl Marx, "The Eighteenth Brumaire of Louis Bonaparte," in *The Marx-Engels Reader*, 2nd ed., ed. Robert C. Tucker (New York: Norton, 1978), 595.

13. Sara Ahmed, *Queer Phenomenology: Orientations, Objects, Others* (Durham, NC: Duke University Press, 2006), 9, 11.

14. Ahmed, *Queer Phenomenology*, 166.

15. Sasha Costanza-Chock, *Design Justice: Community-Led Practices to Build the Worlds We Need* (Cambridge, MA: MIT Press, 2020), 3.

16. Gillespie, "Relevance of Algorithms," 183.

17. Weizenbaum, *Computer Power*, ix.

18. Adam Greenfield, *Everyware: The Dawning Age of Ubiquitous Comput-*
    ing (Berkeley, CA: New Riders, 2006); see also James N. Gilmore,
    "Everywear: The Quantified Self and Wearable Fitness Technologies,"
    New Media & Society 18, no. 11 (December 2016): 2524–39, https://doi
    .org/10.1177/1461444815588768.

19. Michael Kearns and Aaron Roth, *The Ethical Algorithm: The Science of*
    Socially Aware Algorithm Design (New York: Oxford University Press,
    2020); see also Sasha Constanza-Chock's discussion of the work of the
    Algorithmic Justice League in *Design Justice*, 61; on the ideology of
    "technological solutionism," see Evgeny Morozov, *To Save Everything,*
    Click Here: The Folly of Technological Solutionism (New York: Public
    Affairs, 2013).

20. See, e.g., A. L. Kroeber and Clyde Kluckhohn, *Culture: A Critical*
    Review of Concepts and Definitions (New York: Vintage, 1963), 25;
    André Leroi-Gourhan, *Gesture and Speech*, trans. Anna Bostock Berger
    (Cambridge, MA: MIT Press, 1993).

21. Raymond Williams, *Keywords: A Vocabulary of Culture and Society*, rev.
    ed. (New York: Oxford University Press, 1983), 87; see also Vilém
    Flusser, *Natural: Mind*, trans. Rodrigo Maltez Novaes (Minneapolis,
    MN: Univocal, 2013), 89–96; Nicholas A. John, "Sharing," in *Digital*
    Keywords: A Vocabulary of Information Society and Culture, ed. Benja-
    min Peters (Princeton, NJ: Princeton University Press, 2016), 272–73.

22. Matthew Arnold, *Culture and Anarchy and Other Writings*, ed. Stefan
    Collini (Cambridge: Cambridge University Press, 1993), esp. 63, 78, 94;
    Horkheimer and Adorno, "Culture Industry"; Herbert Marcuse, *One-*
    Dimensional Man: Studies in the Ideology of Advanced Industrial Society,
    2nd ed. (Boston: Beacon Press, 1991).

23. Lewis Mumford, *Technics and Civilization* (Chicago and London: Uni-
    versity of Chicago Press, 2010), 204; Gilbert Simondon, *On the Mode*
    of Existence of Technical Objects, trans. Cecile Malaspina and John
    Rogove (Minneapolis, MN: Univocal Publishing, 2017), 16; see also
    Williams, *Keywords*, 89.

24. I define *context* as a network of relationships within which something
    becomes thinkable, articulable, and practicable. For more on the con-
    cept of context, which I am implicitly invoking here, and on the theory
    of articulation in which it is grounded, see Stuart Hall and Lawrence

Grossberg, "On Postmodernism and Articulation: An Interview With Stuart Hall," in *Stuart Hall: Critical Dialogues in Cultural Studies*, ed. David Morley and Kuan-Hsing Chen (London: Routledge, 1996), 141; Jennifer Daryl Slack, "The Theory and Method of Articulation in Cultural Studies," in *Stuart Hall: Critical Dialogues in Cultural Studies*, ed. David Morley and Kuan-Hsing Chen (London: Routledge, 1996), 112–27; Lawrence Grossberg, "Cultural Studies: What's in a Name (One More Time)," in *Bringing It All Back Home: Essays on Cultural Studies* (Durham, NC: Duke University Press, 1997), 254–62. My point about the non-necessity of the culture-technology relationship echoes Jennifer Daryl Slack and J. Macgregor Wise, *Culture and Technology: A Primer*, 2nd ed. (New York: Peter Lang, 2015).

25. Qadri Ismail, *Culture and Eurocentrism* (London: Rowman & Littlefield International, 2015), 2.

26. Williams, *Keywords*, 87.

27. Williams, *Keywords*; Raymond Williams, *Culture and Society, 1780–1950* (New York: Columbia University Press, 1958); Raymond Williams, *The Long Revolution* (Orchard Park, NY: Broadview Press, 2001); Raymond Williams, *The Sociology of Culture* (Chicago: University of Chicago Press, 1981); see also Chris Jenks, *Culture*, 1st ed. (London: Routledge, 1993); Adam Kuper, *Culture: The Anthropologists' Account* (Cambridge, MA: Harvard University Press, 1999); Francis Mulhern, *Culture/Metaculture* (London: Routledge, 2000); Marc Manganaro, *Culture, 1922: The Emergence of a Concept* (Princeton, NJ: Princeton University Press, 2002).

28. Kroeber and Kluckhohn, *Culture*; Williams, *Long Revolution*, 57; Williams, *Culture and Society*, xviii; on culture as "ambiance," see E. P. Thompson, "Custom and Culture," in *Customs in Common: Studies in Traditional Popular Culture* (New York: New Press, 1993), 8.

29. Mario Vargas Llosa, *Notes on the Death of Culture: Essays on Spectacle and Society*, trans. John King (New York: Picador, 2015).

30. Tony Bennett, "Culture," in *New Keywords: A Revised Vocabulary of Culture and Society*, ed. Tony Bennett, Lawrence Grossberg, and Meaghan Morris (Malden, MA: Blackwell, 2005), 68. Bennett, to be fair, composed this chapter in the early years of algorithmic culture. Amazon, for example, was only about a decade old when it was

published, Google was seven, and Facebook was in its infancy. As such, he should be lauded for having recognized the growing proximity of culture and computation in the early twenty-first century.

31. Lawrence Grossberg, "Does Cultural Studies Have Futures? Should It? (Or What's the Matter with New York?)," *Cultural Studies* 20, no. 1 (2006): 17.

32. Bruno Latour, *We Have Never Been Modern* (Cambridge, MA: Harvard University Press, 1993), 104; Williams, *Keywords*, 89; Leo Marx, *The Machine in the Garden: Technology and the Pastoral Ideal in America* (New York: Oxford University Press, 1964); Raymond Williams, *The Country and the City* (New York: Oxford University Press, 1973).

33. Williams, *Culture and Society*, xviii; Williams, *Keywords*, 150; Friedrich Kittler, "Thinking Colours and/or Machines," *Theory, Culture & Society* 23, nos. 7–8 (December 1, 2006): 39–50, doi:10.1177/02632764 06069881, 40–42.

34. Ted Striphas, *The Late Age of Print: Everyday Book Culture from Consumerism to Control* (New York: Columbia University Press, 2009), 81–109.

35. Gerard Genette, *Paratexts: Thresholds of Interpretation*, trans. Jane E. Lewin (Cambridge: Cambridge University Press, 1997).

36. Edward T. Hall, *The Hidden Dimension* (Garden City, NY: Doubleday, 1966); see also Hallinan and Striphas, "Recommended for You," 125; Félix Guattari, *Chaosmosis: An Ethico-Aesthetic Paradigm*, trans. Paul Bains and Julian Pefanis (Bloomington: Indiana University Press, 1995), 24.

37. Hallinan and Striphas, "Recommended for You," 129.

38. Andrea James, "Amazon Calls Mistake 'Embarassing and Ham-Fisted,'" *Seattle Post Intelligencer Blog*, April 13, 2009; Andrea James, "AmazonFail: An inside Look at What Happened," *Seattle Post Intelligencer Blog*, April 13, 2009, http://blog.seattlepi.com/amazon/2009/04 /13/amazonfail-an-inside-look-at-what-happened/; Larry Kramer, quoted in Motoko Rich, "Amazon Says Error Removed Listings," *New York Times*, April 14, 2009, http://www.nytimes.com/2009/04/14 /technology/internet/14amazon.html.

39. Michael Bhaskar, *Curation: The Power of Selection in a World of Excess* (London: Piatkus Books, 2016), 67, 112–19.

40. Safiya Umoja Noble, *Algorithms of Oppression: How Search Engines Reinforce Racism* (New York: New York University Press, 2018), 80–81; Mike Ananny, "The Curious Connection Between Apps for Gay Men and Sex Offenders," *The Atlantic*, April 14, 2011, https://www.theatlantic.com/technology/archive/2011/04/the-curious-connection-between-apps-for-gay-men-and-sex-offenders/237340/.

41. "Algorithmic Justice League—Unmasking AI Harms and Biases," accessed August 16, 2021, https://www.ajl.org/.

42. Noble, *Algorithms of Oppression*; Ananny, "Curious Connection"; Costanza-Chock, *Design Justice*; Ruha Benjamin, *Race After Technology: Abolitionist Tools for the New Jim Code* (Cambridge: Polity, 2019), esp. 97–136; Simone Browne, *Dark Matters: On the Surveillance of Blackness* (Durham, NC: Duke University Press, 2015); Bucher, *If . . . Then*; John Cheney-Lippold, *We Are Data: Algorithms and the Making of Our Digital Selves* (New York: NYU Press, 2017); Wendy Hui Kyong Chun, *Discriminating Data: Correlation, Neighborhoods, and the New Politics of Recognition* (Cambridge, MA: MIT Press, 2021); Kate Crawford, "Can an Algorithm Be Agonistic? Ten Scenes from Life in Calculated Publics," *Science, Technology, & Human Values* 41, no. 1 (January 2016): 77–92, https://doi.org/10.1177/0162243915589635; Virginia Eubanks, *Automating Inequality: How High-Tech Tools Profile, Police, and Punish the Poor* (New York: Picador, 2018); Oscar H. Gandy, "It's Discrimination, Stupid!," in *Resisting the Virtual Life: The Culture and Politics of Information*, ed. James Brook and Iain Boal (San Francisco, CA: City Lights Publishers, 1995), 35–47; Lisa Nakamura, *Cybertypes: Race, Ethnicity, and Identity on the Internet*, (New York: Routledge, 2002); Cathy O'Neil, *Weapons of Math Destruction: How Big Data Increases Inequality and Threatens Democracy* (New York: Crown, 2016); Siva Vaidhyanathan, *Antisocial Media: How Facebook Disconnects Us and Undermines Democracy* (New York: Oxford University Press, 2018); Jacqueline Wernimont, *Numbered Lives: Life and Death in Quantum Media* (Cambridge, MA: MIT Press, 2018), 155–59. See also: Eli Pariser, *The Filter Bubble: What the Internet Is Hiding From You* (New York: Penguin Press, 2011); Christian Sandvig et al., "When the Algorithm Itself Is a Racist: Diagnosing Ethical Harm in the Basic Components of Software," *International Journal of Communication* 10 (2016): 4972–4990; and Tarleton Gillespie, "Algorithmically

Recognizable: Santorum's Google Problem, and Google's Santorum Problem," *Information, Communication & Society* 20, no. 1 (2017): 63–80, doi:10.1080/1369118X.2016.1199721. For a compendium of citations on the subject of algorithmic politics, see Tarleton Gillespie and Nick Seaver, "Critical Algorithm Studies: A Reading List," *Social Media Collective Research Blog*, December 15, 2016, https://socialmedia collective.org/reading-lists/critical-algorithm-studies/, particularly §1 and §2.

43. James Gleick, *The Information: A History, a Theory, a Flood* (New York: Pantheon Books, 2011), 280; O'Neil, *Weapons of Math Destruction*, 3; Chun, *Discriminating Data*, 52. To preserve syntax, I've slightly modified the quotation from O'Neil.

44. On the other-than-human implementation of algorithmic systems, see Christopher Miles, "The Combine Will Tell the Truth: On Precision Agriculture and Algorithmic Rationality," *Big Data & Society* 6, no. 1 (January 1, 2019): https://doi.org/10.1177/2053951719849444.

45. Julia Angwin et al., "Machine Bias," *ProPublica*, May 23, 2016, https://www.propublica.org/article/machine-bias-risk-assessments-in-criminal-sentencing?token=M28Yt5CCtbKAxQp99Ick5WRwgYR keCZw; O'Neil, *Weapons of Math Destruction*; Mark Andrejevic, *Automated Media* (London: Routledge, 2020), 9, 44–72.

46. Siva Vaidhyanathan, *The Googlization of Everything (And Why We Should Worry)* (Berkeley: University of California Press, 2011).

47. Kevin Slavin, "How Algorithms Shape Our World," *TED: Ideas Worth Spreading*, July 2011, http://www.ted.com/talks/kevin_slavin_how _algorithms_shape_our_world.

48. On the historicity of automation, see Mark Seltzer, *Bodies and Machines* (New York: Routledge, 1992), 144; and James R. Beniger, *The Control Revolution: Technological and Economic Origins of the Information Society* (Cambridge, MA: Harvard University Press, 1986). For an example of neo-behavioristic approaches to digital technology, see Shoshana Zuboff, *The Age of Surveillance Capitalism: The Fight for a Human Future at the New Frontier of Power* (New York: Public Affairs, 2019), esp. 449. There, Zuboff argues: "The magnetic pull that social media exerts on young people drives them toward more automatic and less voluntary behavior." Elsewhere, she refers to "a new day of behavioral control," 215.

49. Indeed, Vaidhyanathan is careful not to reduce power simply to its economic or corporate dimensions. Siva Vaidhyanathan, "Afterword: Critical Information Studies—A Bibliographic Manifesto," *Cultural Studies* 20, nos. 2–3 (March 1, 2006): 292–315, https://doi.org/10.1080 /09502380500521091. My concern stems only from a naming convention that might lend itself to just such a reduction. On the critique of political economy, see, e.g.: Lawrence Grossberg, "Cultural Studies vs. Political Economy: Is Anybody Else Bored with This Debate?," *Critical Studies in Mass Communication* 12, no. 1 (March 1995): 72–81; J. K. Gibson-Graham, *The End of Capitalism (As We Knew It): A Feminist Critique of Political Economy* (Oxford: Blackwell, 1996); and Judith Butler, "Merely Cultural," *Social Text*, nos. 52–53 (Autumn–Winter 1997): 265–77.

50. Robert Seyfert and Jonathan Roberge, eds., "What Are Algorithmic Cultures?," in *Algorithmic Cultures: Essays on Meaning, Performance and New Technologies* (London: Routledge, 2016), 5.

51. On homophily, see danah boyd, *It's Complicated: The Social Lives of Networked Teens* (New Haven, CT: Yale University Press, 2014), 166. On filter bubbles, see Pariser, *Filter Bubble.*

52. Fred Turner, *The Democratic Surround: Multimedia and American Liberalism from World War II to the Psychedelic Sixties* (Chicago: University of Chicago Press, 2013).

53. Turner, *Democratic Surround*, 70, 74.

54. Fred Turner, *From Counterculture to Cyberculture: Stewart Brand, the Whole Earth Network, and the Rise of Digital Utopianism* (Chicago: University of Chicago Press, 2006).

55. Turner, *Democratic Surround*, 160.

56. Park Honan, *Matthew Arnold: A Life* (New York: McGraw-Hill, 1981), 396–407.

57. D. W. Brogan, "The Working Class Simply Isn't What It Used to Be: *The Long Revolution*, by Raymond Williams," *New York Times*, August 27, 1961, BR3, BR32; see also John Clive, "*Culture and Society, 1780–1950* (Book Review)," *American Historical Review* 64, no. 4 (July 1959): 934–35, https://doi.org/10.2307/1905142; J. Jean Hecht, "*Culture and Society, 1780–1950* (Book Review)," *American Sociological Review* 24, no. 5 (October 1959): 746; M. S. Wilkins, "*Culture and*

Society, 1780–1950 (Book Review)," *Political Science Quarterly* 75, no. 2 (June 1960): 302–3, https://doi.org/10.2307/2146178; Robert E. Spiller, "*The Long Revolution*, by Raymond Williams," *Annals of the American Academy of Political and Social Science* 339 (January 1962): 217.

58. Williams, *Long Revolution*, 101; see also 63.

59. Friedrich Kittler, "Rock Music: A Misuse of Military Equipment," in *The Truth of the Technological World: Essays on the Genealogy of Presence*, trans. Erik Butler (Stanford, CA: Stanford University Press, 2013), 152–64.

60. See, e.g., Susan Hockey, "The History of Humanities Computing," in *A Companion to Digital Humanities*, ed. Susan Schreibman, Ray Siemens, and John Unsworth (Oxford: Blackwell, 2004), https://ebookcentral.proquest.com/lib/ucb/detail.action?docID=350868; Stephen Ramsay, *Reading Machines: Toward an Algorithmic Criticism* (Urbana: University of Illinois Press, 2011), 1; Anne Burdick et al., *Digital_Humanities* (Cambridge, MA: MIT Press, 2012), 123. See also Angelo Stagnaro, "The Italian Jesuit Who Taught Computers to Talk to Us," *National Catholic Register* (blog), January 28, 2017, https://www.ncregister.com/blog/the-italian-jesuit-who-taught-computers-to-talk-to-us.

61. Roberto Busa, "The Annals of Humanities Computing: The Index Thomisticus," *Computers and the Humanities* 14, no. 2 (October 1980): 83; Thomas N. Winter, "Roberto Busa, S.J., and the Invention of the Machine-Generated Concordance," *The Classical Bulletin* 75, no. 1 (1999): 6.

62. Winter, "Roberto Busa, S.J.," 12.

63. Busa, "Annals of Humanities Computing," 84.

64. David Link, "Traces of the Mouth: Andrei Andreyevich Markov's Mathematization of Writing," *History of Science* 44 (2006): 324. Link goes even further back in his history of the mathematization of writing to the cryptanalytical work of al-Kindi, who was a contemporary and coworker of Moḥammed ibn-Mūsā al-Khwārizmī, the primary subject of chapter 2.

65. Claude Elwood Shannon and Warren Weaver, *The Mathematical Theory of Communication* (Champaign-Urbana: University of Illinois, 1964), 45; Armand Mattelart and Michèle Mattelart, *Theories of*

Communication: A Short Introduction, trans. Susan Gruenheck Taponier
and James A. Cohen (Thousand Oaks, CA: Sage, 1998), 44; Brian
Hayes, "First Links in the Markov Chain," American Scientist,
April 2013, https://www.americanscientist.org/article/first-links-in
-the-markov-chain; Hari Balasubramanian, "Where Probability
Meets Literature and Language: Markov Models for Text Analysis,"
3 Quarks Daily (blog), March 14, 2016, https://3quarksdaily.com
/3quarksdaily/2016/03/where-probability-meets-literature-and
-language-markov-models-for-text-analysis.html.

66. Busa, "Annals of Humanities Computing," 84.

67. David M. Berry, "The Computational Turn: Thinking About the
Digital Humanities," *Culture Machine* 12 (2011): 2.

68. Berry, "Computational Turn," 3. See also Lev Manovich, *Software
Takes Command* (New York and London: Bloomsbury, 2013), 21. There,
Manovich refers to "cultural software," by which he refers to applica-
tions "that support actions we normally associate with 'culture.'" Berry
seems to take the idea one step further—appropriately, I believe—in
collapsing the two categories. He develops the argument further in
David M. Berry, *Critical Theory and the Digital* (London: Bloomsbury
Academic, 2015), 53–87.

69. Lori Emerson, *Reading Writing Interfaces: From the Digital to the Book-
bound* (Minneapolis: University of Minnesota Press, 2014).

70. Lydia H. Liu, "The Cybernetic Unconscious: Rethinking Lacan, Poe,
and French Theory," *Critical Inquiry* 36, no. 2 (Winter 2010): 291. See
also Gibson-Graham, *End of Capitalism*.

71. Lawrence Grossberg, *Caught in the Crossfire: Kids, Politics, and America's Future* (Boulder, CO: Paradigm Publishers, 2005), vi. The irony is
that the epigraph repeats a common misquotation of this passage from
Twain: "Truth is stranger than fiction, but it is because Fiction is
obliged to stick to possibilities; Truth isn't." Mark Twain, *Following
the Equator: A Journey Around the World*, rev. ed. (New York: Dover,
1989), 156. See also Garson O'Toole, "Truth Is Stranger than Fiction,
But It Is Because Fiction Is Obliged to Stick to Possibilities; Truth
Isn't," *Quote Investigator*, accessed July 17, 2017, http://quoteinvestigator
.com/2015/07/15/truth-stranger/.

72. Grossberg, *Bringing It All Back*, 259, and passim. Grossberg borrows
the phrase "without guarantees" from Stuart Hall. Stuart Hall, "The

Problem of Ideology: Marxism Without Guarantees," in *Stuart Hall: Critical Dialogues in Cultural Studies*, ed. David Morley and Kuan-Hsing Chen (London: Routledge, 1996), 25–46.

73. Karl Marx, *Grundrisse: Foundations of the Critique of Political Economy*, trans. Martin Nicolaus (London: Penguin Books, 1973), 90.

74. Dipesh Chakrabarty, *Provincializing Europe: Postcolonial Thought and Historical Difference*, new ed. (Princeton, NJ: Princeton University Press, 2007), xiv. On the critique of history/historiography/historicism, see also: Walter Benjamin, "Theses on the Philosophy of History," in *Illuminations: Essays and Reflections*, ed. Hannah Arendt, trans. Harry Zohn (New York: Schocken Books, 1968), 253–64; Hayden White, *Metahistory: The Historical Imagination in Nineteenth-Century Europe* (Baltimore, MD: Johns Hopkins University Press, 1973); and Michel de Certeau, *The Writing of History*, trans. Tom Conley (New York: Columbia University Press, 1988).

75. I've borrowed the phrase "teeth-gritting harmony" from Louis Althusser, "Ideology and Ideological State Apparatuses (Notes Toward an Investigation)," in *Lenin and Philosophy and Other Essays*, trans. Ben Brewster (New York: Monthly Review Press, 1971), 142.

76. Stuart Hall, "Cultural Studies: Two Paradigms," *Media, Culture, and Society* 2, no. 1 (1980): 57–58, https://doi.org/10.1177/016344378000200106 (emphasis in original).

77. Williams, *Culture and Society*, ix–xx.

78. See, e.g., John Storey, ed., "Introduction to Part I: The 'Culture and Civilization' Tradition," in *Cultural Theory and Popular Culture: A Reader*, 3rd ed. (Athens: University of Georgia Press, 2006), 3–5.

79. Raphael Samuel, "'Philosophy Teaching by Example': Past and Present in Raymond Williams," *History Workshop*, no. 27 (Spring 1989): 145.

80. On the concept of "assemblage," see Gilles Deleuze and Félix Guattari, *A Thousand Plateaus: Capitalism and Schizophrenia*, trans. Brian Massumi (Minneapolis: University of Minnesota Press, 1987); Bruno Latour, *Reassembling the Social: An Introduction to Actor-Network Theory* (Oxford: Oxford University Press, 2005); Jasbir Puar, *Terrorist Assemblages: Homonationalism in Queer Times* (Durham, NC: Duke University Press, 2007); and Judith Butler, *Notes Toward a Performative Theory of Assembly* (Cambridge, MA: Harvard University Press, 2015).

81. Williams, *Culture and Society*, vii.

82. Carolyn Steedman, "Culture, Cultural Studies, and the Historians,"
    in *Cultural Studies*, ed. Lawrence Grossberg, Cary Nelson, and Paula
    Treichler (New York: Routledge, 1992), 621; see also Richard Johnson,
    "Historical Returns: Transdisciplinarity, Cultural Studies, and His-
    tory," *European Journal of Cultural Studies* 4, no. 3 (August 2001): 262.
83. Gary Hall, *Culture in Bits: The Monstrous Future of Theory* (London:
    Continuum, 2002), 126.
84. Friedrich A. Kittler, *Gramophone, Film, Typewriter*, trans. Geoffrey
    Winthrop-Young and Michael Wutz (Stanford, CA: Stanford Univer-
    sity Press, 1999), xxxix. I have modified the translation based on the
    advice of Florian Cramer, whom I thank. On "discourse networks,"
    see Friedrich A. Kittler, *Discourse Networks, 1800/1900*, trans. Michael
    Metteer and Chris Cullens (Stanford, CA: Stanford University Press,
    1990), 369. See also John Durham Peters, *The Marvelous Clouds: Toward
    a Philosophy of Elemental Media* (Chicago: University of Chicago Press,
    2015).
85. Arnold, *Culture and Anarchy*, 190. See also Ann M. Blair, *Too Much to
    Know: Managing Scholarly Information before the Modern Age* (New
    Haven, CT: Yale University Press, 2011).
86. Latour, *Reassembling the Social*, 95.
87. As Mehdi Semati (personal communication, December 2021) has
    pointed out to me: "In writing his [al-Khwārizmī's] name, a system of
    transliteration is used. That system (devised by 'Westerners,' I assume,
    since it renders the name/writing phonetically in recognizable sounds/
    letters) already creates a problem in that the pronunciation it produces
    Arabizes the Persian sounds (in Persian, it is Kharazmi, whereas Kha-
    warizmi is a rendering of what sounds to Westerners as Arabic)." I
    continue using the "standard" orthography only for purposes of legi-
    bility, and with due acknowledgment of the ethnocentrism of my doing
    so. Moreover, I've left unaltered alternative spellings of the name
    appearing in the literature, as a way of drawing attention to the poli-
    tics of translation/transliteration.

1. KEY-WORDS

1. Laurence Rose et al., "Reconnecting Kids with Nature Is Vital, and
   Needs Cultural Leadership," January 12, 2015, https://www.nature

musicpoetry.com/uploads/2/9/3/8/29384149/letter_to_oup_final.pdf;
Julie Henry, "Words Associated with Christianity and British History
Taken Out of Children's Dictionary," *The Telegraph*, December 6,
2008, https://www.telegraph.co.uk/education/3569045/Words-associ
ated-with-Christianity-and-British-history-taken-out-of-childrens
-dictionary.html; Alison Flood, "Oxford Junior Dictionary's Replacement of 'Natural' Words with 21st-Century Terms Sparks Outcry,"
The Guardian, January 13, 2015, https://www.theguardian.com/books
/2015/jan/13/oxford-junior-dictionary-replacement-natural-words;
Laurence Rose, "Literary Stars Support #Naturewords Campaign,"
Natural Light (blog), January 12, 2015, https://www.naturemusicpoetry
.com/news-and-blog/literary-stars-support-naturewords-campaign.
I find it ironic that an essay questioning the addition of *blog* and
other terms associated with digital technology appeared, in all places,
on a blog. For the Oxford University Press response, see "Nature
Words and the Oxford Junior Dictionary," *Oxford Education Blog*
(blog), January 12, 2018, https://educationblog.oup.com/childrens
/nature-words-and-the-oxford-junior-dictionary; and Katherine
Barber, "Dictionary Leaves Out Thousands of Words!," *Wordlady*
(blog), January 3, 2018, https://katherinebarber.blogspot.com/2018
/01/dictionary-leaves-out-thousands-of-words.html.
2. Henry, "Words Associated with Christianity."
3. *Oxford Corpus and ReadOxford, Oxford University* (Oxford Education,
2017), https://www.youtube.com/watch?v=ok-50GVxyMw&t=11s.
4. Alan Durant, "Raymond Williams's Keywords: Investigating Meanings 'Offered, Felt for, Tested, Confirmed, Asserted, Qualified,
Changed,'" *Critical Quarterly* 48, no. 4 (December 2006): 7–8, https://doi
.org/10.1111/j.1467-8705.2006.00743.x. See also Raymond Williams, *Culture and Society, 1780–1950* (New York: Columbia University Press, 1983),
xiin, xiii–xx; Raymond Williams, *Keywords: A Vocabulary of Culture and
Society*, rev. ed. (New York: Oxford University Press, 1983), 13; The Keywords Project, "Introduction," in *Keywords for Today: A 21st Century
Vocabulary*, ed. Colin MacCabe and Holly Yanacek (New York: Oxford
University Press, 2018), ix.
5. On Williams's war service, see Fred Inglis, *Raymond Williams* (London: Routledge, 1995) 86–106; and Dai Smith, *Raymond Williams: A
Warrior's Tale* (Cardigan, UK: Parthian Books, 2008), 131–97.

6. Williams, *Keywords* (1983), 11. On the identity of his anonymous interlocutor, see Ben Highmore, *"Keywords* and Keywording," *Cultural Studies*, 2021, 5, 21n5, https://doi.org/10.1080/09502386.2021.1947336.

7. Williams, *Culture and Society*, xiii.

8. Williams, *Keywords* (1983), 14; Williams, *Culture and Society*, xii. For more on Williams's two parallel keywords projects, see Ted Striphas, "Culture," in *Digital Keywords: A Vocabulary of Information Society and Culture*, ed. Benjamin Peters (Princeton, NJ: Princeton University Press, 2016), 70–71. On the characterization of keywords as "historical semantics," see Stephen Heath, "Raymond Williams and Keywords," Keywords Project, n.d., https://keywords.pitt.edu/williams_keywords.html.

9. Jan Zita Grover, "AIDS: Keywords," *October* 43 (1987): 17–30, https://doi.org/10.2307/3397563; Alan Durant and Colin MacCabe, "Compacted Doctrines: Empson and the Meanings of Words," in *William Empson: The Critical Achievement*, ed. Christopher Norris and Nigel Mapp (Cambridge: Cambridge University Press, 1993), 170–95; Tony Bennett, Lawrence Grossberg, and Meaghan Morris, eds., *New Keywords: A Revised Vocabulary of Culture and Society* (Malden, MA: Blackwell, 2005); Durant, "Raymond Williams's Keywords"; Barbie Zelizer and Stuart Allan, eds., *Keywords in News and Journalism Studies* (New York: McGraw-Hill, 2010); Nancy Lesko and Susan Talburt, eds., *Keywords in Youth Studies: Tracing Affects, Movements, Knowledges* (New York: Routledge, 2012); Paisley Currah and Susan Stryker, eds., "Postposttranssexual: Key Concepts for a Twenty-First-Century Transgender Studies," Special Issue of *Transgender Studies Quarterly* 1, nos. 1–2 (May 2014); Rachel Adams, Benjamin Reiss, and David Serlin, eds., *Keywords for Disability Studies* (New York: NYU Press, 2015); Colin MacCabe, "Foreword," in *Keywords: A Vocabulary of Culture and Society*, new ed. (New York: Oxford University Press, 2015); David Novak and Matt Sakakeeny, eds., *Keywords in Sound* (Durham, NC: Duke University Press, 2015); Cathy J. Schlund-Vials, K. Scott Wong, and Linda Trinh Võ, eds., *Keywords for Asian American Studies* (New York: NYU Press, 2015); Joni Adamson, William A. Gleason, and David Pellow, eds., *Keywords for Environmental Studies* (New York: NYU Press, 2016); Benjamin Peters, ed., *Digital Keywords: A*

Vocabulary of Information Society and Culture (Princeton, NJ: Princeton University Press, 2016); Laurie Ouellette and Jonathan Gray, eds., *Keywords for Media Studies* (New York: NYU Press, 2017); Deborah R. Vargas, Lawrence La Fountain-Stokes, and Nancy Raquel Mirabal, eds., *Keywords for Latina/o Studies* (New York: NYU Press, 2017); Erica R. Edwards, Roderick A. Ferguson, and Jeffrey O. G. Ogbar, eds., *Keywords for African American Studies* (New York: NYU Press, 2018); Colin MacCabe and Holly Yanacek, eds., *Keywords for Today: A 21st Century Vocabulary* (New York: Oxford University Press, 2018); Bruce Burgett and Glenn Hendler, eds., *Keywords for American Cultural Studies*, 3rd ed. (New York: NYU Press, 2020); Ramzi Fawaz, Shelley Streeby, and Deborah Elizabeth Whaley, eds., *Keywords for Comics Studies* (New York: NYU Press, 2021); Highmore, "*Keywords* and Keywording"; Michele Kennerly, Samuel Frederick, and Jonathan E. Abel, eds., *Information: Keywords* (New York: Columbia University Press, 2021); Marie Moran, "Keywords as Method," *European Journal of Cultural Studies* 24, no. 4 (June 17, 2021), https://doi.org/10.1177/13675494211016858; and Philip Nel, Lissa Paul, and Nina Christensen, eds., *Keywords for Children's Literature*, 2nd ed. (New York: NYU Press, 2021).

10. Joachim Gentz, *Keywords Re-Oriented* (Göttingen, Germany: Universitätsverlag Göttingen, 2009), https://univerlag.uni-goettingen.de/handle/3/isbn-978-3-940344-88-5.

11. Ashish Kothari et al., eds., *Pluriverse: A Post-Development Dictionary* (New Delhi: Tulika Books, 2019), xi.

12. Durant, "Raymond Williams's Keywords," 2–3.

13. Tony Bennett, Lawrence Grossberg, and Meaghan Morris, "Introduction," in *New Keywords: A Revised Vocabulary of Culture and Society*, ed. Tony Bennett, Lawrence Grossberg, and Meaghan Morris (Malden, MA: Blackwell, 2005), xviii (emphasis in original).

14. Stuart Hall, "Cultural Studies: Two Paradigms," *Media, Culture, and Society* 2, no. 1 (1980): 69, https://doi.org/10.1177/016344378000200106. My thanks to Megan Wood and Bernard Dionysus Geoghegan for helping me to track down the citation.

15. Important exceptions include Highmore, "*Keywords* and Keywording," and Gentz, *Keywords Re-Oriented*.

16. Gary Hall, *Culture in Bits: The Monstrous Future of Theory* (London: Continuum, 2002), 126.

17. Moses Boudourides, "The Graph of Raymond Williams' 'Keywords,'" *Moses Boudourides* (blog), September 13, 2018, https://medium.com/@mosabou/the-graph-of-raymond-williams-keywords-de7bb0e0a9f8. Scott Weingart and I (unpublished) have created a similar, although far less detailed, map of the internal structure of *Keywords*.

18. Williams, *Culture and Society*, xiii–xx; Williams, *Keywords* (1983), 11–26; Raymond Williams, *Marxism and Literature* (Oxford: Oxford University Press, 1977), 133; Raymond Williams and New Left Review, *Politics and Letters: Interviews with New Left Review* (London: Verso Books, 1979), 175–85.

19. Williams, *Keywords* (1983), 25–26.

20. Williams, *Keywords* (1983), 25.

21. Williams, *Keywords* (1983), 25.

22. My inspiration for using *key words* as the inclusive term lies, in part, with the journal *Key Words: A Journal of Cultural Materialism*, published by the Raymond Williams society: https://raymondwilliams.co.uk/journal/.

23. "Keyword, n.," in *OED Online* (Oxford University Press), accessed October 7, 2022, http://www.oed.com/view/Entry/312961; "Zero, n. and Adj.," in *OED Online* (Oxford University Press), accessed September 15, 2021, http://www.oed.com/view/Entry/232803; "Algorism, n.," in *OED Online* (Oxford University Press), accessed September 15, 2021, http://www.oed.com/view/Entry/4956.

24. For further detail, see Claude Shannon, "A Mathematical Theory of Cryptography" (New Jersey: Bell Labs, September 1, 1945), https://www.iacr.org/museum/shannon/shannon45.pdf; Claude Elwood Shannon and Warren Weaver, *The Mathematical Theory of Communication* (Champaign-Urbana: University of Illinois, 1964); and Ted Striphas, "The Shannon and Weaver Model," *The Late Age of Print* (blog), accessed September 15, 2021, https://www.thelateageofprint.org/2012/02/20/the-shannon-and-weaver-model/. See also Brian Lennon, *Passwords: Philology, Security, Authentication* (Cambridge, MA: Belknap Press of Harvard University Press, 2018).

25. This is what Marx is essentially saying when he remarks, "humankind sets itself only such tasks as it can solve." Karl Marx, "Marx on the

History of His Opinions," in *The Marx-Engels Reader*, ed. Robert C. Tucker, 2nd ed. (New York: Norton, 1978), 5, translation modified. See also Gilles Deleuze, *Bergsonism*, trans. Hugh Tomlinson and Barbara Habberjam (New York: Zone Books, 1988), 15–16.

26. "Keyword, n.," 1b, 2, *OED Online*, accessed October 7, 2022.

27. "Keyword, n.," *OED Online*, accessed October 7, 2022.

28. Janice A. Radway, *Reading the Romance: Women, Patriarchy, and Popular Literature* (Chapel Hill: University of North Carolina Press, 1984), 21–22; Raymond Williams, *The Long Revolution* (Orchard Park, NY: Broadview Press, 2001), esp. 177–253.

29. See, e.g., Sarah Zhang, "The Pitfalls of Using Google Ngram to Study Language," *Wired*, October 12, 2015, http://www.wired.com/2015/10 /pitfalls-of-studying-language-with-google-ngram/.

30. "Key-word, key word, keyword," *Google NGram Viewer*, accessed January 11, 2016. https://books.google.com/ngrams/graph?content =keyword%2C+key+word%2C+key-word&year_start=1800&year _end=2000&corpus=15&smoothing=3&share=&direct_url=t1%3 B%2Ckeyword%3B%2Cc0%3B.t1%3B%2Ckey%20word%3B%2 Cc0%3B.t1%3B%2Ckey%20-%20word%3B%2Cc0.

31. "Keyword, n.," *OED Online*, accessed October 7, 2022. "In later use in sense 1b ["A word or idea that serves as a solution or explanation for something; a word, expression, or concept of particular importance or significance."] the first element may be understood as a use of key *adj.*"

32. Williams, *Culture and Society*, iii; Williams, *Long Revolution*, 25.

33. Anatoly Liberman, "Keys and Bolts: The Etymology of 'Key,'" *OUPblog*, accessed January 13, 2016, http://blog.oup.com/2015/03/key -etymology-word-origin/; Anatoly Liberman, *An Analytic Dictionary of English Etymology: An Introduction* (Minneapolis: University of Minnesota Press, 2008), 132.

34. "Key, n.1 and adj.," *OED Online*, accessed January 12, 2016, https:// www.oed.com/view/Entry/103130.

35. "Key (n.1)," accessed January 13, 2016, http://etymonline.com/index .php?term=key&allowed_in_frame=0.

36. Liberman, "Keys and Bolts." See also "kay | key, adj.," *OED Online*, for a related discussion of the terms "kay-fisted" and "key-pawed." Accessed January 13, 2016.

37. Liberman, *Analytic Dictionary*, 131.

38. "Key, n.1 and adj.," *OED Online*, accessed January 12, 2016; see also "clef (n.)," accessed January 13, 2016, http://etymonline.com/index.php?allowed_in_frame=0&search=clef.

39. Carol J. Adams, *The Sexual Politics of Meat: A Feminist-Vegetarian Critical Theory*, 10th anniversary ed. (New York: Continuum, 2003).

40. Liberman, *Analytic Dictionary*, 130.

41. "Word, n. and int.," *OED Online*, accessed January 14, 2016, www.oed.com/view/Entry/230192.

42. "wer-5," *American Heritage Dictionary of Indo-European Roots Appendix*, accessed January 15, 2016, https://www.ahdictionary.com/word/indoeurop.html#IR123200; Francis P. Dinneen, *General Linguistics* (Washington, DC: Georgetown University Press, 1995), 118–19.

43. "Word, n. and int.," *OED Online*. Note that this usage is of a different line than the authoritative sense of *word*, as in "the divine Word," which hails from the Greek λόγος (*logos*) connoting not only words but also logic and truth.

44. Geneva Smitherman, *Black Talk: Words and Phrases from the Hood to the Amen Corner* (Boston: Houghton Mifflin, 1994), 240.

45. Gilles Deleuze and Félix Guattari, *A Thousand Plateaus: Capitalism and Schizophrenia*, trans. Brian Massumi (Minneapolis: University of Minnesota Press, 1987), 79.

46. Deleuze and Guattari, *Thousand Plateaus*, 523n1; "Word, n. and int." 1e, *OED Online*. See also Ronald Bogue, *Deleuze and Guattari* (London: Routledge, 1989), 136–37.

47. For a masterclass on the concept of catachresis, see Michael Kaplan, "The Rhetoric of Hegemony: Laclau, Radical Democracy, and the Rule of Tropes," *Philosophy and Rhetoric* 43, no. 3 (2010): 253–83.

48. C.f. Kory Stamper, *Word by Word: The Secret Life of Dictionaries* (New York: Pantheon Books, 2017), 35. Lexicographer Kory Stamper claims that "'prescriptivism' . . . is unfortunately not how dictionaries work at all." I see the point in principle, but I cannot abide by the categorical nature of the claim given the numerous ways, both subtle and explicit, dictionaries cue readers to proper usage.

49. Williams, *Marxism and Literature*, 122. Williams, for his part, is careful to differentiate the archaic, or that which is definitively of and existentially left in the past, from the residual, or an element hailing from the past that nonetheless remains effective in the present day.

50. Raymond Williams, "Base and Superstructure in Marxist Cultural Theory," *New Left Review* 82 (1973): 9.

51. Williams, *Marxism and Literature*, 123–25.

52. Williams, *Keywords* (1983), 22, 50–52. See also Fernand Braudel, *The Wheels of Commerce: Civilization and Capitalism 15th–18th Century*, trans. Siân Reynolds, vol. 2, 3 vols. (New York: Harper & Row, 1986), 232–39.

53. Williams, *Marxism and Literature*, 126. See also Williams, *Politics and Letters*, 167.

54. Vilém Flusser, *On Doubt*, ed. Siegfried Zielinski, trans. Rodrigo Novaes (Minneapolis, MN: Univocal Publishing, 2014), 53.

55. Williams, *Marxism and Literature*, 132; Norbert Elias, *The Civilizing Process: Sociogenetic and Psychogenetic Investigations*, trans. Edmund Jephcott, rev. ed. (Oxford: Blackwell, 2000), 58. Norbert Elias introduced the phrase "structure of feelings" in 1939, although it's unclear if Elias's usage was the source that inspired Williams. If it wasn't, then it's an intriguing instance of how the phrase itself may have resulted from exactly what it set out to describe.

56. Ben Anderson, "Affective Atmospheres," *Emotion, Space, and Society* 2, no. 2 (2009): 78; Kathleen Stewart, "Atmospheric Attunements," *Environment and Planning D: Society and Space* 29 (2011): 452; Dora Zhang, "Notes on Atmosphere," *Qui Parle* 27, no. 1 (June 2018): 121. The language of "atmospheres" shares an affinity with the language of "solutions" and "precipitates" Williams sometimes used to explain structures of feeling. See also Michael Orrom and Raymond Williams, *Preface to Film* (London: Film Drama Ltd., 1954), 21–22; and Williams, *Marxism and Literature*, 133–34. I'm grateful for Greg Seigworth for directing me to this work.

57. Williams, *Politics and Letters*, 159.

58. Williams, *Keywords* (1983), 175. Williams goes on to discuss how *jargon* developed "a specialized meaning [in English] close to *cipher* and the later (C19) *code*," thus linking it, albeit unwittingly, to the algorithmic inflection of *key-word*.

59. Williams, *Keywords* (1983), 22.

60. Gilles Deleuze, *Proust and Signs: The Complete Text*, trans. Richard Howard (Minneapolis: University of Minnesota Press, 2004), 29 (emphasis in original); on the "worldly," see 5–7 and passim.

61. On implication, explication, and complication, see Deleuze, *Proust and Signs*, 45, and passim. See also Gilles Deleuze, *The Fold: Leibniz and the Baroque*, trans. Tom Conley (Minneapolis: University of Minnesota Press, 1992).

62. Williams, *Keywords* (1983), 15.

63. Kothari et al., *Pluriverse*.

64. Félix Guattari, *The Three Ecologies*, trans. Ian Pindar and Paul Sutton (London; New Brunswick, NJ: Althone Press, 2000), 44–46.

65. Williams, *Keywords* (1983), 27.

66. Michel Foucault, "Questions of Method," in *The Foucault Effect: Studies in Governmentality*, ed. Graham Burchell, Colin Gordon, and Peter Miller (Chicago: University of Chicago Press, 1991), 82.

67. MacCabe, "Foreword," xv.

68. Williams, *Keywords* (1983), 20.

69. Williams, *Keywords* (1983), 20.

70. Williams, *Politics and Letters*, 164; Williams, *Marxism and Literature*, 133–34.

71. "A Noun Is a Person, Place, or Thing," *Schoolhouse Rock!* (American Broadcasting Company, 1973), https://www.youtube.com/watch?v=hom89e9oZko; "Verb: That's What's Happening," *Schoolhouse Rock!* (American Broadcasting Company, 1974), https://www.youtube.com/watch?v=5EicxQxzsW4; "Conjunction Junction," *Schoolhouse Rock!* (American Broadcasting Company, 1973), https://www.youtube.com/watch?v=rHcNOIZJ2Js.

72. Flusser, *On Doubt*, 52. See also Michel Foucault, *The Order of Things: An Archaeology of the Human Sciences* (New York: Vintage Books, 1970).

73. See Robert Harriman and John Louis Lucaites, *No Caption Needed: Iconic Photographs, Public Culture, and Liberal Democracy* (Chicago: University of Chicago Press, 2011). There are intriguing, if indirect, resonances between Williams's work on keywords and Harriman and Lucaites's conceptualization of iconic photographs.

74. Miriam Joseph, *The Trivium: The Liberal Arts of Logic, Grammar, and Rhetoric*, ed. Marguerite McGlinn (Philadelphia: Paul Dry Books, 2002).

75. Williams, *Keywords* (1983), 16.

76. Meaghan Morris, *Identity Anecdotes: Translation and Media Culture* (London: Sage Publications, 2006), 210.

77. Helen Rosner, "The Meaning of California's Bill Against Nonconsensual Condom Removal," *New Yorker*, September 16, 2021, https://www.newyorker.com/news/q-and-a/the-meaning-of-californias-anti-stealthing-bill.

78. Williams, *Politics and Letters*, 182 (emphasis in original).

79. Antonio Gramsci, *Selections from the Prison Notebooks*, repr. ed., ed. Quintin Hoare and Geoffrey Nowell Smith (New York: International Publishers, 1971), 276.

80. Zygmunt Bauman, "Times of Interregnum," *Ethics & Global Politics* 5, no. 1 (February 27, 2012), accessed February 18, 2016, https://doi.org/10.3402/egp.v5i1.17200.

81. Paul Gilroy, *There Ain't No Black in the Union Jack: The Cultural Politics of Race and Nation* (Chicago: University of Chicago Press, 1991), 53.

82. On the origins of the name "Wales," see William Cran, "The Mother Tongue," *The Story of English* (PBS, 1986), https://www.youtube.com/watch?v=p3q95Mg2i7c. On Williams's complex and shifting relationship to Wales, see Raymond Williams, *Who Speaks for Wales? Nation, Culture, Identity*, centenary ed., ed. Daniel G. Williams (Cardiff: University of Wales Press, 2021).

83. Friedrich A. Kittler, *Discourse Networks, 1800/1900*, trans. Michael Metteer and Chris Cullens (Stanford, CA: Stanford University Press, 1990), 369.

84. The historical timeframe of *Culture and Society, 1790–1950* is bookended by the arrival of mass literacy, on the one side, and by the start of the computer revolution, on the other. This is where the project of keywords essentially operates, give or take a few decades on either end.

85. Anderson, "Affective Atmospheres," 79.

86. Deborah Cameron, "Dreaming the Dictionary: Keywords and Corpus Linguistics," *Key Words: A Journal of Cultural Materialism*, no. 1 (1998): 44; Highmore, "*Keywords* and Keywording," 13–14.

2. ALGORITHM

1. Virginia Eubanks, *Automating Inequality: How High-Tech Tools Profile, Police, and Punish the Poor* (New York: Picador, 2018), 183. Eubanks goes on to note important differences in these systems, observing, for

instance, how the poorhouse system worked in conjunction with the surpluses and deficits of industrial laborers.

2. Eubanks, *Automating Inequality*, 37.

3. Eubanks, *Automating Inequality*, 3, 5.

4. Raymond Williams, *Keywords: A Vocabulary of Culture and Society*, rev. ed. (New York: Oxford University Press, 1983), 131.

5. David Fincher, *The Social Network* (Columbia Pictures, 2010).

6. Eubanks, *Automating Inequality*, 181.

7. Williams, *Keywords*; Wilhelm Dilthey, *Selected Works Volume I: Introduction to the Human Sciences*, ed. Rudolf A. Makkreel and Frithjof Rodi (Princeton, NJ: Princeton University Press, 1989), 439.

8. Williams, *Keywords*, 117, 119.

9. Michel de Certeau, *The Practice of Everyday Life*, trans. Steven Rendall (Berkeley: University of California Press, 1984), v.

10. James Gleick, *The Information: A History, a Theory, a Flood* (New York: Pantheon Books, 2011), 51–77; Elizabeth L. Eisenstein, *The Printing Revolution in Early Modern Europe* (Cambridge: Cambridge University Press, 1983), 78–91; Walter J. Ong, *Orality and Literacy: The Technologizing of the Word* (London: Routledge, 1982), 38, 78–116.

11. Joseph Mazur, *Enlightening Symbols: A Short History of Mathematical Notation and Its Hidden Powers* (Princeton, NJ: Princeton University Press, 2014), 167–68; Friedrich Kittler, "Number and Numeral," *Theory, Culture & Society* 23, nos. 7–8 (December 1, 2006): 53, https://doi.org/10.1177/0263276406069882. See also Jeff Scheible, *Digital Shift: The Cultural Logic of Punctuation* (Minneapolis and London: University of Minnesota Press, 2015).

12. Martin Heidegger, "Modern Science, Metaphysics, and Mathematics," in *Basic Writings*, 2nd ed. (New York: HarperCollins, 1993), 273–74; "Mathematic, N. and Adj.," *OED Online* (Oxford University Press), accessed April 6, 2018, http://www.oed.com.colorado.idm.oclc.org/view/Entry/114965; Douglas Harper, "Mathematic (N.)," *Online Etymology Dictionary*, accessed April 6, 2018, https://www.etymonline.com/word/mathematic; Douglas Harper, "*mendh-," *Online Etymology Dictionary*, accessed April 6, 2018, https://www.etymonline.com/word/*mendh-.

13. Helen Verran, *Science and an African Logic* (Chicago: University of Chicago Press, 2001), 18.

14. Jens Høyrup, "Sub-Scientific Mathematics: Observations on a Pre-Modern Phenomenon," *History of Science* 28, no. 1 (March 1990): 64, https://doi.org/10.1177/007327539002800102 (emphasis removed from the original).

15. Høyrup, "Sub-Scientific Mathematics," 75.

16. Jens Høyrup, "Practitioners—School Teachers—'Mathematicians': The Divisions of Pre-Modern Mathematics and Its Actors" (Writing and Rewriting the History of Science, 1900–2000, Les Treilles, France, 2003), 1–3, http://akira.ruc.dk/~jensh/Publications/2003%7BK%7D04_LesTreilles.PDF.

17. Høyrup, "Sub-Scientific Mathematics," 75.

18. Mazur, *Enlightening Symbols*, x, 56, 167–68. On the relationship between print media and mathematical notation, see also: Vilém Flusser, *Does Writing Have a Future?*, trans. Nancy Ann Roth (Minneapolis: University of Minnesota Press, 2011), 23–35; and Robin Rider, "Shaping Information: Mathematics, Computing, and Typography," in *Inscribing Science: Scientific Texts and the Materiality of Communication*, ed. Timothy Lenoir (Stanford, CA: Stanford University Press, 1998), 39–54.

19. Mazur, *Enlightening Symbols*, 112.

20. Mazur, *Enlightening Symbols*, 129. My calculus teacher Don Lester Lyons, who called himself DL², used to refer to mathematical variables as "stuff." Only now do I understand that he was, inadvertently, channeling the sensibilities of early modern mathematics.

21. Gleick, *Information*, 152. "Entirely because of the telegraph," argues James Gleick, "by the late nineteenth century people grew comfortable, or at least familiar, with the idea of codes." The point I'm raising, though speculative, suggests mathematics may well have prepared the ground far earlier for the acceptance of codes and coding, and possibly for the telegraph.

22. See, e.g., Jens Høyrup, "Al-Khwârizmî, Ibn Turk, and the Liber Mensurationum: On the Origins of Islamic Algebra," *Erdem* 2, no. 5 (May 1986): 445–84; Jens Høyrup, "The Formation of 'Islamic Mathematics': Sources and Conditions," *Science in Context* 1, no. 2

(September 1987), 281–329. https://pdfs.semanticscholar.org/6208/b2a 92303c32d61e49c4c865610f30da8bdof.pdf; and Mazur, *Enlightening Symbols*. See also Philip J. Davis and Reuben Hersh, "Rhetoric and Mathematics," in *The Rhetoric of the Human Sciences: Language and Argument in Scholarship and Public Affairs* (Madison: University of Wisconsin Press, 1987), 53–68; and Mitchell G. Reyes, "The Rhetoric in Mathematics: Newton, Leibniz, the Calculus, and the Rhetorical Force of the Infinitesimal," *Quarterly Journal of Speech* 90, no. 2 (May 2004): 163–88, https://doi.org/10.1080/0033563042000227427. These and other scholars discuss the suasive dimensions of mathematical communication without fully appreciating the broader history of "rhetorical mathematics."

23. Mohammed ibn Musa al-Khwarīzmī, *The Algebra of Mohammed Ben Musa*, trans. Frederic Rosen (London: J. L. Cox, 1831), 6, https:// archive.org/details/algebraofmohammeookhuwuoft.

24. Al-Khwarīzmī, *Algebra of Mohammed Ben Musa*, 6n. The three statements end up looking like this, respectively: $x^2 = 5x$; $x^2/3 = 4x$; and $5x^2 = 10x$.

25. Frederic Rosen, "Preface," in *The Algebra of Mohammed Ben Musa* (London: J. L. Cox, 1831), x, https://archive.org/details/algebraofmohamm eookhuwuoft. On the mnemotechnics of primary oral cultures, see Ong, *Orality and Literacy*, 34–35.

26. Mazur, *Enlightening Symbols*, 109. According to Mazur, the *Brāhmasphuṭasiddhānta* "not only advanced the mathematical role of zero, but also introduced rules for manipulating negative and positive numbers, methods for computing square roots, and systematic methods for solving linear and limited types of quadratic equations." See also Acharyavara Ram Swarup Sharma, ed., *Brahmagupta's Brāhmasphuṭasiddhānta*, vol. I (New Delhi: Indian Institute of Astronomical and Sanskrit Research, 1966), https://archive.org/details /Brahmasphutasiddhanta_Vol_1; Tom Yohe, "My Hero, Zero," *Schoolhouse Rock!* (American Broadcasting Company, 1973), https://www .youtube.com/watch?v=6eh8Ml-ruOo.

27. Sarah Glaz, "Poetry Inspired by Mathematics: A Brief Journey Through History," *Journal of Mathematics and the Arts* 5, no. 4 (December 2011): 171–83, https://doi.org/10.1080/17513472.2011.599019. See also Louis C. Karpinski and E. G. R. Waters, "A Thirteenth Century

Algorism in French Verse," *Isis* 11, no. 1 (September 1928): 45–84. Though uncommon, mathematical verse existed in Europe during the Middle Ages.

28. A compilation of mathematical learning rhymes can be found here: Florida Center for Instructional Technology, "Counting and Math Rhymes," *Lit2Go*, 2012, http://etc.usf.edu/lit2go/66/counting-and -math-rhymes/. A quotation from John Durham Peters also seems apropos: "Those who say that the mathematical or technical miss all that is most soulful miss the point: we are most human in our relations to the sky and to time." John Durham Peters, *The Marvelous Clouds: Toward a Philosophy of Elemental Media* (Chicago: University of Chicago Press, 2015), 178. For a discussion of the "sounds of the body" as they relate to "counting jingles," see Certeau, *Practice of Everyday Life*, 162–63.

29. On recreational mathematics and mathematical riddles, see Jens Høyrup, "What Is Mathematics? Perspectives Inspired by Anthropology" (Emergent Mathematics Workshop, Durham University, Stockton on Tees, UK, 2015), 4, https://rucforsk.ruc.dk/ws/portalfiles /portal/59976727; and Høyrup, "Sub-Scientific Mathematics," 66–67, 74. On "lived ideas," see Régis Debray, *Transmitting Culture*, trans. Eric Rauth (New York: Columbia University Press, 2000), 2.

30. Raymond Williams, "Culture Is Ordinary," in *Resources of Hope: Culture, Democracy, Socialism* (London: Verso, 1989), 3–18.

31. Marcia Ascher and Robert Ascher, "Ethnomathematics," *History of Science* 24, no. 2 (June 1986): 131–32, https://doi.org/10.1177/00732753 8602400202.

32. Ascher and Ascher, "Ethnomathematics," 132.

33. Ascher and Ascher, "Ethnomathematics," 135.

34. On the tendency to adopt culturally laden assumptions to "explain away" relevant anthropological data, particularly where mathematical concepts, figures, and modes of reasoning are concerned, see Verran, *Science and an African Logic*, 23 and passim.

35. Stuart Hall, "The West and the Rest: Discourse and Power," in *Modernity: An Introduction to Modern Societies*, ed. Stuart Hall et al. (Malden, MA: Blackwell, 1996), 184–227; see also Nick Seaver, "Algorithms as Culture: Some Tactics for the Ethnography of Algorithmic

Systems," *Big Data & Society* 4, no. 2 (December 2017): 1–12, https://doi.org/10.1177/2053951717738104.

The tendency to subsume mathematics under the rubric of culture has a long history, dating back at least to the early days of anthropology. Edward Burnett Tylor, one of the more vexing characters in the discipline's pantheon of founding figures, devoted an entire chapter of *Primitive Culture* (1871) to "The Art of Counting." In characteristic style, he detailed a series of words, gestures, and techniques "savage or barbaric peoples" used to quantify the world around them. The endeavor, added Tylor, was more "etymological" than descriptive—an effort to glimpse the elementary forms of "higher" mathematics in the "childish" practices of the "lower races." Moreover, Wilhelm von Humboldt, architect of the modern German research university and an early evangelist for culture, studied the metaphorics of numeration present within the ancient Kawi language of Indonesia (the word *lima* denoting both "five" and "hand," for instance). The endeavor was part of a larger effort to understand both the origins of language and the emergence of distinct cultural worldviews. Edward Burnett Tylor, *Primitive Culture: Researches into the Development of Mythology, Philosophy, Religion, Language, Art, and Custom*, 2nd ed., vol. I, 2 vols. (Mineola, NY: Dover Publications, 2016), 241, 253, 271–72; Wilhelm von Humboldt, *Humboldt on Language: On the Diversity of Human Language Construction and Its Influence on the Mental Development of the Human Species*, 2nd ed., ed. Michael Losonsky, trans. Peter Heath (New York: Cambridge University Press, 2000), 286–87. On Humboldt's relationship to *culture*, see Bill Readings, *The University in Ruins* (Cambridge, MA: Harvard University Press, 1996), 69.

36. Eubanks, *Automating Inequality*, 5.
37. On the prevalence of algorithms in popular culture, see Ted Striphas, "Algorithms," in *Information: A Historical Companion*, ed. Ann Blair et al. (Princeton, NJ: Princeton University Press, 2021), 298.
38. Ed Finn, *What Algorithms Want: Imagination in the Age of Computing* (Cambridge, MA: MIT Press, 2017), 185.
39. C. Wright Mills, *The Sociological Imagination* (New York: Oxford University Press, 1959), 5–8.
40. Taina Bucher, *If . . . Then: Algorithmic Power and Politics* (New York: Oxford University Press, 2018), 114. See also Taina Bucher, "The

Algorithmic Imaginary: Exploring the Affects of Facebook Algorithms," *Information, Communication & Society* 20, no. 1 (2017): 30–44, https://doi.org/10.1080/1369118X.2016.1154086.

41. Ted Striphas, "Algorithmic Culture," *European Journal of Cultural Studies* 18, nos. 4–5 (August 2015): 395–412, https://doi.org/10.1177/1367549415577392. The research for this publication began in 2010.

42. See, e.g., Christopher Steiner, *Automate This: How Algorithms Took Over Our Markets, Our Jobs, and the World* (New York: Portfolio/Penguin, 2012), 54–55; Finn, *What Algorithms Want*, 17; and Tarleton Gillespie, "Algorithm," in *Digital Keywords: A Vocabulary of Information Society and Culture*, ed. Benjamin Peters (Princeton, NJ: Princeton University Press, 2016), 18–19. See also Jean-Luc Chabert, ed., *A History of Algorithms: From the Pebble to the Microchip*, trans. Chris Weeks (Berlin: Springer, 1999), 1–2. Chabert dives more deeply, if briefly, into the figure of al-Khwārizmī.

43. Gillespie, "Algorithm," 19.

44. See Striphas, "Algorithmic Culture," 403–4. I, too, count among the guilty parties here, although I continue to stand by the broader argument.

45. On "fixity," see Eisenstein, *Printing Revolution*, 113–26; see also Ong, *Orality and Literacy*, 78–116; Gleick, *Information*, 51–77; and Adrian Johns, *The Nature of the Book: Print and Knowledge in the Making* (Chicago: University of Chicago Press, 2000), 10–11 and passim. Note that Johns contests the narrative of print's tendency to fix knowledge, information, definitions, etc.

46. George A. Saliba, "The Meaning of Al-Jabr Wa'l-Muqābalah," *Centaurus* 17, no. 3 (September 1973): 190.

47. Asuman Güven Aksoy, "Al-Khwarizmı and the Hermeneutic Circle: Reflections on a Trip to Samarkand," *Journal of Humanistic Mathematics* 6, no. 2 (July 2016): 124, https://doi.org/10.5642/jhummath.201602 .09; Jeffrey A. Oaks and Haitham M. Alkhateeb, "Simplifying Equations in Arabic Algebra," *Historia Mathematica* 34, no. 1 (2007): 58. The difference in spelling—*muqābalah* vs. *muqābala*—reflects different frameworks for transliterating Arabic into English.

48. Wendy Hui Kyong Chun, "Race and/as Technology or How to Do Things to Race," in *Race After the Internet*, ed. Lisa Nakamura and Peter A. Chow-White (New York: Routledge, 2012), 49.

49. Finn, *What Algorithms Want*, 17.

50. Steiner, *Automate This*, 54–55.

51. Høyrup, "Practitioners—School Teachers—'Mathematicians,'" 4; Bruno Latour, *Reassembling the Social: An Introduction to Actor-Network Theory* (Oxford: Oxford University Press, 2005), 95.

52. Stuart Hall, "Race, Culture, and Communications: Looking Backward and Forward at Cultural Studies," *Rethinking Marxism* 5, no. 1 (Spring 1992): 15, https://doi.org/10.1080/08935699208657998.

53. See Oaks and Alkhateeb, "Simplifying Equations," 53. Apropos, Moḥammed ibn-Mūsā al-Khwārizmī isn't the only historical figure bearing the surname, "al-Khwārizmī." It also belongs to Muḥammad ibn-Aḥmad al-Khwārizmī, a lexicographer who lived during the tenth century CE/the fourth century AH.

54. D. N. MacKenzie, "Khwarazmian Language and Literature," in *The Cambridge History of Iran: The Seleucid, Parthian, and Sasanid Periods*, ed. E. Yarshater, vol. 3, 7 vols. (Cambridge: Cambridge University Press, 1983), 1244; "Chorasmia," in *Encyclopædia Iranica*, online ed., 2011, https://www.iranicaonline.org/articles/chorasmia-index; Heinz Zemanek, "Al-Khorezmi: His Background, His Personality, His Work, and His Influence," in *Algorithms in Modern Mathematics and Computer Science (Proceedings, Urgench, Uzbek SSR, September 16–22, 1979)*, ed. A. P. Ershov and Donald E. Knuth, Springer Lecture Notes in Computer Science (Berlin: Springer, 1981), 32.

55. W. Barthold, "Khwārizm," in *Encyclopaedia of Islam (1913–1936)*, ed. M. Th. Houtsma et al., 1st ed. (Brill Online), accessed April 19, 2019, https://referenceworks.brillonline.com/browse/encyclopaedia-of -islam-1/alpha/c.

56. Corona Brezina, *Al-Khwarizmi: The Inventor of Algebra* (New York: Rosen Publishing Group, 2006), 32.

57. Brezina, *Al-Khwarizmi*, 41.

58. D. N. MacKenzie, "Chorasmia iii.: The Chorasmian Language," in *Encyclopædia Iranica*, online ed., 2011, https://www.iranicaonline.org /articles/chorasmia-iii; V. A. Livshits, "The Khwarezmian Calendar and the Eras of Ancient Chorasmia," *Acta Antiqua Academiae Scientiarum Hungaricae* 16 (1968): 435. There is a significant discrepancy in the dating across these two sources. The latter dates the introduction

of Khwarezmian script to the second century BCE, while the former says the second century CE. Livshits appears to be more aware of the subtleties of the archaeological evidence, for whatever it's worth. A note of caution from Certeau is worth adding here: "It is . . . useless to set off in quest of this voice that has been simultaneously colonized and mythified by recent Western history. There is . . . no 'pure' voice." Certeau, *Practice of Everyday Life*, 132.

59. Michel de Certeau, *The Writing of History*, trans. Tom Conley (New York: Columbia University Press, 1988), 216. "The power that writing's expansionism leaves intact is colonial in principle." See also Siraj Ahmed, *Archaeology of Babel: The Colonial Foundation of the Humanities* (Stanford, CA: Stanford University Press, 2018), passim; Certeau, *Practice of Everyday Life*, 131–53.

60. C. E. Bosworth, "Āl-e Afrīg," in *Encyclopædia Iranica*, online ed., 2011, https://www.iranicaonline.org/articles/al-e-afrig.

61. Yuri Aleksandrovich Rapoport, "Chorasmia i.: Archaeology and Pre-Islamic History," in *Encyclopædia Iranica*, online ed., 2011, https://www.iranicaonline.org/articles/chorasmia-index.

62. Peters, *Marvelous Clouds*, 177. "Calendars and clocks negotiate between the heavens and the state, orient us to time and eternity, and thus fulfill . . . the classical function of providing a meaningful orientation to the universe."

63. MacKenzie, "Chorasmia iii." Note the following, however, from MacKenzie, "Khwarazmian Language and Literature," 1245: "As in all Iranian languages using the Aramaic script, ideograms . . . still conceal a number of indigenous words, and even those spelt 'phonetically' may in fact enshrine an earlier pronunciation, though there is no contemporary evidence to prove this."

64. C. E. Bosworth, "Āl-e Afrīg," in *Encyclopædia Iranica*, online ed., 2011, https://www.iranicaonline.org/articles/al-e-afrig; C. E. Bosworth, "Chorasmia ii.: In Islamic Times," in *Encyclopædia Iranica*, online ed., 2011, https://www.iranicaonline.org/articles/chorasmia-ii; Georges Ifrah, *The Universal History of Numbers: From Prehistory to the Invention of the Computer*, trans. David Bellos et al. (New York: John Wiley & Sons, 2000), 513.

65. Ifrah, *Universal History of Numbers*, 513.

66. Quoted in Ifrah, *Universal History of Numbers*, 513. But also see C. E. Bosworth, "Āl-e Afrīg." Bosworth questions Al-Bīrunī's allegations, calling them an "exaggeration." Similarly, see Zemanek, "Al-Khorezmi," 6. Zemanek states: "Later reports about the killing of all priests and scientists and the burning of all books by the Arab conquerors are probably a fiction—the old habits and books simply lost their meaning and use in the Arab culture and disappeared gradually, but not completely." Perhaps—but that does little to explain the near-total disappearance of the Khwārazmian language and calendar, much less the conversion of both the leadership and broad swaths of the Khwārazmian population to Islam. Al-Bīrunī himself, along with other intellectuals, was forced to relocate to the city of Ghazna (located in present-day Afghanistan), having been pressed into the service of the Ghaznavid Emperor Mahmud, for whom he was considered a spoil of war. It's unclear whether the relationship was one of patronage or bondage—or both. E. S. Kennedy, "The Exact Sciences," in *The Cambridge History of Iran*, ed. R. N. Frye (Cambridge: Cambridge University Press, 1975), 394.

67. Zemanek, "Al-Khorezmi," 35. The claim that he was born in Qutrub-bull seems to be dubious, appearing in only one account of al-Khwārizmī's life. The area was, however, "inhabited by the Khorezmi-ans, famous for its restaurants and cellars (where people certainly, in spite of the Prophet's rules, drank wine), famous for its music and singing, a district preferred by artists and poets."

68. Gerald J. Toomer, "Al-Khwārizmī, Abu Ja'far Muḥammad Ibn Mūsā," in *Complete Dictionary of Scientific Biography*, vol. 7 (New York: Charles Scribner's Sons, 2008), 358; Ifrah, *Universal History of Numbers*, 531.

69. Toomer, "Al-Khwārizmī," 358; Brezina, *Al-Khwarizmi*, 21, 40, 43; John N. Crossley and Alan S. Henry, "Thus Spake Al-Khwārizmī: A Translation of the Text of Cambridge University Library Ms. Ii.vi.5," *Historia Mathematica* 17, no. 2 (May 1990): 104, https://doi.org/10.1016/0315-0860(90)90048-I.

70. Zemanek, "Al-Khorezmi," 34. Zemanek notes this detail in connection with Al-Khwārizmī's having written a treatise on the Jewish calendar.

71. Ong, *Orality and Literacy*, 98.

72. Edward W. Said, *Orientalism* (New York: Vintage, 1979).

73. E. P. Thompson, *Customs in Common: Studies in Traditional Popular Culture* (New York: The New Press, 1993), 354; Peters, *Marvelous Clouds*, 189; Stephen Nissenbaum, *The Battle for Christmas* (New York: Vintage, 1996), 13 (emphasis in original).

74. Zemanek, "Al-Khorezmi," 34. "He was known as a Khorezmian and it was the tolerance of the Baghdad court which permitted him to identify himself during his lifetime with the conquered country."

75. Ahmed, *Archaeology of Babel*, 41, 44. I'm paraphrasing Ahmed's own words very closely here.

76. Crossley and Henry, "Thus Spake Al-Khwārizmī," 110–11; L. C. Karpinski, "Augrim-Stones," *Modern Language Notes* 27, no. 7 (November 1912): 207.

77. "History of Paper," *Wikipedia*, accessed June 7, 2019, https://en.wikipedia.org/wiki/History_of_paper.

78. Brezina, *Al-Khwarizmi*, 27; Salim Quraishi, "A Survey of the Development of Papermaking in Islamic Countries," *Bookbinder—Journal of the Society of Bookbinders and Book Restorers* 3 (1989): 29–36.

79. Hala Khalidi and Basma Ahmad Sedki Dajani, "Facets from the Translation Movement in Classic Arab Culture," *Procedia—Social and Behavioral Sciences* 205 (October 2015): 571, https://doi.org/10.1016/j.sbspro.2015.09.080. See also Harold A. Innis and Mary Q. Innis, *Empire and Communications*, rev. ed. (Toronto: University of Toronto Press, 1972), 126–27; Aksoy, "Al-Khwārizmī and the Hermeneutic Circle," 118; Brezina, *Al-Khwarizmi*, 21; Crossley and Henry, "Thus Spake Al-Khwārizmī," 104. See also Peter E. Pormann and Emilie Savage-Smith, *Medieval Islamic Medicine* (Edinburgh, Scotland: Edinburgh University Press, 2007), 29. Pormann and Savage-Smith dispute the existence of the House of Wisdom, describing it more as a library than a scholarly institution per se.

On the reasons for listing Mary Q. Innis as co-author of *Empire and Communications*, see Donica Belisle and Kiera Mitchell, "Mary Quayle Innis: Faculty Wives' Contributions and the Making of Academic Celebrity," *Canadian Historical Review* 99, no. 3 (2018): 456–86, https://doi.org/10.3138/chr.2017-0108https://doi.org/10.3138/chr.2017-0108.

80. Crossley and Henry, "Thus Spake Al-Khwārizmī," 107.

81. On the binding together of multiple manuscripts, see Elizabeth Eisenstein, *The Printing Press as an Agent of Change: Communications and Cultural Transformations in Early-Modern Europe* (Cambridge: Cambridge University Press, 1979), 45; and Ted Striphas, *The Late Age of Print: Everyday Book Culture from Consumerism to Control* (New York: Columbia University Press, 2009), 11. On the status of the manuscript on numeration, see Crossley and Henry, "Thus Spake Al-Khwārizmī," 106.

82. A. P. Ershov and Donald E. Knuth, eds., *Algorithms in Modern Mathematics and Computer Science (Proceedings, Urgench, Uzbek SSR, September 16–22, 1979)*, Springer Lecture Notes in Computer Science (Berlin: Springer, 1981), 32, quoted in Crossley and Henry, "Thus Spake Al-Khwārizmī," 106; see also 107.

83. Jeffrey A. Oaks and Haitham M. Alkhateeb, "*Māl*, Enunciations, and the Prehistory of Arabic Algebra," *Historia Mathematica* 32, no. 4 (November 2005), 404.

84. Rosen, "Preface," xiii–xiv.

85. Zemanek, "Al-Khorezmi," 30.

86. Oaks and Alkhateeb, "Prehistory of Arabic Algebra," 404.

87. Barnabas Hughes, "The Medieval Latin Translations of Al-Khwarizmi's Al-Jabr," *Manuscripta* 26, no. 1 (1982): 31.

88. Guillaume de Lorris and Jean de Meung, *Le Roman de La Rose*, trans. Pierre Marteau, vol. IV, 4 vols. (Orléans, France, 1879), 35–36, http://www.gutenberg.org/files/44713/44713-h/44713-h.htm; English-language translation: Guillaume de Lorris and Jean de Meun, *The Romance of the Rose*, trans. Charles Dahlberg, 3rd ed. (Princeton, NJ: Princeton University Press, 1995), 273–74.

89. Geoffrey Chaucer, "The Book of the Duchess," ed. Librarius, n.d., http://www.librarius.com/duchessfs.htm; Geoffrey Chaucer, *The Book of the Duchess*, trans. A. S. Kline, 2007, https://www.poetryintranslation.com/PITBR/English/Duchess.php.

90. Geoffrey Chaucer, "The Miller's Prologue and Tale—an Interlineal Translation," https://chaucer.fas.harvard.edu/pages/millers-prologue-and-tale, translation slightly modified. I am indebted to the following piece for alerting me to the existence of the relevant passages in *Le Roman de la Rose* and *The Canterbury Tales*: Karpinski, "Augrim-Stones."

91. For a critique of the Proto-Indo-European hypothesis, see Ahmed, *Archaeology of Babel.*

92. Stanley Lane-Poole and J. B. Katz, "Rosen, Friedrich August (1805–1837)," in *Oxford Dictionary of National Biography* (Oxford: Oxford University Press, 2004), https://doi.org/10.1093/ref:odnb/24104.

93. Rosane Rocher and Ludo Rocher, *The Making of Western Indology: Henry Thomas Colebrooke and the East India Company* (London: Routledge, 2012), 14.

94. Rocher and Rocher, *Making of Western Indology*, 96–98.

95. Rocher and Rocher, *Making of Western Indology*, 97.

96. I use the word "concubine" here and later in this chapter with some trepidation, as it's difficult to assess the status of the women to whom this label is often applied in the historical record, or the nature of their relationship to the men in question. Other names I've considered are "mistress," "sex-slave," and "enslaved sex-worker." The reader should bear this ambiguity in mind.

97. Rocher and Rocher, *Making of Western Indology*, 118–20.

98. Ahmed, *Archaeology of Babel*, 2, 107. On the continuation of Jones's work, see "Notices of the Life of Henry Thomas Colebrooke, Esq., by His Son," *Journal of the Royal Asiatic Society of Great Britain and Ireland* 5, no. 1 (1839): 22–23. See also Rocher and Rocher, *Making of Western Indology*, 113–14.

99. Stanley Lane-Poole, "Colebrooke, Henry Thomas (1765–1837)," in *Dictionary of National Biography*, ed. Leslie Stephen, vol. 11 (Clater-Condell), 63 vols. (London: Smith Elder & Co., 1887), 283.

100. Brahmegupta and Bháscara, *Algebra, With Arithmetic and Mensuration, from the Sanscrit*, trans. Henry Thomas Colebrooke (London: John Murray, 1817).

101. Lane-Poole, "Colebrooke, Henry Thomas," 283; R. Chakrabarty, "The Asiatic Society, 1784–2008: An Overview," in *Time Past and Time Present: Two Hundred and Twenty-Five Years of the Asiatic Society* (Kolkata, India: Asiatic Society, 2008), 2–24.

102. "Appendix, No. II: Oriental Translation Fund," *Transactions of the Royal Asiatic Society of Great Britain and Ireland* 2, no. 1 (1829): xxiv; on the founding of the Royal Asiatic Society, see also Said, *Orientalism*, 79.

103. For extended treatments of this theme, see Said, *Orientalism*; Johannes Fabian, *Time and the Other: How Anthropology Makes Its Object* (New

York: Columbia University Press, 1983); Gauri Viswanathan, *Masks of Conquest: Literary Study and British Rule in India*, 25th anniversary ed. (New York: Columbia University Press, 2014); Dipesh Chakrabarty, *Provincializing Europe: Postcolonial Thought and Historical Difference*, new ed. (Princeton, NJ: Princeton University Press, 2007); and *Ahmed*, Archaeology of Babel.

104. "Appendix, No. II," xxiv.

105. Lane-Poole and Katz, "Rosen, Friedrich August"; Rosen, "Preface," xv. Rosen indicates he came to the manuscript through an unnamed intermediary.

106. Henry Thomas Colebrooke, "Dissertation," in *Algebra, With Arithmetic and Mensuration, from the Sanscrit*, trans. Henry Thomas Colebrooke (London: John Murray, 1817), lxiv–lxxx, specifically lxxv–lxxix.

107. Colebrooke, "Dissertation," lxxiii.

108. Further to this point, see Peters, *Marvelous Clouds*.

109. Colebrooke, "Dissertation," lxxiv, lxxix. See also Rocher and Rocher, *Making of Western Indology*, 21.

110. Rosen, "Preface," xv–xvi.

111. Al-Khwarīzmī, *Algebra of Mohammed Ben Musa*, 3; Colebrooke, "Dissertation," lxxiv.

112. Rosen, "Preface," xviii; Colebrooke, "Dissertation," lxxiv.

113. Rosen, "Preface," x–xi.

114. Colebrooke, "Dissertation," vii.

115. Oaks and Alkhateeb, "Simplifying Equations," 55n74; Høyrup, "Al-Khwârizmî, Ibn Turk," 471 (emphasis in original).

116. Høyrup, "Al-Khwârizmi, Ibn Turk," 471 (emphasis in original).

117. Roland Barthes, "The Death of the Author," in *Image-Music-Text*, trans. Stephen Heath (New York: Hill and Wang, 1977), 146.

118. Eubanks, *Automating Inequality*, 181.

119. Al-Khwarīzmī, *Algebra of Mohammed Ben Musa*, 86.

120. Al-Khwarīzmī, *Algebra of Mohammed Ben Musa*, 125–26.

121. Al-Khwarīzmī, *Algebra of Mohammed Ben Musa*, 133–40.

122. Al-Khwarīzmī, *Algebra of Mohammed Ben Musa*, 140. Here, I have chosen to preserve the language of "slave" rather than the preferred form, "enslaved person," given the appearance of the former term in the quoted passage.

123. Colebrooke, "Dissertation," lxxv–lxxix.

124. Rosen, "Preface," v–xvi.

125. Armond Towns, *On Black Media Philosophy* (Berkeley: University of California Press, 2022).

126. On enslavement in the plural, see Abdul Sheriff, "The Zanj Rebellion and the Transition from Plantation to Military Slavery," *Comparative Studies of South Asia, Africa and the Middle East* 38, no. 2 (2018): 246, https://doi.org/10.1215/1089201x-6982029.

127. Sheriff, "Zanj Rebellion," 251.

128. R. Brunschvig, "ʿAbd," in *Encyclopædia of Islam*, ed. P. Bearman et al. (Leiden: Brill, 2007 1960), http://dx.doi.org/10.1163/1573-3912_islam_COM_0003.

129. Sheriff, "Zanj Rebellion," 251.

130. Brunschvig, "ʿAbd"; Sheriff, "Zanj Rebellion," 248.

131. Patricia Hill Collins, *Fighting Words: Black Women and the Search for Justice* (Minneapolis: University of Minnesota Press, 1998), 21; Simone Browne, *Dark Matters: On the Surveillance of Blackness* (Durham, NC: Duke University Press, 2015), 57; Alice Childress and Roxane Gay, *Like One of the Family: Conversations from a Domestic's Life*, repr. ed. (Boston: Beacon Press, 2017); Ena Jansen, *Like Family: Domestic Workers in South African History and Literature* (Johannesburg: Wits University Press, 2019).

132. Al-Khwārizmī, *Algebra of Mohammed Ben Musa*, 150–51.

133. Al-Khwārizmī, *Algebra of Mohammed Ben Musa*, 133n.

134. E. P. Thompson, "The Long Revolution (Review, Parts I & II)," *New Left Review*, nos. 9–10 (August 1961): 33.

135. Verran, *African Logic*, 15–18.

136. Patricia Cline Cohen, *A Calculating People: The Spread of Numeracy in Early America* (New York: Routledge, 1999), 19. I am grateful to Nathan Ensmenger for first pointing out to me, in 2013, that numbers and number systems are a technology.

137. Sara Ahmed, *Queer Phenomenology: Orientations, Objects, Others* (Durham, NC: Duke University Press, 2006), 112–20.

138. Seaver, "Algorithms as Culture," 5.

139. Certeau, *Practice of Everyday Life*, 163.

140. Bernard Dionysius Geoghegan, "Orientalism and Informatics: Alterity from the Chess-Playing Turk to Amazon's Mechanical Turk," *Ex-Position*, no. 43 (June 2020): 45–90.

141. Joel Dias-Porter, "The Al Khwarizmi in You," *Black Renaissance/Renaissance Noire* 16, no. 1 (Winter/Spring 2016): 108.

3. CULTURE

1. "Judeo-Boasian Anthropology Is Subversive and Psychological Racial Warfare," *Smash Cultural Marxism*, April 1, 2015, https://smashcult uralmarxism.wordpress.com/2015/04/01/boasian-anthropology-is-sub versive-and-psychological-racial-warfare/.

2. See, e.g., Patrick Langridge, "The 11 Most Infamous Google Bombs in History," *The Screaming Frog*, October 18, 2012, https://www .screamingfrog.co.uk/google-bombs/.

3. Amar Toor, "White Nationalists Seem to Have Manipulated Google Search Results for 'Boasian Anthropology,'" *The Verge*, February 27, 2017, http://www.theverge.com/2017/2/27/14748690/google-white-natio nalist-boasian-anthropology-search-result.

4. Francis Mulhern, *Culture/Metaculture* (London: Routledge, 2000), xiv.

5. "Media determine our situation." Friedrich A. Kittler, *Gramophone, Film, Typewriter*, trans. Geoffrey Winthrop-Young and Michael Wutz (Stanford, CA: Stanford University Press, 1999), xxxiv.

6. Raymond Williams, *The Long Revolution* (Orchard Park, NY: Broadview Press, 2001), 177–94.

7. Kittler, *Gramophone, Film, Typewriter*, 210 and passim. Friedrich A. Kittler, *Discourse Networks, 1800/1900*, trans. Michael Metteer and Chris Cullens (Stanford, CA: Stanford University Press, 1990), 192–205.

8. Kittler, *Gramophone, Film, Typewriter*, 229; Raymond Williams, *Culture and Society, 1780–1950* (New York: Columbia University Press, 1983), 227–43.

9. On the philosophy of everyday life, see, among other notable works: Henri Lefebvre, *Critique of Everyday Life: Introduction*, trans. John Moore, vol. 1, 3 vols. (London: Verso, 1991); Henri Lefebvre, *Critique of Everyday Life: Foundations for a Sociology of the Everyday*, vol. 2, trans. John Moore (London: Verso, 2002); Henri Lefebvre, *Critique of Everyday Life: From Modernity to Modernism (Towards a Metaphilosophy of Daily Life)*, vol. 3, trans. Gregory Elliott (London: Verso, 2005); Henri Lefebvre, *Everyday Life in the Modern World*, ed. Philip Wander, trans. Sacha Rabinovitch (New Brunswick, NJ: Transaction Publishers, 1984); Michel de Certeau, *The Practice of Everyday Life*, trans. Steven

Rendall (Berkeley: University of California Press, 1984); Rita Felski, "The Invention of Everyday Life," in *Doing Time: Feminist Theory and Postmodern Culture* (New York: NYU Press, 2000), 77–98; Michael Gardiner, *Critiques of Everyday Life: An Introduction* (London: Routledge, 2000); and Ben Highmore, ed., *The Everyday Life Reader* (London: Routledge, 2001).

10. Ben Highmore, "*Keywords* and Keywording," *Cultural Studies* (2021), 5, https://doi.org/10.1080/09502386.2021.1947336; Raymond Williams, *Keywords: A Vocabulary of Culture and Society*, rev. ed. (New York: Oxford University Press, 1983), 11–12.

11. Highmore, "*Keywords* and Keywording," 5.

12. Raymond Williams, *Border Country*, repr. ed. (Cardigan, UK: Parthian, 2021), 8.

13. Raymond Williams, "Seeing a Man Running," in *What I Came to Say* (London: Hutchinson Radius, 1989), 22.

14. Raymond Williams, *The Country and the City* (New York: Oxford University Press, 1973), 4.

15. Highmore, "*Keywords* and Keywording," 6.

16. "Anecdote, n.," in *Oxford English Dictionary* (Oxford: Oxford University Press, 2021), https://www.oed.com/view/Entry/7367; see also: "Anecdote, n.," *Merriam-Webster*, accessed August 10, 2021, https://www.merriam-webster.com/dictionary/anecdote; "Anecdote, n.," *Dictionary.com*, accessed August 10, 2021, https://www.dictionary.com/browse/anecdote; and "Anecdote, n.," *Cambridge Dictionary*, accessed August 10, 2021, https://dictionary.cambridge.org/us/dictionary/english/anecdote.

17. Meaghan Morris, *Identity Anecdotes: Translation and Media Culture* (London: Sage, 2006), 8.

18. "Anecdote, n.," *Oxford English Dictionary*, online.

19. Certeau, *Practice of Everyday Life*, 131–53, 158; Michel de Certeau, *The Writing of History*, trans. Tom Conley (New York: Columbia University Press, 1988), 216.

20. On the critique and rehabilitation of anecdotes, see Joel Fineman, "The History of the Anecdote: Fiction and Fiction 1," in *The New Historicism*, ed. Harold Veeser (New York: Routledge, 1989), 49–76; Jane Gallop, *Anecdotal Theory* (Durham, NC: Duke University Press Books, 2002); Meaghan Morris, "Banality in Cultural Studies," in *Logics of*

Television: Essays in Cultural Criticism, ed. Patricia Mellencamp (Bloomington: Indiana University Press, 1990), 14–43; and Morris, *Identity Anecdotes*, esp. 1–28.

21. Kathleen Stewart, "Atmospheric Attunements," *Environment and Planning D: Society and Space* 29, no. 3 (2011): 452.
22. Tony Pinkney, *Raymond Williams* (Bridgend, UK: Seren Books, 1991), 135; see also 14, 32, 52, 55, and 110.
23. "Anecdote, n.," *Oxford English Dictionary*, online.
24. Morris, "Banality in Cultural Studies," 15.
25. Certeau, *Practice of Everyday Life*, 11–12, 23. Certeau's discussion of "the prose of the world" (a phrase he nicks from Maurice Merleau-Ponty) resonates with the idea of atmospheres. Moreover, Certeau's discussion of folktales and legends, as instances of the prose of the world, shares much in common with what I'm saying about anecdotes.
26. Morris, *Identity Anecdotes*, 8.
27. Kittler, *Gramophone, Film, Typewriter*, 221. The passage reads: "The good fortune of media is the negation of their hardware."
28. Raymond Williams, "Culture Is Ordinary," in *Resources of Hope: Culture, Democracy, Socialism* (London: Verso, 1989), 5.
29. Thorstein Veblen, *The Theory of the Leisure Class* (New York: Dover, 1994).
30. Norbert Elias, *The Civilizing Process: Sociogenetic and Psychogenetic Investigations*, trans. Edmund Jephcott, rev. ed. (Oxford: Blackwell, 2000), 11.
31. Elias, *Civilizing Process*, 15.
32. Elias, *Civilizing Process*, 12; see also Lionel Trilling, *Matthew Arnold*, 2nd ed. (New York: Meridian Books, 1955), 206.
33. Elias, *Civilizing Process*, 24.
34. Elias, *Civilizing Process*, 6.
35. Pierre Bourdieu, *Distinction: A Social Critique of the Judgment of Taste*, trans. Richard Nice (Cambridge, MA: Harvard University Press, 1984), 54, 173.
36. Elias, *Civilizing Process*, 47–48; see also 144, where Elias calls the book "a kind of standard work for a very considerable number of people."
37. Desiderius Erasmus, *The Education of Children*, trans. Richard Sherry (Project Gutenberg, 2009), passim, https://www.gutenberg.org/files

/28338/28338-h/28338-h.htm, quoted in Elias, *Civilizing Process*, 76, 110, 122, 136.

38. Elias, *Civilizing Process*, 70; Achille Mbembe, *Necropolitics*, trans. Steven Corcoran (Durham, NC: Duke University Press, 2019); Dierk Walter, *Colonial Violence: European Empires and the Use of Force*, trans. Peter Lewis (New York: Oxford University Press, 2017).

39. Elias, *Civilizing Process*, 10; emphasis in original.

40. A. L. Kroeber and Clyde Kluckhohn, *Culture: A Critical Review of Concepts and Definitions* (New York: Vintage, 1963), 28; see also Oswald Spengler, *The Decline of the West*, trans. Charles Atkinson, abridged ed. (New York: Oxford University Press, 1991), 24.

41. Samuel Taylor Coleridge, *On the Constitution of the Church and State According to the Idea of Each* (London: William Pickering, 1839), 46 [accessed March 3, 2016], http://archive.org/details/cu31924105501906; see also Williams, *Culture and Society*, 61; Williams, *Keywords*, 59.

42. Marc Manganaro, *Culture, 1922: The Emergence of a Concept* (Princeton, NJ: Princeton University Press, 2002), 13; see also Qadri Ismail, *Culture and Eurocentrism* (London: Rowman & Littlefield, 2015), 7. There, Ismail calls *culture* "a labyrinthely networked concept."

43. Vilém Flusser, *Natural:Mind*, trans. Rodrigo Maltez Novaes (Minneapolis, MN: Univocal Publishing, 2013), 90; see also Kroeber and Kluckhohn, *Culture*, 15; Williams, *Keywords*, 87.

44. Lucien Febvre, "Civilisation: Evolution of a Word and a Group of Ideas," in *A New Kind of History: From the Writings of Febvre*, ed. Peter Burke, trans. K. Folea (London: Routledge & Kegan Paul, 1973), 243. Earlier in the piece (p. 225), Febvre locates evidence from the late-eighteenth century of pitting *culture* over and against *civilization* in the French language, much as it would come to be in German.

45. Williams, *Keywords*, 57.

46. Ismail, *Culture and Eurocentrism*, 5, 17; Mbembe, *Necropolitics*, passim. This taxonomy appears to have been inaugurated by Tylor. See Edward Burnett Tylor, *Anthropology: An Introduction to the Study of Man and Civilization* (New York: D. Appleton & Co., 1881).

47. Ismail, *Culture and Eurocentrism*, 10; Kroeber and Kluckhohn, *Culture*, 25.

48. On Arnold's racism, elitism, etc., see Ismail, *Culture and Eurocentrism*, 13–37.

49. Raymond Williams, *Politics and Letters: Interviews with New Left Review* (London: New Left Books, 1979), 109.

50. Stuart Hall, *The Hard Road to Renewal: Thatcherism and the Crisis of the Left* (London: Verso, 1988); Lawrence Grossberg, *We Gotta Get Out of This Place: Popular Conservatism and Postmodern Culture* (New York: Routledge, 1992); Lawrence Grossberg, *Caught in the Crossfire: Kids, Politics, and America's Future* (Boulder, CO: Paradigm, 2005); Lawrence Grossberg, *Under the Cover of Chaos: Trump and the Battle for the American Right* (London: Pluto Press, 2018).

51. Park Honan, *Matthew Arnold: A Life* (New York: McGraw-Hill, 1981), 115.

52. Honan, *Matthew Arnold*, viii, 32; David Nicholls, "The Totalitarianism of Thomas Arnold," *Review of Politics* 29, no. 4 (October 1967): 518–25.

53. Honan, *Matthew Arnold*, 78.

54. Matthew Arnold, "Empedocles on Etna," in *Empedocles on Etna and Other Poems* (London: B. Fellowes, 1852), 3–70.

55. John Coates, "Two Versions of the Problem of the Modern Intellectual: 'Empedocles on Etna' and 'Cleon,'" *Modern Language Review* 79, no. 4 (October 1984): 769. See also Manfred Dietrich, "Arnold's 'Empedocles on Etna' and the 1853 Preface," *Victorian Poetry* 14, no. 4 (Winter 1976): 318, 320; Walter E. Houghton, "Arnold's 'Empedocles on Etna,'" *Victorian Studies* 1, no. 4 (June 1958): 313; Trilling, *Matthew Arnold*, 103; Honan, *Matthew Arnold*, 207; Matthew Arnold, "Author's Preface," in *The Poems of Matthew Arnold, 1840–1867* (London: Oxford University Press, 1909), https://www.bartleby.com/254/1002.html.

56. Arnold, "Empedocles on Etna," 66–67.

57. Arnold, "Empedocles on Etna," 21–22, 50.

58. Honan, *Matthew Arnold*, 210. On steam printing, see Williams, *Long Revolution*, 186–87, 216–17.

59. Arnold, "Empedocles on Etna," 25.

60. Ann M. Blair, *Too Much to Know: Managing Scholarly Information before the Modern Age* (New Haven, CT: Yale University Press, 2011).

61. Sidney M. B. Coulling, "Matthew Arnold's 1853 Preface: Its Origins and Aftermath," *Victorian Studies* 7, no. 3 (March 1964): 245.

62. Only to reappear in 1867. See Dietrich, "Arnold's 'Empedocles on Etna,'" 311.

63. Matthew Arnold, "Author's Preface," n.p.

64. Matthew Arnold, "Author's Preface," n.p. (emphasis added).

65. Matthew Arnold, *Culture and Anarchy and Other Writings*, ed. Stefan Collini (Cambridge: Cambridge University Press, 1993), 79, 190.

66. Gauri Viswanathan, "Raymond Williams and British Colonialism: The Limits of Metropolitan Cultural Theory," in *Views Beyond the Border Country: Raymond Williams and Cultural Politics*, ed. Dennis Dworkin and Leslie Roman (New York: Routledge, 1993), 228–29; see also Gauri Viswanathan, *Masks of Conquest: Literary Study and British Rule in India*, 25th anniversary ed. (New York: Columbia University Press, 2014), 2–3; Ismail, *Culture and Eurocentrism*, 72; Trilling, *Matthew Arnold*, 62.

67. Arnold, *Culture and Anarchy*, 89.

68. Matthew Arnold, "Culture and Its Enemies," *The Cornhill Magazine* 16 (July–December 1867): 36–57. For more on the book's publication history, see Stefan Collini, "Note on the Texts and Acknowledgments," in Matthew Arnold, *Culture and Anarchy and Other Writings*, ed. Stefan Collini (Cambridge: Cambridge University Press, 1993), xxxii–xxxiii.

69. Matthew Arnold, "Anarchy and Authority" (Part I), *The Cornhill Magazine* 17, (January–June 1868): 30–47, 239–56, 745–60; Matthew Arnold, "Anarchy and Authority" (Part II), *The Cornhill Magazine* 18, (July–December 1868): 91–107, 239–56.

70. Raymond Williams, "A Hundred Years of Culture and Anarchy," in *Culture and Materialism: Selected Essays* (London: Verso, 2005), 3–8; Arnold, *Culture and Anarchy*, 85–88.

71. According to family lore, Bright may have been a distant relative of mine. My uncle, cousin, grandfather, and great-grandfather, all maternal, share the name John Bright, apparently in honor of the famous MP. I have yet to verify the claims of a familial connection.

72. Quoted in Arnold, *Culture and Anarchy*, 55.

73. Arnold, *Culture and Anarchy*, 151.

74. Arnold, *Culture and Anarchy*, 151, 157, 184, 186, 190, and passim; see also Williams, *Culture and Society*, 115.

75. Arnold, *Culture and Anarchy*, 106.

76. Matthew Arnold, "Democracy," in *Culture and Anarchy and Other Writings*, ed. Stefan Collini (Cambridge: Cambridge University Press, 1993), 21.

77. Arnold, *Culture and Anarchy*, 65. See also Trilling, *Matthew Arnold*, 149–50.

78. Arnold, *Culture and Anarchy*, 63 (emphasis in original).

79. Arnold, *Culture and Anarchy*, 63, 71.

80. Williams, *Long Revolution*, 48.

81. Trilling, *Matthew Arnold*, 230.

82. Williams, *Culture and Society*, 118; Williams, "Hundred Years," 3–8.

83. Arnold, *Culture and Anarchy*, 66. This is, essentially, the "well-tempered self" Toby Miller would rediscover in the 1990s, in his study of cultural citizenship. Toby Miller, *The Well-Tempered Self: Citizenship, Culture, and the Postmodern Subject* (Baltimore, MD: Johns Hopkins University Press, 1993).

84. Paul Gilroy, *The Black Atlantic: Modernity and Double Consciousness* (Cambridge, MA: Harvard University Press, 1993), 11.

85. Honan, *Matthew Arnold*, 339–40.

86. Williams, "Hundred Years," 6–7.

87. Matthew Arnold, "Numbers," in *Discourses in America* (New York: Macmillan, 1912), 34, 37. See also Honan, *Matthew Arnold*, 117–18. Honan notes that Arnold's concern for Ireland first emerged when he was a young man, prompted by the Great Irish Famine (1845–1849).

88. Arnold, "Numbers," 22–23.

89. Arnold, "Numbers," 32.

90. Honan, *Matthew Arnold*, 307, 387.

91. Arnold, *Culture and Anarchy*, 79. "The men of culture are the true apostles of equality. The great men of culture are those who have had a passion for diffusing, for making prevail, for carrying from one end of society to the other, the best knowledge, the best ideas of their time."

92. Tony Bennett, *Culture: A Reformer's Science* (London: Sage Publications, 1998), 11, 153. I have modified the quotation slightly to preserve syntax. Beyond the matter of "goodness" and "purity," another major difference between Arnold and Bennett is that Arnold held onto interiority (psychology, etc.), whereas Bennett seems only concerned with externalized behavior. On the relationship of culture, cultural

institutions, and governance, see also: Dee Garrison, *Apostles of Culture: The Public Librarian and American Society, 1876–1920* (New York: Macmillan, 1977); Lawrence W. Levine, *Highbrow/Lowbrow: The Emergence of Cultural Hierarchy in America* (Cambridge, MA: Harvard University Press, 1988); and Tony Bennett, *The Birth of the Museum: History, Theory, Politics* (London: Routledge, 1995).

93. Bill Bell, "Beyond the Death of the Author: Matthew Arnold's Two Audiences, 1888–1930," *Book History* 3, no. 1 (2000): 158, https://doi.org/10.1353/bh.2000.0002.

94. Bell, "Death of the Author," 159.

95. Honan, *Matthew Arnold*, 396–407.

96. Honan, *Matthew Arnold*, viii.

97. Williams, *Long Revolution*, 66–70.

98. See Janice A. Radway, *A Feeling for Books: The Book-of-the-Month Club, Literary Taste, and Middle-Class Desire* (Chapel Hill: University of North Carolina Press, 1997), 197, for the following example. "I think it might be argued, therefore, that through the introduction of the negative option and the reply coupon the Book-of-the-Month Club was instructing large numbers of Americans in how to take up appropriate roles in vast, integrated systems for the production and circulation of both goods and information. It was teaching them, in effect, how to perform the kinds of work that would increasingly be asked of them by a consumer-oriented and information-dominated society, the work of sorting, representing, and passing on materials and information which, of necessity, circulated throughout the larger system."

99. Williams, "Seeing a Man Running," 22–23.

100. Ian MacKillop, *F. R. Leavis: A Life in Criticism* (London: Allen Lane/Penguin Press, 1995), 44.

101. Q. D. Leavis, quoted in G. Singh, *F. R. Leavis: A Literary Biography* (London: Duckworth, 1995), 19; see also 20.

102. Michael Black, "The Long Pursuit," in *The Leavises: Recollections and Impressions*, ed. Denys Thompson (Cambridge: Cambridge University Press, 1984), 101.

103. Q. D. Leavis, quoted in Singh, *F. R. Leavis*, 19. See also Mary Pitter, "6, Chesterton Hall Crescent," in *The Leavises: Recollections and Impressions*, ed. Denys Thompson (Cambridge: Cambridge University Press,

1984), 27–28; John Harvey, "Leavis: An Appreciation," in *The Leavises: Recollections and Impressions*, ed. Denys Thompson (Cambridge: Cambridge University Press, 1984), 174; D. W. Harding, "No Compromise," in *The Leavises: Recollections and Impressions*, ed. Denys Thompson (Cambridge: Cambridge University Press, 1984), 199–200.

104. MacKillop, *F. R. Leavis*, 35.

105. MacKillop, *F. R. Leavis*, 37–39; Harvey, "Leavis," 171.

106. MacKillop, *F. R. Leavis*, 38, 41–42.

107. David Frum, "The Lessons of the Somme," *The Atlantic*, July 1, 2016, http://www.theatlantic.com/international/archive/2016/07/somme-centennial/489656/.

108. Joseph Loconte, "How J.R.R. Tolkien Found Mordor on the Western Front," *New York Times*, June 30, 2016, http://www.nytimes.com/2016/07/03/opinion/sunday/how-jrr-tolkien-found-mordor-on-the-western-front.html; John Garth, "Battle of the Somme: The 'Animal Horror' that Inspired J.R.R. Tolkien," *The Telegraph*, October 4, 2013.

109. MacKillop, *F. R. Leavis*, 39–44.

110. MacKillop, *F. R. Leavis*, 38.

111. MacKillop, *F. R. Leavis*, 44; Harvey, "Leavis," 171; Harding, "No Compromise," 199.

112. See Judith Butler and Athena Athanasiou, *Dispossession: The Performative in the Political* (Cambridge, UK: Polity Press, 2013).

113. MacKillop, *F. R. Leavis*, 38; Singh, *F. R. Leavis*, 11; Raymond O'Malley, "Charisma?," in *The Leavises: Recollections and Impressions*, ed. Denys Thompson (Cambridge: Cambridge University Press, 1984), 58.

114. Williams, "Seeing a Man Running," 17.

115. Carl Krockel, *War Trauma and English Modernism: T. S. Eliot and D. H. Lawrence* (Houndmills, UK: Palgrave Macmillan, 2011), 206.

116. F. R. Leavis, *Mass Civilization and Minority Culture* (Cambridge: Minority Press, 1930).

117. Williams, *Culture and Society*, 254. The quote goes on to acknowledge the part played by I. A. Richards in helping to secure Arnold's intellectual legacy.

118. Leavis, *Mass Civilization*, 3–5.

119. MacKillop, *F. R. Leavis*, 73.

120. MacKillop, *F. R. Leavis*, 72–73.

121. Stefan Collini, "Introduction," in *Two Cultures? The Significance of C. P. Snow*, by F. R. Leavis (Cambridge: Cambridge University Press, 2013), 5.

122. Collini, "Introduction," 5; MacKillop, *F. R. Leavis*, 92–93, 225–28; Francis Mulhern, *The Moment of "Scrutiny"* (London: New Left Books, 1979), 31.

123. Q. D. Leavis, *Fiction and the Reading Public* (London: Chatto & Windus, 1932).

124. MacKillop, *F. R. Leavis*, 132; see also 131.

125. Q. D. Leavis, *Reading Public*, quoted in Singh, *F. R. Leavis*, 20; see also Pitter, "6, Chesterton Hall Crescent," 32; Kate Varney and Jan Montefiore, "A Conversation About Q. D. Leavis," *Women: A Cultural Review* 19, no. 2 (August 1, 2008): 182, https://doi.org/10.1080/09574040802137276.

126. Varney and Montefiore, "Conversation About Q. D. Leavis," 176; Denys Thompson, "Introduction," in *The Leavises: Recollections and Impressions*, ed. Denys Thompson (Cambridge: Cambridge University Press, 1984), 2.

127. MacKillop, *F. R. Leavis*, 28–29; Singh, *F. R. Leavis*, 17.

128. O'Malley, "Charisma?," 58.

129. F. R. Leavis, "What's Wrong With Criticism?," *Scrutiny* 1, no. 2 (September 1932): 135. Two years earlier, in *Mass Civilization and Minority Culture*, Leavis used the language of "fine living" (p. 5). Evidently, he felt compelled to lower the bar.

130. "Editorial," *Scrutiny* 2, no. 4 (March 1934): 332.

131. "Editorial," 332.

132. "Editorial," 332.

133. Jürgen Habermas, *The Structural Transformation of the Public Sphere: An Inquiry into a Category of Bourgeois Society*, trans. Thomas Burger and Frederick Lawrence (Cambridge, MA: MIT Press, 1989), 29, 33.

134. F. R. Leavis, "'The Literary Mind,'" *Scrutiny* 1, no. 1 (May 1932): 30; see also F. R. Leavis, "'Under Which King, Bezonian?,'" *Scrutiny* 1, no. 3 (December 1932): 208. The "standard of living" question persists throughout Leavis's career, bookended by the *Scrutiny* material at the beginning and, near the end, his critique of C. P. Snow. See F. R.

Leavis, "Luddites? Or, There Is Only One Culture," in *Two Cultures? The Significance of C. P. Snow* (Cambridge: Cambridge University Press, 2013), 99.

135. F. R. Leavis and Denys Thompson, *Culture and Environment: The Training of Critical Awareness* (London: Chatto & Windus, 1964), 105.

136. Leavis and Thompson, *Culture and Environment*, 58.

137. George Sturt, *The Wheelwright's Shop* (Cambridge: Cambridge University Press, 1923), quoted in Leavis and Thompson, *Culture and Environment*, 76. The passage anticipates, by almost twenty-five years, Martin Heidegger's *Question Concerning Technology*, specifically the claim that the essence of technology is *alētheia*, or the revelation of truth. See Martin Heidegger, *The Question Concerning Technology and Other Essays*, trans. William Lovitt (New York: Harper Torchbooks, 1977), 12.

138. Q. D. Leavis, quoted in Singh, *F. R. Leavis*, 19. This vignette is included in a memoir authored by Q. D. Leavis, fragments of which appear in the Singh book. On Leavis's decline, see MacKillop, *F. R. Leavis*, 406–7.

139. See, e.g., Williams, *Culture and Society*, 259.

140. Leavis and Thompson, *Culture and Environment*, 96. Leavis would reaffirm the point, in no uncertain terms, later in his career: "I am not a Luddite." See Leavis, *Two Cultures?*, 73.

141. Leavis, *Two Cultures?*, 71.

142. Leavis, *Mass Civilization*, 6, 32. It's worth mentioning that, even there, Leavis states that "it is vain to resist the triumph of the machine" (31).

143. F. R. Leavis, "The Irony of Swift," *Scrutiny* 2, no. 4 (March 1934): 364–78.

144. Leavis, "'Literary Mind'," 24; Mulhern, *Moment of "Scrutiny*," 117.

145. Stuart Hall, *Cultural Studies 1983: A Theoretical History*, ed. Jennifer Daryl Slack and Lawrence Grossberg (Durham, NC: Duke University Press, 2016), 12.

146. Leavis, "'Under Which King, Bezonian?,'" 205.

147. F. R. Leavis, "Restatement for Critics," *Scrutiny* 1, no. 4 (March 1933): 321.

148. Leavis, "'Under Which King, Bezonian?,'" 206; see also Leavis, "Restatement for Critics," 320.

149. Leavis, *Two Cultures?*, 73, 89–112.

150. F. R. Leavis, "Luddites?," 103. Huxley intended "literarism" to be the counterpart to another term of disparagement, "scientism."

151. D. H. Lawrence, "Study of Thomas Hardy," in *Phoenix: The Posthumous Papers of D. H. Lawrence*, ed. Edward D. McDonald (London: Heinemann, 1936), 425, quoted in F. R. Leavis, "Luddites?," 92.

152. Kittler, *Discourse Networks*, 369.

153. Matthew Arnold, *Sohrab and Rustum and Other Poems*, ed. Justus Collins Castleman, E-book (Project Gutenberg, 1905/2004), https://www.gutenberg.org/ebooks/13364.

154. Kate Teltscher, "'The Rubicon Between Empires': The River Oxus in the Nineteenth-Century British Geographical Imaginary," in *Writing Travel in Central Asia*, ed. Nile Green (Bloomington: Indiana University Press, 2014), 142, 144; Reza Taher-Kermani, "Why the Oxus? On the Majestic River of Arnold's 'Sohrab and Rustum,'" *Review of English Studies* 69, no. 289 (2018): 319–20.

155. Teltscher, "'Rubicon Between Empires,'" 135.

4. ALGORITHMIC CULTURE

1. "Impact of Algorithms and Algorithmic Decision-Making," accessed July 18, 2022, https://www.ukessays.com/essays/sciences/impact-of-algorithms-and-algorithmic-decision-making.php.

2. Thao Phan, "Amazon Echo and the Aesthetics of Whiteness," *Catalyst: Feminism, Theory, Technoscience* 5, no. 1 (2019): 1–39, https://doi.org/10.28968/cftt.v5i1.29586.

3. Phan, "Aesthetics of Whiteness," 25; see also Heather Suzanne Woods, "Asking More of Siri and Alexa: Feminine Persona in Service of Surveillance Capitalism," *Critical Studies in Media Communication* 35, no. 4 (August 2018): 334–49, https://doi.org/10.1080/15295036.2018.1488082.

4. Kathryn Stockett, *The Help: A Novel* (New York: Berkeley, 2009).

5. Phan, "Aesthetics of Whiteness," 19–21.

6. Raymond Williams, *Keywords: A Vocabulary of Culture and Society*, rev. ed. (New York: Oxford University Press, 1983), 243.

7. Geoffrey A. Fowler, "Alexa Has Been Eavesdropping on You This Whole Time," *Washington Post*, May 6, 2019, https://www.washingtonpost.com/technology/2019/05/06/alexa-has-been-eavesdropping -you-this-whole-time/; Sidney Fussell, "Police Want Your Smart Speaker—Here's Why," *Wired*, August 23, 2020, https://www.wired .com/story/star-witness-your-smart-speaker/.

8. Williams, *Keywords*, 14; Raymond Williams, *Culture and Society, 1780– 1950* (New York: Columbia University Press, 1958), xii. On Williams's struggles with publisher word counts, see Raymond Williams, *Politics and Letters: Interviews with New Left Review* (London: New Left Books, 1979), 300.

9. Williams, *Culture and Society*, v–vi, 87–92. Race, gender, and sexuality all play a role in *Keywords*, yet for the most part they arrive late to the project. The word *native* appeared in the 1976 edition, but the words *ethnic*, *racial*, and *sex* were not added until the revised edition, issued in 1983. All the entries are relatively short: *ethnic* (one half-page); *native* (one page); *racial* (two and a half pages); and *sex* (also two and a half pages). C.f.: the entry on *class* (nine pages in the 1983 ed.). Raymond Williams, *Keywords: A Vocabulary of Culture and Society*, 1st ed. (New York: Oxford University Press, 1976), 180–81; Williams, *Keywords*, rev. ed., 60–69, 119–20, 215–16, 248–50, 283–86.

    In response to a question about the absence of *race* from the original edition of *Keywords*, Williams states, rather vaguely: "I did a lot of reading on the term, and I don't know why in the end it was omitted." Equally vaguely, he adds: "Another very important related term is 'sex,' which was also excluded. . . . I suspect there's a lot of social history in that one." Williams, *Politics and Letters*, 180.

10. On "paratexts," see Gerard Genette, *Paratexts: Thresholds of Interpretation*, trans. Jane E. Lewin (Cambridge: Cambridge University Press, 1997).

11. See, e.g., *Culture and Society*, 342–43.

12. For a parallel case, see Friedrich A. Kittler, *Discourse Networks, 1800/1900*, trans. Michael Metteer and Chris Cullens (Stanford, CA: Stanford University Press, 1990), esp. 369–72. Here, Kittler explores questions of mediality as they relate to Michel Foucault's archaeological method, which takes for granted its own embeddedness in print culture. See also the preceding chapter in *Algorithmic Culture Before the Internet*.

13. I realize one could make the argument that all of the words appearing in *Keywords* are gendered. I would not disagree, hence my stress on *"explicitly* gendered terminology."

14. Williams, *Keywords*, 1st ed., 155; see also 44–45, 108–11, 121–24, 155–56.

15. Douglas Harper, "Feminism (n.)," *Online Etymology Dictionary*, accessed January 31, 2020, https://www.etymonline.com/word/fem inism#etymonline_v_32935.

16. Williams, *Keywords*, rev. ed., 140–42, 283–86.

17. See Tony Bennett, Lawrence Grossberg, and Meaghan Morris, eds., *New Keywords: A Revised Vocabulary of Culture and Society* (Malden, MA: Blackwell, 2005), which includes entries for *body, difference, family, feminism, gay and lesbian, gender, generation, human, person, pornography, private, public, queer*, and *sexuality*; and Colin MacCabe and Holly Yanacek, eds., *Keywords for Today: A 21st Century Vocabulary* (New York: Oxford University Press, 2018), which includes entries for *feminist, gender, humanity, private, public*, and *sexuality*.

18. Dorothy E. Smith, *The Conceptual Practices of Power: A Feminist Sociology of Knowledge* (Boston: Northeastern University Press, 1990), 12–13; see also Karen Lee Ashcraft and Peter Simonson, "Gender, Work, and the History of Communication Research: Figures, Formations, and Flows," in *The International History of Communication Study*, ed. Peter Simonson and David W. Park (New York: Routledge, 2016), 47–68, esp. 55.

19. Smith, *Conceptual Practices of Power*. To be clear, Williams was no fan of the sociology of knowledge. He described the field as "bourgeois sociology" owing to its propensity to jettison the category of ideology, and hence the assumption that ruling-class ideas tended to prevail in society. While the general critique is perhaps correct, Williams would have done well to engage more closely with the substance of the work in this field, particularly that of Karl Mannheim. Raymond Williams, *Marxism and Literature* (Oxford: Oxford University Press, 1977), 138–39; Karl Mannheim, *Ideology and Utopia: An Introduction to the Sociology of Knowledge*, trans. Louis Wirth and Edward Shils (San Diego: Harcourt, 1955), 285.

20. Michael Gardiner, *Critiques of Everyday Life* (London: Routledge, 2000), 192; Kimberlé Crenshaw, "Demarginalizing the Intersection of Race and Sex: A Black Feminist Critique of Antidiscrimination

Doctrine, Feminist Theory, and Antiracist Politics," *University of Chicago Legal Forum*, no. 1 (1989): 139–67.

21. Smith, *Conceptual Practices of Power*, 4, 15.

22. Williams, *Keywords*, rev. ed., 131–34. The quotation appears on 133 (emphasis in original).

23. Dorothy Smith, "Women, the Family, and Corporate Capitalism," *Berkeley Journal of Sociology* 20 (1975–1976): 56.

24. Smith, "Women, the Family," 66. See also Sarah Sharma, *In the Meantime: Temporality and Cultural Politics* (Durham, NC: Duke University Press, 2014). Williams himself benefitted professionally, materially, and personally from gendered "sub-contractual" labor, which was carried out throughout his career by his wife, Joy. See Fred Inglis, *Raymond Williams* (London: Routledge, 1995), 215–16; and Williams, *Culture and Society*, vii.

25. Smith, "Women, the Family," 60; Smith, *Conceptual Practices of Power*, 45.

26. On patriarchalism in the academy, particularly in the latter half of the twentieth century, see Marilyn Hoder-Salmon, "Collecting Scholar's Wives," *Feminist Studies* 4, no. 3 (1978): 107–14, https://doi.org/10.2307/3177543; Hilary Callan and Shirley Ardener, eds., *The Incorporated Wife* (London: Croom Helm, 1984), 1–66; Margaret W. Rossiter, "The ~~Matthew~~ Matilda Effect in Science," *Social Studies of Science* 23, no. 2 (1993): 325–41; Alison Prentice, "Boosting Husbands and Building Community: The Work of Twentieth-Century Faculty Wives," in *Historical Identities: The Professoriate in Canada*, ed. Paul Stortz and E. Lisa Panayotidis (Toronto: University of Toronto Press, 2006), 271–96; Allison L. Rowland and Peter Simonson, "The Founding Mothers of Communication Research: Toward a History of a Gendered Assemblage," *Critical Studies in Media Communication* 31, no. 1 (March 2014): 3–26, https://doi.org/10.1080/15295036.2013.849355; Ashcraft and Simonson, "Gender, Work, and the History of Communication Research," 47–68; Donica Belisle and Kiera Mitchell, "Mary Quayle Innis: Faculty Wives' Contributions and the Making of Academic Celebrity," *Canadian Historical Review* 99, no. 3 (2018): 456–86, https://doi.org/10.3138/chr.2017-0108.

27. Smith, *Conceptual Practices of Power*, 74. On the concept of "chronotope," see M. M. Bakhtin, "Forms of Time and of the Chronotope in

the Novel," in *The Dialogic Imagination: Four Essays*, ed. Michael Holquist, trans. Caryl Emerson and Michael Holquist (Austin: University of Texas Press, 1981), 84–258.

28. Ted Striphas and Mark Hayward, "Working Papers in Cultural Studies, or, the Virtues of Grey Literature," *New Formations*, no. 78 (Summer 2013): 103, https://doi.org/10.3898/NewF.78.05.2013; see also Kevin Walby and Alex Luscombe, "Freedom of Information Research and Cultural Studies: A Subterranean Affinity," *Cultural Studies ↔ Critical Methodologies* 21, no. 1 (February 1, 2021): 70–79, https://doi.org/10 .1177/1532708620917421.

29. James C. Scott, *Domination and the Arts of Resistance: Hidden Transcripts* (New Haven, CT: Yale University Press, 1990), xii.

30. Smith, *Conceptual Practices of Power*, 67.

31. Correspondence from Clyde Kluckhohn to Talcott Parsons, 16 December 1948, HUGFP 42.8.4 Box 18, Folder—Russian Research Center, 1948–1949, Harvard University Archives, Cambridge, MA, USA; Melissa Bauman, "Studying Soviets, Not Sex: Margaret Mead's Research at RAND," *RAND Blog*, March 7, 2018, https://www.rand .org/blog/rand-review/2018/03/studying-soviets-not-sex-margaret -meads-research-at.html.

32. Elaine Tyler May, *Homeward Bound: American Families in the Cold War Era*, 4th rev. ed. (New York: Basic Books, 2017), 9.

33. "Helen Bancroft Walker," *Abbot Circle* (Andover, MA: Abbot Academy, 1920), 47; *Bulletin of Abbot Academy* (October 1940): 35.

34. "Parsons," *Boston Globe*, April 10, 1993; "Obituary—Helen Parsons, Administrative Assistant," *Boston Herald*, April 10, 1993.

35. Landon R. Y. Storrs, *Civilizing Capitalism: The National Consumers' League, Women's Activism, and Labor Standards in the New Deal Era* (Chapel Hill: University of North Carolina Press, 2000), 145; Christina Looper Baker, *In a Generous Spirit: A First-Person Biography of Myra Page* (Champaign: University of Illinois Press, 1996), 76; Cynthia Neverdon-Morton, *Afro-American Women of the South and the Advancement of the Race, 1895–1925* (Knoxville: University of Tennessee Press, 1989), 219–20. The quotation is drawn from "Group Work with Girls," *News-Bulletin of the Bureau of Vocational Information* 2, no. 13 (September 1, 1924): 98.

36. *Bulletin of Abbot Academy* (May 1937): 34; *Bulletin of Abbot Academy* (October 1940): 35–36; Carl Joachim Friedrich, *Constitutional Government and Democracy: Theory and Practice in Europe and America* (New York: Little, Brown, 1941), ix; *Andover Bulletin* (February 1981): 17.

37. Rowland and Simonson, "The Founding Mothers of Communication Research," 4; Genette, *Paratexts*; Hoder-Salmon, "Collecting Scholar's Wives," 107; Ashcraft and Simonson, "Gender, Work, and the History of Communication Research," 53 (emphasis in original).

38. On the "functional" pull of female domesticity and normative conceptions of family within structural functionalism, see Smith, "Women, the Family," 59; and Rossiter, "~~Matthew~~ Matilda Effect," 326.

39. *Bryn Mawr Alumnae Bulletin* 8, no. 1 (January 1928): 35. The reference to Goodhart Hall pertains to Helen's fundraising efforts for the college.

40. Hilary Callan, "Introduction," in *The Incorporated Wife*, ed. Hilary Callan and Shirley Ardener (London: Croom Helm, 1984), 1.

41. Prentice, "Boosting Husbands," 271–96. See also Callan, "Introduction"; and Belisle and Mitchell, "Mary Quayle Innis."

42. See *Historical Statistics of the United States: Colonial Times to 1970*, bicentennial ed. (U.S. Department of Commerce: Bureau of the Census, 1975), 363. For instance, the number of four-year colleges and universities in the United States increased by about 65% between 1920 and 1970, from 989 to 1,639. The number of faculty increased from 48,615 to 729,000—about fifteen-fold—over the same period of time, while the number of students (undergraduate and graduate) increased from about 600,000 to 6.3 million.

43. Prentice, "Boosting Husbands," 277–78. Here, the author is in conversation with Judith Fingard, "Gender and Inequality at Dalhousie: Faculty Women Before 1950," *Dalhousie Review* 64, no. 4 (1985): 687–703.

44. Margot Lee Shetterly, *Hidden Figures: The American Dream and the Untold Story of the Black Women Mathematicians Who Helped Win the Space Race*, E-Book (New York: William Morrow, 2016), n.p; Nathan Ensmenger, *The Computer Boys Take Over: Computers, Programmers, and the Politics of Technical Expertise* (Cambridge, MA: MIT Press, 2010), 15. See also: Janet Abbate, *Recoding Gender: Women's Changing*

Participation in Computing (Cambridge, MA: MIT Press, 2012); Marie Hicks, *Programmed Inequality: How Britain Discarded Women Technologists and Lost Its Edge in Computing* (Cambridge, MA: MIT Press, 2017); and Charlton D. McIlwain, *Black Software: The Internet and Racial Justice, from the AfroNet to Black Lives Matter* (New York: Oxford University Press, 2020).

45. Kathleen F. McConnell, "The Profound Sound of Ernest Hemingway's Typist: Gendered Typewriting as a Solution to the Problems of Communication," *Communication and Critical/Cultural Studies* 5, no. 4 (December 2008): 328, https://doi.org/10.1080/14791420802412407; Carolyn Marvin, *When Old Technologies Were New: Thinking About Electric Communication in the Late Nineteenth Century* (New York: Oxford University Press, 1988), 26–30; Jeff Scheible, *Digital Shift: The Cultural Logic of Punctuation* (Minneapolis: University Of Minnesota Press, 2015), 120.

46. Ensmenger, *Computer Boys Take Over*, 15; McConnell, "Ernest Hemingway's Typist," 328–35.

47. Smith, "Women, the Family," 66. On incorporation, see Callan, "Introduction."

48. Hicks, *Programmed Inequality*, 5.

49. May, *Homeward Bound*, 3.

50. May, *Homeward Bound*, 24.

51. May, *Homeward Bound*, 9, 12, 16, 31; see also Adam Curtis, *The Century of the Self*, DVD (RDF Television/BBC, 2002), which explores (among other topics) the role psychoanalysis played in maintaining family stability throughout the twentieth century.

52. For memos written by Helen Parsons to her husband, see Correspondence from Helen Parsons to Talcott Parsons, 24 September 1948, HUGFP 42.8.4 Box 18, Folder—Russian Research Center, 1948–1949, Harvard University Archives, Cambridge, MA, USA; and Correspondence from Helen Parsons to Talcott Parsons, 21 September 1948, HUGFP 42.8.4 Box 18, Folder—Russian Research Center, 1948–1949, Harvard University Archives, Cambridge, MA, USA.

53. U.S. Federal Bureau of Investigation, Office Memorandum—SAC Boston to Director, FBI, Concerning Russian Research Center, Harvard University, Cambridge, Mass. (Bureau File 100–360557–14), 5 May 1949: 5.

54. Talcott Parsons and Evon Z. Vogt, "Clyde Kay Maben Kluckhohn 1905–1960," *American Anthropologist* 64, no. 1 (February 1962): 141, https://doi.org/10.1525/aa.1962.64.1.02a00130.

55. U.S. Federal Bureau of Investigation, Memorandum of Facts Revealed in an Intensive Investigation of Charges Made [Redacted] Against Dr. Clyde Kluckhohn of Harvard University (Bureau File 121–32118–9), 17 November 1943: 1, 12; U.S. Federal Bureau of Investigation, Office Memorandum—SAC Boston to Director, FBI, Concerning Russian Research Unit, Harvard University, Cambridge, Mass. (Bureau File 100–360557–1), 12 December 1947: 3; U.S. Federal Bureau of Investigation, Enclosures to Bureau—Clyde Kay Kluckhohn, Concerning Loyalty of Government Employees (Bureau File 121–32118–9), 16 December 1953.

56. U.S. Federal Bureau of Investigation, Statement of [Redacted], Census No. [Redacted] (Bureau File 100–360557–1), 12 June 1943. References to monetary "gifts" appear on pp. 1–3, and 5. In one instance, Kluckhohn allegedly paid the young man in liquor. The "hovering" is recounted on p. 5.

57. U.S. Federal Bureau of Investigation, Memorandum of Facts Revealed in an Intensive Investigation of Charges Against Dr. Clyde Kluckhohn, 7.

58. U.S. Federal Bureau of Investigation, Memorandum of Facts Revealed in an Intensive Investigation of Charges Against Dr. Clyde Kluckhohn, 6.

59. U.S. Federal Bureau of Investigation, Memorandum of Facts Revealed in an Intensive Investigation of Charges Against Dr. Clyde Kluckhohn, 11, 12. Voting age in the United States did not drop from twenty-one to eighteen until the passage of the Twenty-Sixth Amendment, in 1971. Having noted that, the context surrounding instances of the term "boy" in the report suggests its invocation was highly racialized.

60. "Anthropologist Tells Rotarians of the Myth of the Race Theory," *The Gallup Independent*, June 24, 1943: 1.

61. Ann Cvetkovich, *An Archive of Feelings: Trauma, Sexuality, and Lesbian Public Cultures*, Kindle ed. (Durham, NC: Duke University Press, 2003), Kindle Locations 4511–4513. I thank my former student Joe Hatfield for directing me to this and other helpful sources on queer archives.

62. Charles E. Morris III, "Archival Queer," *Rhetoric and Public Affairs* 9, no. 1 (Spring 2006), 146.

63. Charles E. Morris III, "Contextual Twilight/Critical Liminality: J. M. Barrie's Courage at St. Andrews, 1922," *Quarterly Journal of Speech* 82, no. 3 (August 1996): 207–27; Morris, "Archival Queer," 147.

64. Jacob Bagoury, "A Queer History of Computing: Part Two," Rhizome .org, March 19, 2013, https://rhizome.org/editorial/2013/mar/19/queer -computing-2/.

65. Alan McFarlane, *Full Interview with Clifford Geertz, Part I* (Cambridge, UK, 2004), https://www.youtube.com/watch?v=3dQDx3axrDs (the comments occur at approximately the 25:30, 26:30, and 27:15 marks); Clifford Geertz, "An Inconstant Profession: The Anthropological Life in Interesting Times," *Annual Review of Anthropology* 31 (2002): 4; David K. Johnson, *The Lavender Scare: The Cold War Persecution of Gays and Lesbians in the Federal Government* (Chicago: University of Chicago Press, 2004), 5–6; Forrest G. Robinson, *Love's Story Told: A Life of Henry A. Murray* (Cambridge, MA: Harvard University Press, 1992), 423n230.3; Ira Bashkow, "The Dynamics of Rapport in a Colonial Situation: David Schneider's Fieldwork on the Islands of Yap," in *Colonial Situations: Essays on the Contextualization of Ethnographic Knowledge*, ed. George Stocking (Madison: University of Wisconsin Press, 1993), 176.

66. On the matter of sex and anthropological fieldwork, see Don Kulick and Margaret Willson, eds., *Taboo: Sex, Identity, and Erotic Subjectivity in Anthropological Fieldwork*, (London: Routledge, 1995).

67. On this tendency to label, see David H. Price's otherwise highly admirable book, *Cold War Anthropology: The CIA, the Pentagon, and the Growth of Dual Use Anthropology* (Durham, NC: Duke University Press, 2016), xxi, xxiii. Price uses the categories "victims" and "perpetrators," specifically, in reference to anthropologists' involvement with the U.S. government during the Cold War.

68. Parsons and Vogt, "Clyde Kay Maben Kluckhohn," 146–47. I have altered the quotation slightly to preserve syntax.

69. David C. Engerman, *Know Your Enemy: The Rise and Fall of America's Soviet Experts* (Oxford: Oxford University Press, 2009), 44. Ruth Benedict, *The Chrysanthemum and the Sword: Patterns of Japanese Culture* (Boston: Mariner Books, 2006) is the major work in which the

OWI's studies of Japanese morale were published. The first edition of the book appeared in 1946.

70. Geertz, "Inconstant Profession," 4.

71. Martin Oppenheimer, "Footnote to the Cold War: The Harvard Russian Research Center," *Monthly Review* 48, no. 11 (April 1997): 10–11, https://doi.org/10.14452/MR-048-11-1997-04_2; Gene Lyons, *The Uneasy Partnership: Social Science and the Federal Government in the Twentieth Century* (New York: Russell Sage Foundation, 1969), 81.

72. Oppenheimer, "Cold War," 9–10, 13.

73. Oppenheimer, "Cold War," 11–12; Price, *Cold War Anthropology*, 84.

74. Sigmund Diamond, "The Arrangement: The FBI and Harvard University in the McCarthy Period," in *Beyond the Hiss Case: The FBI, Congress, and the Cold War*, ed. Athan G. Theoharis (Philadelphia: Temple University Press, 1982), 341–71.

75. U.S. Federal Bureau of Investigation, Memorandum from V. P. Keay to Mr. Laid (Bureau File 100–360557–15), 17 March 1949: 3; U.S. Federal Bureau of Investigation, Letter from Director, FBI, to SAC Boston (Bureau File 100–360557–17), 11 May 1949: 1; see also U.S. Federal Bureau of Investigation, Memorandum from Mr. F. J. Baumgardner to Mr. H. B. Fletcher (Bureau File 100–360557–17), 23 March 1949: 2.

76. Oppenheimer, "Cold War," 14.

77. U.S. Federal Bureau of Investigation, Memorandum from SAC Boston to Director, FBI, Concerning Russian Research Center, Cambridge, Mass. (Bureau File 100–360557–39), 17 August 1951: 2.

78. The date (1944) is referenced in U.S. Federal Bureau of Investigation, Memorandum from SAC Boston to Director, FBI, Concerning Clyde Kay Kluckhohn (Bureau File 121–32118–5), 7 September 1951: 1.

79. Price, *Cold War Anthropology*, 85; Diamond, "Arrangement," 347.

80. Memorandum from SAC Boston to Director, FBI, 7 September 1951: 1. On the Bureau's handling of the allegation against Kluckhohn, see U.S. Federal Bureau of Investigation, Memorandum from John Edgar Hoover, Director, Federal Bureau of Investigation to Assistant Chief of Staff, Department of the Army, Concerning Clyde Kay Kluckhohn (Bureau File 121–32118–5), 27 September 1951: 3.

81. William Wright, *Harvard's Secret Court: The Savage 1920 Purge of Campus Homosexuals* (New York: St. Martin's Press, 2005); Margaret A.

Nash and Jennifer A. R. Silverman, "'An Indelible Mark': Gay Purges in Higher Education in the 1940s," *History of Education Quarterly* 55, no. 4 (November 2015): 441–59.

82. Johnson, *Lavender Scare*, 4.

83. May, *Homeward Bound*, 91.

84. Johnson, *Lavender Scare*, 3.

85. Christina Dunbar-Hester, "Geek," in *Digital Keywords: A Vocabulary of Information Society and Culture*, ed. Benjamin Peters (Princeton, NJ: Princeton University Press, 2016), 150; Johnson, *Lavender Scare*, 93, 96.

86. Jerome Karabel, *The Chosen: The Hidden History of Admission and Exclusion at Harvard, Yale, and Princeton* (New York: Mariner Books, 2006), 253.

87. U.S. Federal Bureau of Investigation, Memorandum from John Edgar Hoover, Director, Federal Bureau of Investigation to Assistant Chief of Staff, Department of the Army, Concerning Clyde Kay Kluckhohn: 1.

88. Correspondence from Samuel Stouffer to Talcott Parsons, 5 February 1954, HUGFP 42.8.4 Box 13, Folder—Loyalty Investigation Papers & Correspondence, Harvard University Archives, Cambridge, MA, USA: 2–3. See also Mike F. Keen, "No One Above Suspicion: Talcott Parsons Under Surveillance," *The American Sociologist* 24, nos. 3–4 (Fall–Winter 1993): 45.

89. U.S. Federal Bureau of Investigation, Memorandum from SAC, Boston to Director, FBI, Concerning TALCOTT PARSONS—SM-C (Bureau File 100–390459–2), 12 May 1952. The unnamed informant is identified with the pronoun "he" throughout the document.

90. U.S. Federal Bureau of Investigation, Memorandum from SAC, Boston to Director, FBI, Concerning TALCOTT PARSONS—SECURITY MATTER-C (Bureau File 100–390459–3), 21 August 1952: 6.

91. There are two primary pieces of evidence that support the identification of Zimmerman. First, there is a reference in the Parsons FBI file to the informant's listing in the Harvard University *Directory of University Officers and Students*: "[Redacted], S.M., Ph.D., S.D. (honorary), Associate Professor of Sociology and Tutor in the Department of Social Relations." The listing in the *Official Register of Harvard*

University—Department of Social Relations, July 1951, reads: "Carle Clark Zimmerman, Ph.D., D.S. (hon.), *Associate Professor of Sociology* and *Tutor in the Department of Social Relations.*" No other entry for a Social Relations faculty member more closely resembles that of the FBI file. I have also confirmed with Harvard University Libraries that Zimmerman indeed held an SM degree from North Carolina State College, which is listed in the *Directory of University Officers and Students* of 1951. U.S. Federal Bureau of Investigation, Memorandum from SAC, Boston to Director, FBI, Concerning TALCOTT PARSONS, 21 August 1952: 1; *Official Register of Harvard University—Department of Social Relations* 48, no. 16 (July 1951): 8.

Second, there is a reference in Parsons's FBI file to the principal players in the loyalty case: "The 1946–1947 edition of 'Who's Who in America' contains the following information concerning ALLPORT, PARSONS, STOUFFER and [Redacted]." The write-ups from "Who's Who" then follow for Allport, Parsons, Stouffer, and Zimmerman. U.S. Federal Bureau of Investigation, Memorandum from SAC, Boston to Director, FBI, Concerning TALCOTT PARSONS— SECURITY MATTER-C (Bureau File 100–390459–3), 21 August 1952: 3, 5.

On the relationship between Zimmerman and Sorokin, see Patrick L. Schmidt, "Towards a History of the Department of Social Relations—Harvard University, 1946–1972" (Undergraduate Honors Thesis, Cambridge, MA, Harvard University, 1978), 18–19; see also Talcott Parsons, "Department and Laboratory of Social Relations: The First Decade, 1946–1956" (Cambridge, MA: Harvard University, December 31, 1956), 11.

92. U.S. Federal Bureau of Investigation, Memorandum from SAC, Boston to Director, FBI, Concerning TALCOTT PARSONS, 21 August 1952: 6–13; U.S. Federal Bureau of Investigation, Enclosure to Memorandum from SAC, Boston to Director, FBI, Concerning TALCOTT PARSONS, 12 May 1952: 1.

93. U.S. Federal Bureau of Investigation, Memorandum from SAC, Boston to Director, FBI, Concerning TALCOTT PARSONS, 21 August 1952: 8, 10. The file notes that Sullivan had been a student of Parsons at one point, and of Zimmerman (p. 1).

94. U.S. Federal Bureau of Investigation, Memorandum from Director, FBI, to SAC, Boston, Concerning TALCOTT PARSONS— SECURITY MATTER-C (Bureau File 100–390459–3), 27 October 1952: 2.

95. U.S. Federal Bureau of Investigation, Enclosure to Memorandum from SAC, Boston to Director, FBI, Concerning TALCOTT PARSONS, 12 May 1952: 1; U.S. Federal Bureau of Investigation, Memorandum from SAC, Boston to Director, FBI, Concerning TALCOTT PARSONS, 21 August 1952: 10.

    Zimmerman also seems to have noted Talcott Parsons's relationship with Florence Kluckhohn, Clyde Kluckhohn's wife, who had received a PhD in sociology from Harvard and was a lecturer in sociology in Soc-Rel during the time of the investigation. Because the passages are heavily redacted, it is difficult to know for sure, but Zimmerman seems to have been hinting at the possibility of a broader conspiracy involving Soc-Rel faculty and associated family members.

96. U.S. Federal Bureau of Investigation, Memorandum from Director, FBI, to SAC, Boston, Concerning TALCOTT PARSONS— SECURITY MATTER-C (Bureau File 100–390459–7), 2 April 1953; U.S. Federal Bureau of Investigation, Memorandum from Director, FBI, to SAC, Boston, Concerning TALCOTT PARSONS— SECURITY MATTER-C (Bureau File 100–390459–8), 8 May 1953: 1; U.S. Federal Bureau of Investigation, Memorandum from SAC, Mobile to Director, FBI, Concerning TALCOTT PARSONS— SM-C (Bureau File 100–390459–11), 15 May 1953; U.S. Federal Bureau of Investigation, Memorandum from SAC, Chicago to Director, FBI, Concerning TALCOTT PARSONS—SECURITY MATTER-C (Bureau File 100–390459–12), 18 May 1953; U.S. Federal Bureau of Investigation, SAC, Los Angeles to Director, FBI, Concerning TALCOTT PARSONS—SECURITY MATTER-C (Bureau File 100–390459–14), 11 June 1953; U.S. Federal Bureau of Investigation, SAC, Washington, DC to Director, FBI, Concerning TALCOTT PARSONS—SECURITY MATTER-C (Bureau File 100–390459–41), 4 March 1954. See also Keen, "No One Above Suspicion," 45.

97. U.S. Federal Bureau of Investigation, SAC, Boston to DIRECTOR, FBI, Concerning TALCOTT PARSONS—SECURITY MAT-TER-C (Bureau File 100-390459-46), 29 July 1954; U.S. Federal Bureau of Investigation, FBI, to White House (Bureau File 100-390459-7), 14 February 1968.

98. Correspondence from Talcott Parsons to McGeorge Bundy, 24 February 1954, HUGFP 42.8.4 Box 13, Folder—Loyalty Investigation Papers & Correspondence, Harvard University Archives, Cambridge, MA, USA: 2; see also Correspondence from McGeorge Bundy to Talcott Parsons, 2 March 1954, HUGFP 42.8.4 Box 13, Folder—Loyalty Investigation Papers & Correspondence, Harvard University Archives, Cambridge, MA, USA; Correspondence from Talcott Parsons to McGeorge Bundy, 25 May, 1954, HUGFP 42.8.4 Box 13, Folder—Loyalty Investigation Papers & Correspondence, Harvard University Archives, Cambridge, MA, USA.

99. Correspondence from Samuel Stouffer to Talcott Parsons, 21 May, 1954, HUGFP 42.8.4 Box 13, Folder—Loyalty Investigation Papers & Correspondence, Harvard University Archives, Cambridge, MA, USA: 1.

100. International Organizations Employees Loyalty Board—Interrogatory of Mr. Talcott Parsons, 17 May, 1954, HUGFP 42.8.4 Box 13, Folder—Loyalty Investigation Papers & Correspondence, Harvard University Archives, Cambridge, MA, USA: VII-5.

101. Correspondence from Talcott Parsons to Samuel Stouffer, 12 February 1954, HUGFP 42.8.4 Box 13, Folder—Loyalty Investigation Papers & Correspondence, Harvard University Archives, Cambridge, MA, USA: 1. On Anne Parsons's life, mental illness, and tragic suicide in 1964 at the age of 33, see Winifred Breines, "Alone in the 1950s: Anne Parsons and the Feminine Mystique," *Theory and Society* 15, no. 6 (November 1986): 805–43.

102. Smith, "Women, the Family," 84; emphasis added.

103. Johnson, *Lavender Scare*, 95.

104. I use the word "threatened" here with caution. Talcott Parsons's own white-male-professional privilege was threatened in the sense that it could potentially be revoked on the basis of the allegation he was a communist—at least, that's what he believed. The broader system of privilege that had been invested in him, however, was—and

remains—far more resilient. For a parallel case, see Robin DiAngelo, *White Fragility: Why It's So Hard for White People to Talk About Racism* (Boston: Beacon Press, 2018).

105. Talcott Parsons, "Theory in the Humanities and Sociology," *Daedalus* 99, no. 2 (1970): 517.

106. Smith, "Women, the Family," 71. "Masculine authority in the home is conditional upon [the husband's] employment and because it is conditional, it can be separated from him. If he loses his job, his rights to sexual access to his wife, his privileges as master in the home are undermined. Long periods of unemployment characteristically result in changes in the husband's status in the home."

107. U.S. Federal Bureau of Investigation, Affidavit of Talcott Parsons before the Eastern Industrial Personnel Security Board—Matter of Samuel Andrew Stouffer (Enclosure to Memorandum from Legal Attaché, London, England to Director, FBI—(Bureau File 100–390459–42), 11 March 1954: 1.

108. Affidavit of Talcott Parsons (Bureau File 100–390459–42), 11 March 1954: 2.

109. Talcott Parsons, "McCarthyism and American Social Tension: A Sociologist's View," *Yale Review* 44, no. 2 (1954): 226–45; Talcott Parsons, "On Building Social Systems Theory: A Personal History," *Daedalus* 99, no. 4 (Spring 1970): 841.

110. See Uta Gerhardt, ed., *Talcott Parsons on National Socialism* (New York: Aldine de Gruyter, 1993), esp. chapters 1, 2, and 11.

111. J. T. Dunlop et al., "Toward a Common Language for the Area of Social Science," White Paper, Harvard University, Cambridge, MA, 1941.

112. See Talcott Parsons, *Essays in Sociological Theory, Pure and Applied* (Glencoe, IL: Free Press, 1949); Arthur J. Vidich, "The Department of Social Relations and 'Systems Theory' at Harvard: 1948–50," *International Journal of Politics, Culture, and Society* 13, no. 4 (June 2000): 617, https://doi.org/10.1023/A:1022923107834. I make this inference on the following basis: (1) *Parsons* is the only name spelled out fully in the author line of the document; (2) a large segment of the piece was included in the first edition of a collection of Parsons's essays; (3) Vidich refers to the essay as a paper written by Parsons; and (4) references to the Zuni Indian tribe appearing in the introduction point to Kluckhohn's imprint.

113. On the rise and fall of Soc-Rel, see Schmidt, "Department of Social Relations." On Leary and Alpert, see Don Lattin, *The Harvard Psychedelic Club: How Timothy Leary, Ram Dass, Huston Smith, and Andrew Weil Killed the Fifties and Ushered in a New Age for America* (New York: HarperOne, 2010), 99–106.

114. Parsons, "Department and Laboratory," 41–45, 55. Notable graduates of the doctoral program in social relations include Robert Bellah, Roy D'Andrade, Renée Fox, Harold Garfinkel, Mark Granovetter, Robert Merton (a holdover from the older sociology department), Stanley Milgram, Michelle Rosaldo, Renato Rosaldo, and Barry Wellman. Dick Price, co-founder of the Esalen Institute, was briefly a Soc-Rel graduate student before flunking out of the program and experiencing a psychotic break.

115. Vidich, "Department of Social Relations," 617.

116. J. T. Dunlop et al., "Toward a Common Language," 16, 17.

117. J. T. Dunlop et al., "Toward a Common Language," 23.

118. J. T. Dunlop et al., "Toward a Common Language," 23.

119. Roy R. Grinker and Helen MacGill Hughes, eds., *Toward a Unified Theory of Human Behavior* (New York: Basic Books, 1956), 154, 210.

120. Parsons, "Social Systems Theory," 831, 878n35.

121. See. e.g., Alfred E. Emerson, "Dynamic Homeostasis: A Unifying Principle in Organic, Social, and Ethical Evolution," *The Scientific Monthly* 78, no. 2 (1954): 67–85; Alfred E. Emerson, "Homeostasis and Comparison of Systems," in *Toward a Unified Theory of Human Behavior*, ed. Roy R. Grinker and Helen MacGill Hughes (New York: Basic Books, 1956), 147–63; and Alfred E. Emerson, "Human Cultural Evolution and Its Relation to Organic Evolution in Insect Societies," in *Social Change in Developing Areas: A Reinterpretation of Evolutionary Theory*, ed. Herbert R. Barringer, George I. Blanksten, and Raymond W. Mack (Cambridge, MA: Schenkman Publishing, 1965), 50–67.

122. Emerson, "Dynamic Homeostasis," 76.

123. Parsons, "Social Systems Theory," 850.

124. Talcott Parsons, "Evolutionary Universals in Society," *American Sociological Review* 29, no. 3 (1964): 341–42.

125. David E. Apter, "On Clifford Geertz," *Daedalus* 136, no. 3 (2007): 111; Fred Inglis, *Clifford Geertz: Culture, Custom, and Ethics* (Cambridge:

Polity Press, 2000), 4; Clifford Geertz, "Passage and Accident: A Life of Learning," in *Available Light: Anthropological Reflections on Philosophical Problems* (Princeton, NJ: Princeton University Press, 2000), 5–6.

126. Geertz, "Passage and Accident," 7.
127. Douglas Oliver, quoted in Price, *Cold War Anthropology*, 94. See also: Peter C. Baker, "Bad Intelligence," *The Nation*, June 16, 2016, https://www.thenation.com/article/archive/bad-intelligence/; Ben White, "Clifford Geertz: Singular Genius of Interpretive Anthropology," *Development and Change* 38, no. 6 (November 1, 2007): 91–1188, https://doi.org/10.1111/j.1467-7660.2007.00460.x. Modjokuto is now Pare, a town located on the island of Java.
128. Geertz, "Inconstant Profession," 5. For details on Geertz's difficult relationship with Kluckhohn, see McFarlane, *Full Interview with Clifford Geertz*, at ±25 minutes.
129. McFarlane, *Clifford Geertz*, at ±28 minutes.
130. Geertz, "Inconstant Profession," 4.
131. Geertz, "Passage and Accident," 8.
132. Quoted in Apter, "On Clifford Geertz," 122. Curiously, toward the end of his life, Geertz claimed that "I myself never really followed his [Parsons's] line of thought." While the claim may be true of Geertz's work after 1970, Parsons's imprint is all over his research before that. McFarlane, *Clifford Geertz*, at ±28 minutes.
133. Clifford Geertz, *The Interpretation of Cultures: Selected Essays* (New York: Basic Books, 1973), 5.
134. Geertz, *Interpretation of Cultures*, v.
135. Geertz, *Interpretation of Cultures*, 39; see also Clyde Kluckhohn, *Mirror for Man: The Relation of Anthropology to Modern Life* (New York: McGraw-Hill, 1949), 8–9.
136. Geertz, *Interpretation of Cultures*, 40.
137. Kenneth Burke, "Definition of Man," *The Hudson Review* 16, no. 4 (1963): 491–514; Kenneth Burke, *Language as Symbolic Action: Essays on Life, Literature, and Method* (Berkeley: University of California Press, 1966), 3–24; Emerson, "Human Cultural Evolution," passim. Burke is well-known, particularly in the discipline of communication, for his claim that human beings are "symbol-using

animals." He first advanced the thesis in the Winter 1963–1964 issue of *The Hudson Review*, and it subsequently appeared in the collection *Language and Symbolic Action*, first published in 1966. This line of argument appeared almost a decade *after* Emerson had introduced it in a 1954 piece he published in *Scientific Monthly*. It's unclear whether Burke read or was aware of Emerson's work, although Burke was unusually reflexive about the nature of his contribution in proposing people as symbol-using animals. "Granted, it doesn't come as much of a surprise" is the line immediately following the definitional statement, as if to suggest the self-evidence of the proposition, its lack of originality, or perhaps both. For whatever it's worth, Burke was a personal friend of Talcott Parsons.

138. Geertz, *Interpretation of Cultures*, 41, 44.

139. Geertz, *Interpretation of Cultures*, 92–93.

140. Geertz, *Interpretation of Cultures*, 44.

141. Geertz, *Interpretation of Cultures*, 199.

142. Geertz, *Interpretation of Cultures*, 50. On information theory, see James Gleick, *The Information: A History, a Theory, a Flood* (New York: Pantheon Books, 2011); and John Durham Peters, "Information: Notes Toward a Critical History," *Journal of Communication Inquiry* 12, no. 2 (1988): 9–23.

143. Geertz, *Interpretation of Cultures*, 44.

144. Geertz, *Interpretation of Cultures*, 44, 50, 92.

145. John MacCormick, *Nine Algorithms That Changed the Future: The Ingenious Ideas That Drive Today's Computers* (Princeton, NJ: Princeton University Press, 2012), 3 (emphasis added).

146. Geertz, *Interpretation of Cultures*, 355, 357.

147. Geertz, *Interpretation of Cultures*, 250.

148. Geertz, *Interpretation of Cultures*, 11, 12.

149. Geertz, *Interpretation of Cultures*, 11.

150. See, e.g., Flo Conway and Jim Siegelman, *Dark Hero of the Information Age: In Search of Norbert Wiener, the Father of Cybernetics* (New York: Basic Books, 2005); Ronald R. Kline, *The Cybernetics Moment: Or Why We Call Our Age the Information Age*, repr. ed. (Baltimore: Johns Hopkins University Press, 2015); Jimmy Soni and Rob Goodman, *A Mind*

at Play: How Claude Shannon Invented the Information Age, repr. ed. (New York: Simon & Schuster, 2017); Gleick, *Information*, 168–268. See also Norbert Wiener, *Cybernetics or, Control and Communication in the Animal and the Machine* (New York: MIT Press, 1961); Norbert Wiener, *The Human Use of Human Beings: Cybernetics and Society*, rev. ed. (Cambridge, MA: Da Capo Press, 1954).

151. See Gilles Deleuze, *Bergsonism*, trans. Hugh Tomlinson and Barbara Habberjam (New York: Zone Books, 1988). Here, I'm using the word "virtually" in the Deleuzian sense, to denote that which is real (i.e., producing effects) without being actual (i.e., fully manifest or articulated). On Gates's college career, see Walter Isaacson, "Bill Gates, Inside the Gates," *Harvard Magazine*, September 20, 2013, https://harvardmagazine.com/2013/09/walter-isaacson-on-bill-gates-at-harvard. Gates took a hiatus from his studies in fall 1975 but returned to Harvard for the subsequent two semesters. He dropped out definitively at the end of fall semester 1976.

152. Raymond Williams, *The Sociology of Culture* (Chicago: University of Chicago Press, 1981), 231–32.

153. Raymond Williams, "Culture and Technology," in Raymond Williams, *Towards 2000* (London: Chatto & Windus, 1983), 128.

154. Williams, *Keywords*, rev. ed., 315–16; see also Williams, *Keywords*, 1st ed. An inkling of his having registered the relationship may be the addition of an entry for technology in the revised edition of *Keywords*. The entry, however, is among the shortest in the volume.

155. Williams, "Culture and Technology," 149.

156. Williams, "Culture and Technology," 147.

157. Williams, "Culture and Technology," 149.

158. Williams, "Culture and Technology," 148.

EPILOGUE: COMING TO TERMS

1. Mario Vargas Llosa, *Notes on the Death of Culture: Essays on Spectacle and Society*, trans. John King (New York: Picador, 2015).

2. On the observation of reactionary political interests, see Raymond Williams, "The Uses of Cultural Theory," in *The Politics of Modernism: Against the New Conformists* (London: Verso, 1989), 172.

3. Sarah Sharma, "A Manifesto for the Broken Machine," *Camera Obscura* 35, no. 2 (September 2020): 173, https://doi.org/10.1215/02705346 -8359652.

4. James Surowiecki, *The Wisdom of Crowds: Why the Many Are Smarter Than the Few and How Collective Wisdom Shapes Business, Economies, Societies and Nations* (New York: Doubleday, 2004); see also Pierre Levy, *Collective Intelligence: Mankind's Emerging World in Cyberspace*, trans. Robert Bononno (Cambridge, MA: Basic Books, 1999); Howard Rheingold, *Smart Mobs: The Next Social Revolution* (Cambridge, MA: Basic Books, 2002); Yochai Benkler, *The Wealth of Networks: How Social Production Transforms Markets and Freedom* (New Haven, CT: Yale University Press, 2006).

5. Zoë Quinn, *Crash Override: How Gamergate (Nearly) Destroyed My Life, and How We Can Win the Fight Against Online Hate* (New York: Public Affairs, 2017); Aja Romano, "What We Still Haven't Learned from Gamergate," *Vox*, January 27, 2021, https://www.vox.com/culture /2020/1/20/20808875/gamergate-lessons-cultural-impact-changes -harassment-laws.

6. Lawrence Grossberg, *Under the Cover of Chaos: Trump and the Battle for the American Right* (London: Pluto Press, 2018), 97.

7. Raymond Williams, *Keywords: A Vocabulary of Culture and Society*, rev. ed. (New York: Oxford University Press, 1983), 23. Williams goes on to observe that *community* is "a difficult word."

8. Raphael Samuel, "'Philosophy Teaching by Example': Past and Present in Raymond Williams," *History Workshop*, no. 27 (Spring 1989): 144. Samuel offers the description specifically in reference to Williams's deployment of the methodology in *The Country and the City*.

9. The line is an homage to Carolyn Steedman, "Culture, Cultural Studies, and the Historians," in *Cultural Studies*, eds. Lawrence Grossberg, Cary Nelson, and Paula Treichler (New York: Routledge, 1992), 621; see also Richard Johnson, "Historical Returns: Transdisciplinarity, Cultural Studies, and History," *European Journal of Cultural Studies* 4, no. 3 (August 2001): 262.

10. Stuart Hall, *Cultural Studies 1983: A Theoretical History*, eds. Jennifer Daryl Slack and Lawrence Grossberg (Durham: Duke University

Press, 2016), 89; Lawrence Grossberg, *Cultural Studies in the Future Tense* (Durham, NC: Duke University Press, 2010), 25. Here, I'm playing on the language of the "detour through theory" in cultural studies.

11. Tony Fry, *Defuturing: A New Design Philosophy* (London: Bloomsbury Visual Arts, 2020), 238. I first encountered Fry in the work of Arturo Escobar, to which this discussion also owes a significant intellectual debt. See Arturo Escobar, *Designs for the Pluriverse: Radical Interdependence, Autonomy, and the Making of Worlds* (Durham, NC: Duke University Press, 2018).

12. Hans-Georg Gadamer, *Truth and Method*, trans. Joel Weinsheimer and Donald G. Marshall, 2nd rev. ed. (New York: Continuum, 1996), 547–48.

13. I am riffing on James Clifford, *The Predicament of Culture: Twentieth-Century Ethnography, Literature, and Art* (Cambridge, MA: Harvard University Press, 1988).

14. Williams, *Keywords*, rev. ed., 12; see also Alan Durant, "Raymond Williams's Keywords: Investigating Meanings 'Offered, Felt For, Tested, Confirmed, Asserted, Qualified, Changed,'" *Critical Quarterly* 48, no. 4 (December 2006): 1–26, https://doi.org/10.1111/j.1467-8705.2006.00743.x.

15. For an excellent synopsis of the cascade of revelations, see Nicholas Confessore, "Cambridge Analytica and Facebook: The Scandal and the Fallout So Far," *New York Times*, April 4, 2018, https://www.nytimes.com/2018/04/04/us/politics/cambridge-analytica-scandal-fallout.html. For additional details, see Christopher Wylie, *Mindfuck: Cambridge Analytica and the Plot to Break America* (New York: Random House, 2019), esp. ch. 6; and Karim Amer and Jehane Noujaim, *The Great Hack* (Netflix, 2019).

16. Wylie, *Mindfuck*, 62.

17. Brittany Kaiser, *Targeted: The Cambridge Analytica Whistleblower's Inside Story of How Big Data, Trump, and Facebook Broke Democracy and How It Can Happen Again* (New York: Harper, 2019); Wylie, *Mindfuck*; Amer and Noujaim, *Great Hack*.

18. See, e.g., Shoshana Zuboff, "You Are Now Remotely Controlled," *New York Times*, January 24, 2020, sec. Opinion, https://www.nytimes.com/2020/01/24/opinion/sunday/surveillance-capitalism.html.

19. Grossberg, *Cover of Chaos*, 132. See also Stuart Hall, "Encoding/ Decoding," in *The Cultural Studies Reader*, ed. Simon During, 2nd ed. (London: Routledge, 1993), 507–17; Langdon Winner, *The Whale and the Reactor: A Search for Limits in an Age of High Technology* (Chicago: University of Chicago Press, 1989), 9–10.

20. Winner, *Whale and the Reactor*, 11.

21. Tara McPherson, "U.S. Operating Systems at Mid-Century: The Intertwining of Race and UNIX," in *Race After the Internet*, ed. Lisa Nakamura and Peter A. Chow-White (New York: Routledge, 2012), 36.

22. Wylie, *Mindfuck*, 47 (emphasis in original).

23. Wylie, *Mindfuck*, 67.

24. Wylie, *Mindfuck*, 64.

25. Wylie, *Mindfuck*, 64 and passim.

26. Angela Chen and Alessandra Potenza, "Cambridge Analytica's Facebook Data Abuse Shouldn't Get Credit for Trump," *The Verge*, March 20, 2018, https://www.theverge.com/2018/3/20/17138854 /cambridge-analytica-facebook-data-trump-campaign-psycho graphic-microtargeting. See also Wendy Hui Kyong Chun, *Discriminating Data: Correlation, Neighborhoods, and the New Politics of Recognition* (Cambridge, MA: MIT Press, 2021), 39.

27. Chen and Potenza, "Cambridge Analytica's Facebook Data Abuse Shouldn't Get Credit for Trump"; Siva Vaidhyanathan, *Antisocial Media: How Facebook Disconnects Us and Undermines Democracy* (New York: Oxford University Press, 2018), 1–30.

28. "#DeleteFacebook Trends Amid Cambridge Analytica Scandal," *CBS News*, March 21, 2018, https://www.cbsnews.com/news/deletefacebook -trends-amid-cambridge-analytica-scandal/.

29. Jerome Teelucksingh, *Labour and Decolonization Struggle in Trinidad and Tobago* (Hampshire, UK: Palgrave Macmillan, 2015), 8. See also Ann Marie Bissessar, "Trinidad and Tobago," in *Ethnic Conflict in Developing Societies: Trinidad and Tobago, Guyana, Fiji, and Suriname* (Cham, Switzerland: Palgrave Macmillan/Springer Nature, 2017), 89–109.

30. Teelucksingh, *Labour and Decolonization Struggle*, 7.

31. Chun, *Discriminating Data*, 41–42.

32. Wylie, *Mindfuck*, 52–53, 55; Amer and Noujaim, *Great Hack*.

33. Aimé Césaire, *Discourse on Colonialism*, trans. Joan Pinkham (New York: Monthly Review Press, 2000), 36 (emphasis in original). See also Achille Mbembe, *Necropolitics*, trans. Steven Corcoran (Durham, NC: Duke University Press, 2019), 72, 76.

34. Raka Shome, "Thinking Culture and Cultural Studies—from/of the Global South," *Communication and Critical/Cultural Studies* 16, no. 3 (July 2019): 205 https://doi.org/10.1080/14791420.2019.1648841; Raymond Williams, "Culture Is Ordinary," in *Resources of Hope: Culture, Democracy, Socialism* (London: Verso, 1989), 3–18.

35. Wylie, *Mindfuck*, 53.

36. Shoshana Zuboff, *The Age of Surveillance Capitalism: The Fight for a Human Future at the New Frontier of Power* (New York: Public Affairs, 2019), 12–14, 351–53.

37. Césaire, *Discourse on Colonialism*; Mbembe, *Necropolitics*; Nick Couldry and Ulises A. Mejias, *The Costs of Connection: How Data Is Colonizing Human Life and Appropriating It for Capitalism* (Stanford, CA: Stanford University Press, 2019), xii.

38. On "roots" and "routes," see Paul Gilroy, *The Black Atlantic: Modernity and Double Consciousness* (Cambridge, MA: Harvard University Press, 1993), 19.

39. McPherson, "U.S. Operating Systems," 24; see also 33.

40. Oscar H. Gandy, *The Panoptic Sort: A Political Economy of Personal Information* (Boulder, CO: Westview Press, 1993), 139; see also Oscar H. Gandy, "It's Discrimination, Stupid!," in *Resisting the Virtual Life: The Culture and Politics of Information*, eds. James Brook and Iain Boal (San Francisco, CA: City Lights Publishers, 1995), 35–47.

41. Safiya Umoja Noble, *Algorithms of Oppression: How Search Engines Reinforce Racism* (New York: New York University Press, 2018), 1; Ruha Benjamin, *Race After Technology: Abolitionist Tools for the New Jim Code* (Cambridge: Polity, 2019), 5–6. See also, among other notable works: Cathy O'Neil, *Weapons of Math Destruction: How Big Data Increases Inequality and Threatens Democracy* (New York: Crown, 2016); John Cheney-Lippold, *We Are Data: Algorithms and the Making of Our Digital Selves* (New York: NYU Press, 2017), especially 15–18; and Virginia

Eubanks, *Automating Inequality: How High-Tech Tools Profile, Police, and Punish the Poor* (New York: Picador, 2018).

42. Kashmir Hill, "Wrongfully Accused by an Algorithm," *New York Times*, June 24, 2020, https://www.nytimes.com/2020/06/24/technology/facial-recognition-arrest.html; Benjamin, *Race After Technology*, 97–136; Simone Browne, *Dark Matters: On the Surveillance of Blackness* (Durham, NC: Duke University Press, 2015), 161.

43. Nabil Echchaibi, "Thou Shalt Not Erase Me," *Al Jazeera*, July 10, 2020, https://www.aljazeera.com/indepth/opinion/thou-erase-20070716 4436376.html.

44. See, e.g., among many other notable works: Homi K. Bhabha, *The Location of Culture*, 2nd ed. (London: Routledge, 2004); James Clifford, *Routes: Travel and Translation in the Late Twentieth Century* (Cambridge, MA: Harvard University Press, 1997); Johannes Fabian, *Time and the Other: How Anthropology Makes Its Object* (New York: Columbia University Press, 1983); Paul Gilroy, *There Ain't No Black in the Union Jack: The Cultural Politics of Race and Nation* (Chicago: University of Chicago Press, 1991); Lawrence Grossberg, "Cultural Studies, Modern Logics, and Theories of Globalisation," in *Back to Reality? Social Experience and Cultural Studies*, ed. Angela McRobbie (Manchester, UK: Manchester University Press, 1997), 7–35; Qadri Ismail, *Culture and Eurocentrism* (London: Rowman & Littlefield International, 2015); and Gauri Viswanathan, *Masks of Conquest: Literary Study and British Rule in India*, 25th anniversary ed. (New York: Columbia University Press, 2014).

45. George Yúdice, *The Expediency of Culture: Uses of Culture in the Global Era* (Durham, NC: Duke University Press, 2004).

46. Kory Stamper, *Word by Word: The Secret Life of Dictionaries* (New York: Pantheon Books, 2017), 248 (emphasis in original).

47. Williams, *Keywords*, rev. ed., 18; Stamper, *Word by Word*, 11 (emphasis in original); see also 126–27.

48. Williams, *Keywords*, rev. ed., 26.

49. "Instagram Changes Algorithm Amid Claims of Anti-Palestinian Bias," Middle East Eye, May 31, 2021, http://www.middleeasteye.net/news/instagram-changes-algorithm-amid-palestinian-activists-allegations-bias.

50. Some of these terms appear in Benjamin Peters, ed., *Digital Keywords: A Vocabulary of Information Society and Culture* (Princeton, NJ: Princeton University Press, 2016). The collection represents an important first step in mapping the idiom of algorithmic culture, and of digital technology more broadly.

INDEX

Arnold, Thomas, 139
artisanship, 162–164
Aryabhaṭa (mathematician), 76
Ascher, Marcia, 77–79
Ascher, Robert, 77–79
Ashcraft, Karen Lee, 183
Asiatic Researches (journal), 100
Asiatic Society of Calcutta, 100
Asiatic Society of Great Britain
    and Ireland, 100
atmospheres, 21, 57, 65, 121, 127,
    265n56, 284n25. *See also*
    structure of feeling
authoritarianism, 18, 20, 139, 212
Automate This (Steiner), 84
automated culture, 16, 17
automated media, 16, 17
automatism, 17

Bannon, Steve, 230, 232
the Barbarians, 102, 146–47, 149
Bayt al-Hakima (House of
    Wisdom), 91–92, 105
Bell, Bill, 151
Benedict, Ruth, 179, 195
Benjamin, Ruha, 15, 238
Bennett, Tony, 150–51
Berry, David M., 23
Big Tech, 2, 17–18, 237
Bildung, 132, 135
Birmingham Centre for
    Contemporary Cultural
    Studies, 28
Black, Michael, 153
Black African diaspora, 109
Black women, 170, 182

Boas, Franz, 18, 117–21, 119*f*, 137,
    165–66
Boasian anthropology, 117–21, 119*f*
Book of the Duchess, The (Chaucer),
    95–97
Bopp, Franz, 97
Border Country (Williams), 124–25
Boston Globe, 181–82
Boston Herald, 182
Boudourides, Moses, 42
Bourdieu, Pierre, 133
Brahmagupta (mathematician), 76
Brand, Stewart, 19
Breitbart, 230–32
Brexit (UK), 34, 230
Bright, John, 145, 287n71
British Empire, 37, 168
Brown, Douglas, 182
Browne, Simone, 15, 238
Bryn Mawr Alumnae Bulletin,
    183–84
Bucher, Taina, 15, 80
Bundy, McGeorge, 205
Burke, Edmund, 26
Burke, Kenneth, 309n137
Busa, Roberto, 21–23
Bush, George W., 138

cæg, defined, 49
California Committee on
    Un-American Activities, 200
Cambridge Analytica scandal, 34,
    229–35
Cambridge University, 129, 154,
    157–59, 201
Cambridge University Press, 153

*Constitutional Government
and Democracy* (Friedrich),
182–83
containment and algorithmic
culture, 181, 187–88, 225
context, defined, 249n24
Cornhill Magazine, 144
Costanza-Chock, Sasha, 6, 15
Couldry, Nick, 236
Coulling, Sidney, 143
Country and the City, The
(Williams), 125
Crawford, Kate, 15
crimes against humanity, 235
criticism and algorithmic culture,
143, 157–58, 164, 225
Crossley, John N., 92
cultivation, 11, 132, 135–36, 143–45,
164, 167–68, 243
cultura, 9
cultural intermediaries, 4, 133
cultural software, 219, 256n68
cultural studies, 7, 24–25, 27, 28, 42,
126, 138, 228
cultural technologies, 151
culture: action systems and, 213;
anecdotes of, 121–28;
anthropology and, 10, 13, 18;
Arnold on, 137–152, 166–169,
210–11; Boasian anthropology,
117–21, 119f; civilization and,
128–37, 217, 225; defined, 4,
10–12, 32–33, 221; defined by
Geertz, 216–17, 240–41;
documentary definition of, 11;
etymology of, 8–9; as

governance, 240; heritage of, 14;
high culture, 33, 130, 151;
historical baggage of, 228–29,
239–40; humanities and, 12–13,
135, 157, 165; ideal definition of,
10; intellectualism and, 11, 24,
122, 132, 134, 153, 157–58;
introduction to, 31; key-words
and, 125, 128, 137, 166, 167;
keywords and, 121–25, 167;
Leavis and, 26, 32–33, 121, 125,
152–165, 156f, 240; mathematical
subtext of, 112–13, 271nn34–35;
metaculture, 120–123, 128, 138,
166–167; politics of race, 121;
semantics of, 39; social
definition of, 11; softwarized,
23–24; symbolic dimensions of
culture, 217–19; technoculture,
11; technology and, 9–10, 240;
totalitarianism and, 33, 167, 181,
208–13, 218, 225–26, 236, 240;
Williams and, 7, 10–11, 20, 32.
See also algorithmic culture
Culture and Anarchy (Arnold),
143–149, 157, 288n91
Culture and Environment (Leavis,
Thompson), 162–63
culture and society tradition,
19–20, 26–28, 38, 44–46, 63–64,
71, 112–13, 121–123, 128, 225
Culture and Society (Williams), 20,
26–27, 30, 39, 41, 43, 46, 49, 112,
123–24, 128–31, 173–76, 225–26,
267n84
Cvetkovich, Ann, 193

industrialization, 26, 47, 162–63, 166
information gap, 218–19
information technology, 170–72, 223
information theory, 22, 46, 142,
    218–21
Inglis, Fred, 214
Instagram, 4, 243
insurance claims algorithm, 68–69
intellectualism: algorithm and, 89,
    92, 97, 239; algorithmic culture
    and, 166, 183, 200, 215–16;
    collective intelligence, 226;
    culture and, 11, 24, 122, 132, 134,
    153, 157–58; literary criticism
    and, 164–65
intelligent technologies, 116
intelligentsia, 131–34, 148
International Organizations
    Employees Loyalty Board, 206
Interpretation of Cultures, The
    (Geertz), 216–17
Islam, 79, 81, 87, 89, 109–10, 225,
    276n66
Ismail, Qadri, 10, 137

jargon, 57, 265n58
Jim Crow laws, 238
John Reed Club, 204, 208
Johnson, David K., 195, 199
Jones, William, 100

Karabel, Jerome, 200
keel, defined, 49
kei, defined, 55
Kennan, George F., 181
Kenneth, Burke, 217

key, defined, 50–53, 58
key-legged, 50
key-words: agnosticism of, 137;
    algorithm and, 71–72;
    algorithmic culture and, 174,
    177–78, 225, 228; anthropology
    and, 59; culture and, 125, 128,
    137, 166, 167; defined, 44–45,
    53–63; as emergent language,
    53–56; epistemology of, 62–63;
    as grammatical undertaking,
    61–62; historical grounds for,
    45–49, 58; introduction to, 7, 30,
    35–38; methodology of, 63–66,
    72, 166–67
key words, defined, 44–45, 47–48
keyness, 48, 65
keynote, 51, 58
keystone, 51, 58
keywords: algorithm and, 71;
    algorithmic culture and, 172–76;
    culture and, 121–25, 167;
    defined, 41, 44–45, 263n31;
    introduction of, 47–48;
    methodology of, 63–66, 167, 237;
    semantic approach to, 39–40;
    standard orthography of, 45
Keywords Re-Oriented (Gentz), 40,
    44
Keywords (Williams), 39–45, 47, 59,
    61, 65, 69–70, 122, 124, 173–76,
    242–43
Khwarizm, 85–87, 168
Kittler, Friedrich, 28, 64, 72, 122–23
Kluckhohn, Clyde, 10, 33, 134–35,
    179–201, 180*f*, 212, 215–17, 240

GPSR Authorized Representative: Easy Access System Europe, Mustamäe tee
50, 10621 Tallinn, Estonia, gpsr.requests@easproject.com

www.ingramcontent.com/pod-product-compliance
Lightning Source LLC
Chambersburg PA
CBHW022135020426
42334CB00015B/903